ALTHOUGH CRITICS in many countries have commented voluminously on the world that Sholom Aleichem created in his stories —that world of simple villages, of humor and wisdom and moral sensitivity—his own life, astonishingly, has never before been fully told. And much of it may come as a surprise to the vast audience that has read his stories in English, in Yiddish, in almost every major language spoken today, or seen them transmuted as *Fiddler on the Roof*. For this man whose writing conjures up the naïve magic of folklore was himself a Kiev stockbroker, urbane, sophisticated, an early supporter of Zionism, a contributor to literary journals—the memoir provides fascinating insights into literary and theatrical circles

intellectual and a man of
irst and foremost, he was
his six children who adored
d entranced to each new
r favorite characters, and
s literary triumphs. His
cts with tenderness the be-
o often wrote through the
ght, but was never too pre-
rate a child's birthday and
argeness of spirit offset the
Jewish life in Russia.

n's ebullient nature and in-
, triumphing over early
health and the anguish of
vaded even his will: he
asked that the anniversary of his death be celebrated by reading "one of the very merry" of his stories, so that his name might be "recalled with laughter." It is with laughter and love that his daughter recalls him, in a book that will move and delight his old admirers and his new.

D1171201

My Father,
SHOLOM ALEICHEM

Marie Waife-Goldberg

Simon and Schuster

New York

SECOND PRINTING

LIBRARY OF CONGRESS CATALOG CARD NUMBER: 68-11011
DESIGNED BY EVE METZ
MANUFACTURED IN THE UNITED STATES OF AMERICA
BY THE BOOK PRESS INCORPORATED, BRATTLEBORO, VERMONT

Grateful acknowledgment is made to Farrar, Straus & Giroux, Inc., the publishers of the only existing English edition of material from From the Fair (*their title,* The Great Fair, Copyright © The Noonday Press, 1955)*, for permission to include new translations of a number of passages included in their book.*

The original Yiddish language edition of From the Fair *Copyright 1918 by Olga Rabinowitz, Copyright renewed 1946 by Marie Waife-Goldberg and Sarah Lila Kaufman.*

To Wendy, Ronald, Sandra, and Robert

Contents

My Father, Sholom Aleichem

Foreword

ALTHOUGH my father, Sholom Aleichem, passed away over fifty years ago, and his popularity at his death has since grown into world fame —his works are now read in some two-score languages—there is not a single book in any language that tells the complete story of his life. Much has been written in books and periodicals about his literary activity, but only a few periods of his eventful life have been treated in print, and mostly only as related to his writing.

For years Sholom Aleichem had wanted to write the story of his life himself. He envisioned it as his magnum opus, running into a number of volumes, and he intended it to be the story of his time and of the people he had met as well. But the pressure of other commitments, and the lack of enthusiasm on the part of the publishers, prevented his undertaking this task. He did finally begin, in the year 1915, to write his autobiography, which he called *From the Fair,* writing about himself in the third person so as to be less inhibited in depicting his inner life. When the first installments appeared in a newspaper the literary community hailed it as a new masterpiece. But only a year and a half later death snatched the pen out of his hand. He had brought his story to his twenty-first year, on the threshold of a most dramatic moment in his personal life, and before he first saw his name in print.

My father had the feeling that no stranger could do justice to the story of his life, perhaps because he lived all his life, except the last year and a half, away from the Jewish literary community, completely immersed in his writing and his immediate family, which he called his Republic. In his introduction to *From the Fair* he quoted the words he had said to himself as the reason for writing his autobiography. "No one knows what the morrow may bring . . . and people will turn up who think they know you and understand you, and they will fabricate stories about you that are untrue and misleading. . . . Better do it yourself. . . ." Unfortunately, this apprehension proved well justified over the years. By word of mouth and also in print stories about my father have been circulated that are not only untrue but entirely out of keeping with his character and misrepresenting his view of life and attitude toward people. There is even a preposterous novel in Russian, purporting to be a fictionalized life of my father, crudely depicting him as an early proletarian partisan, Bolshevik style.

As to the members of our family writing my father's story, my husband kept urging my mother to write the story of her life, which would have been the story of Sholom Aleichem. When she died, in 1942, she left only a brief sketch of her father, a small part of what she hoped would be her memoirs. My late sister Lyala, a short-story writer, published a few vignettes, a personal glimpse of our father, but no more. My late brother-in-law, Isaac Dov Berkowitz, who translated my father's works into Hebrew, was intimately involved with my father's literary activities during the period 1905–1916, and he left behind an exhaustive source book in Yiddish, *Dos Sholom Aleichem Buch,* containing much information about my father and a collection of his letters, also a five-volume memoir, in Yiddish and Hebrew, on the Jewish literary scene during those eleven years, centering about my father. Again, only a specific period, and dealing mostly with the literary phase.

It seemed to me clear that there was need for an available record, be it a cursory one, of my father's life, to which an interested person might turn for enlightenment and guidance.

My mother and I often talked about this as we were wont to reminisce together on family affairs. As the fifth child I had been young enough to keep close to my parents, yet old enough to understand what was going on through the central years of their life. I have therefore been much involved in all our family affairs. When I was invited to a literary club to speak about my father, my mother encouraged me to accept the invitation. She wanted people to hear about my father from a member of our family. She also wanted the story of the life of our father and our family recorded, even if she could not bring herself to do it.

My original idea was to do just a personal memoir, dealing only with the incidents of my own immediate experience. But my husband insisted that I incorporate material from other sources as well, in order to fill the gap in the literature about Sholom Aleichem and present a book that gives a basic record of the entire life of my father. I granted the need for such a book, but, frankly, I did not feel equal to the task. He undertook to provide all the assistance I might need. His help fully warranted the listing of his name as joint author. But he would not hear of it. His argument was that it is the spirit of a book that makes it, and the spirit of this one is all mine. So, all I can do is to thank him here for his consistent help and encouragement, both of which were indispensable to the completion of this book.

In Warsaw (then part of Russia), in 1910, my sister Tissa and I attended a performance of one of my father's plays in Russian. We had seats in the loge and someone reported our presence to the director of the theater. Before the lights were dimmed for the last act the director appeared on stage, announced to the public that two daughters of Sholom Aleichem were in the audience, and pointed to our loge. There was tremendous applause and many people in the audience rose to have a better view of us. Tissa and I stood up to take a bow.

Back home with my parents in Badenweiler, Germany, I told my father what had happened to Tissa and me at his play in Warsaw. This amused him greatly; he beamed with delight. He had me repeat the story to guests visiting us: "Tell them, Maroussia, how you were applauded in Warsaw."

He was happy to have some of his glory radiate upon his children. He wanted members of his family involved in his literary life. He was elated when my brother Misha attempted to translate his stories into Russian. I like to think that if he knew about this effort he would be pleased, and call to my mother: "Olga, look, Maroussia has written a book about me."

New York, April 1967

I
Fragments of Memory

ONCE I HAPPENED to be walking down a long curving corridor. For no reason, it occurred to me to stop and look back. I could see for some distance in clear light, but then the corridor began to dim, and finally it faded into complete darkness. The farthest reaches lay beyond my sight. I often wonder if our memory does not function in the same way. We peer into our past until we reach a point where the light of recollection vanishes, and we are no longer certain whether what we remember is actual experience or imagined experience based on something repeated over and over again in our presence.

Let me begin, then, with a few clear, lighted memories of Sholom Aleichem as father of a family.

I was sleeping on a small iron bed in a corner of my parents' bedroom, since my own room had been given over to a new baby—my brother Numa—and his nurse. On this particular night I woke up, my eyes peering into the darkness. After a while I saw my father getting out of bed, putting on his dressing gown, and lighting a candle. He noticed my head raised from the pillow and whispered, "*Spi! Spi!*" (Sleep!). I closed my eyes, trying to obey him, but half-opened them again and saw him, candle in hand, going to his study. I knew what he would do there—he would stand and write.

My father never wrote seated at his desk. He used it only when correcting a manuscript or pasting together the tiny pages of the notebook he used for his original writing. For this, the more creative work, he stood at a contraption which he had designed himself and had a carpenter build. It resembled a pulpit and was tall enough to rest his elbows on, with a place for the candlestick on the top. He would stand there for hours, so absorbed that he would hardly be aware of the dawn of a new day or of the tumult around him when the children were getting up and dressing, some being sent off to school, others being kept from squabbling. When we banged away at the piano in the living room next to his study, or even when we went into his room and played right there, he never seemed disturbed, and he went on writing.

Now, in the dead of night, probably to avoid disturbing the household by the sound of the door closing, my father left it open a little, and it swung farther out by itself. I could see him walking to his writing stand. The light of his candle quivered, casting a shadow on the side wall and ceiling. He seemed to me taller than in the daytime; his blue eyes were shining with thought, his very thin penpoint swiftly dotting the small pages of his notebook. From time to time he put the pen in its inkwell and rubbed his hands, for it was winter and the fire in the stove had been out for some hours. Then again his hand moved swiftly over the pages of the notebook; he paused to read over what he had written, obviously enjoying it, raising his eyebrows as though in surprise at what he had just put down, barely suppressing a laugh so that he would not wake up his family.

What a strange Papulia! I thought. He gets up in the middle of the night, stands writing by the light of a candle, and has a good time all by himself.

Many years, almost half a century, later, after the Nazis destroyed my father's world and many of his people, and much of the rest of the world as well, I met escapees from ghettos and survivors from labor camps who told me that my father's stories, miraculously retained in captivity and held on to by them as their most precious possessions, were a source of solace, cheer and courage in their misery. One expression that many of them used—that Sholom Aleichem had been the only "ray of light" in their darkest hours—particularly touched my heart. I thought then of my father standing at his wooden contraption, writing by candlelight. Rays from that light brightened the road for many walking in darkness all those years.

Another indelible memory concerns the daily ritual during that early time when I was too young to go to school and my father was still a businessman spending part of every day at the *birzha* (bourse or stock market).

Around noon, he would emerge from his study, through with creative writing for the day. The revising and rewriting would be done later. He always seemed relaxed, in spite of having been on his feet since before dawn, but appeared somewhat distracted too, as though he had been on a long journey to a distant land. Psychologically he had been away; during those hours of writing he lived in another world, seeing, hearing, talking with the characters in his stories. He would begin to talk with my mother, and this helped him make the transition back to the everyday realities he was soon to face.

He would tell her how the writing had gone that morning, and usually the report was favorable—it had flowed easily and freshly, like clear water from a spring. Some days, when he had difficulties, the wrinkles on his face seemed to be cut deeper, and there were shades of fatigue around his eyes. My mother, the guardian angel over every phase of his life, including his writing, would ask him what it was he was trying to write, and was it some character in the story who was giving him trouble? She never asked for specific details, knowing he would read the story aloud to all of us when it was finished.

It was time then for my father to wash, dress and have his breakfast. After that he prepared to leave for the *birzha*. I still have a clear image of the scene at the door. I watch him struggling with his boots, meanwhile smiling at me and asking me questions: "Did you make up with your brother Misha, or are you still enemies?" I answering quickly, "Enemies," and he, laughing, "Then, Musa, what do you think of the Dreyfus affair?"—an important topic in our house then— "Are you for Dreyfus or against him?" "Against Dreyfus," I reply, and he laughs again.

Then I ask him, "When will you be back, Papulia?"

"For dinner, I hope." At this point there comes a pat on my head and a whisper in my ear, "It's time for your haircut," which was his secret with me. (He had a penchant for taking the younger children to the barber and having their hair cut, something my mother did not approve of, for it made the girls look like boys.) I run to the mirror to look at my hair, exactly the color of his, but disheveled, as I have not combed it yet. Then back to the door for one last goodbye.

My father was a man of striking appearance. He was very meticulous about his dress and appearance. At that time, in the nineties, he wore his wavy blond hair long, touching his shoulders. After the turn of the century it was trimmed shorter but still long enough to reach the back of his neck. From behind pince-nez his blue eyes gleamed with warmth and kindness. Even in his youth there were deep lines on each side of his mouth, perhaps from smiling so much. His smile had a great variety of expressions and meanings. There was the full round smile, the real one, when he was happy about something, or for someone. There was the wry smile, when he felt compassion, or angry pity, as for instance when he saw an animal hurt or abused. He had a smile, too, for when we misbehaved—a cross between annoyance and amusement. Then he would admonish but never punish us, perhaps because he remembered that he had done things as bad or worse in his own childhood, or because he couldn't help seeing the humor in our behavior. My father's smile revealed strong, perfect teeth, which served him well to his last day. When he wore his hair long, his face was completely shaven; later, when his hair was shorter, he grew a mustache, always kept elegantly trimmed, and a small goatee.

He liked to have a frequent change of dress—not necessarily requiring many different suits, for even a change of vest would do. Vests were independent garments then, unrelated in color and cloth to coat and trousers. My father had an assortment of them, of velvet, silk, plaid. But sometimes even a set of new buttons for a vest would satisfy his craving for variety. Or it could be a new cravat or tiepin or chain for his watch. He had several watch chains, some of white gold, thin and delicate, and most of them too fragile for his massive gold watch. He would let us handle one, saying, "Just imagine how skillful the hands must be to produce such delicate work!" In a few months the chain would suddenly appear around the neck of one of the girls—a birthday present. Then he would have a new chain to show us, not perhaps as delicate as the last one, but with an even more unusual design. He loved fine work; he loved, too, to share all pleasant objects and thoughts with his children.

At the same time he disliked ostentation in any form, and one of his special smiles would appear whenever he saw a *nouveau riche* flaunting wealth, like the wife who asked her husband, in the presence of her friends, "What time is it on your gold watch?" Once when we were out for a walk, a stranger came over and asked for the time. My father slowly took his watch out of his vest pocket. With a perfectly serious face, he said to the stranger, "On my gold watch it's three o'clock." We had to bite our lips to keep from laughing until the man was far enough away not to hear us.

"This is Number Five," my father would say when introducing me to guests visiting us for the first time. Invariably this introduction produced laughter, and I readily joined in the fun.

But what was so funny about being Number Five? Was it funnier than being Number Four or Number Three? I did not ponder too much over this—the fact was that none of the other children was introduced by number, and this gave me a distinction I enjoyed.

I remember another distinction, however, that was not at all pleasing. This lay only in my own mind, but for the mind of a child it was a heavy stone. Fortunately (or was it unfortunately?) no one ever mentioned this subject except my maternal grandmother, whom we called Babushka, and she spoke of it only at my prodding. Painful as it was, I kept asking her to talk about it, the way one keeps scratching a sore. It was about how poor our family became just before I was born.

Our talk would usually take place in Babushka's bedroom when she was making her morning preparations for the day. Babushka was always groomed as though for a social occasion. Even on first rising, she would emerge from her room wearing not a peignoir, as was the style then, but fully dressed. After the morning chores of running her daughter's household, she would return to her room to put on the finishing touches.

I used to love watching her fix her hair. After pulling back her own short gray hair and tying it up in a bun, she carefully combed and brushed her reddish wig and put it on. Her face would harden slightly. She was always a little angry about having given in to the ancient Jewish custom—still in practice today among the ultra-orthodox—of cutting off the hair of a bride at the marriage ceremony so that she should have her head covered with a *sheitl* (wig), or a shawl for the rest of her life. At the time of her first marriage, Babushka had refused to let anyone cut her hair. But on her second marriage, to my Grandfather Elimelech, though he himself did not care, her *bratova*— a word she coined for her sister-in-law from the Russian *brat* (brother) —raised a terrible rumpus, since she had been forced to cut *her* hair when she was married. So they clipped Babushka's beautiful long thick black braids, and it was like a knife cutting into her heart. "The *bratova*," she would cry, as I listened to the story for perhaps the fiftieth time, "the *bratova* was a mean, jealous cat!"

In this mood, she was easily led to talk about the matter that tormented me constantly.

"And then, Babushka, what happened then?"

"And then? Nothing happened then. All went well with us, very well. Your grandfather was a very wealthy man and we lived like lords of the manor." A smile would come over her face. "I sent word to our coachman and he had a carriage ready in a jiffy. If I wanted a new dress, we ordered the silk from Boguslav and the seamstress came to our estate and made it right there. Then, when your grandfather died, he left us all a great fortune. When we moved to Kiev later, we had money for everything—everything we could want. We were as rich as the Brodskys."

"Then, Babushka, and then?" I worried the sore spot.

Her smile disappeared. "Then came the disaster, the misfortune, and we lost everything! All the money was gone. All of it! And we became poor, very poor."

"When, Babushka, when did this happen?" I asked.

"When? You know when—I've told you many times. It happened just before you were born."

There it was.

"From that time on, your mother was to worry every minute about money, and your father . . ." Babushka paused abruptly, as she always did at that point. "Well, never mind about your father."

Because Babuska always coupled the impoverishment of our family with my arrival into the world, I could never regard the two events as merely coincidental. I came to believe in my deepest heart that I had brought the ill luck to the family. Each telling of the story drove my guilt in deeper, and for years I was sensitive about our financial circumstances. Babushka's thinly repressed references to my father only added to the guilt and made it more painful. In some mysterious way, Papulia was even more of a victim of my arrival than the rest, though my mishap had harmed us all. Could Papulia love me in spite of what I had brought about? How could he?

I am in the living room. It is dark, for the twilight has come, and Babushka has neglected to light the lamps. One of my sisters cries out, "Papulia's coming!" I close my eyes and imagine my father opening the front door with his key, snow on his fur hat and collar; he lifts me up and kisses me, I feel the brush of his frozen mustache . . .

But I know in advance what will really happen. All the other children will crowd around him at once. My sister Tissa, the oldest, will reach him first. Lyala and Emma, both bigger and stronger than I, will get ahead of me, and my older brother, Misha—he will simply push me aside, as he always does. I will come up at the end, and then my father will notice me and say, "Ah, Musa . . ."

So I bite my nails in the darkening living room and dream of a miracle, some miracle in which I restore the finances of the family to the wonderful state Babushka describes as existing before I was born, before I became Number Five.

One strange memory has never left me. It has to do with birthdays —and the birthday of a new century. I remember entering my father's study one evening. The kerosene lamp was lit, its light shining through the colored glass shade. My mother and father were both there, she at his desk writing something on a piece of paper, and he standing behind her, looking over her shoulder. This was an unusual sight; I was used to seeing those positions reversed. After my mother had written several lines, she gave the pen to my father and stood up; he sat down and wrote something below her lines. I edged closer, but all I could read was the number 1900. The rest of it, my father's beautiful handwriting contrasting with the large scrawl of my mother, was too hard to make out. My father carefully folded the paper over and rolled it up until it was as small as possible. Then he put it inside an oval wooden container that looked like a small egg.

"Olga," he said to my mother, "do you realize that we are now entering the twentieth century?"

I did not understand what that meant but assumed it must be something very good, for the customary strain on my mother's face was gone, and the sadness around her eyes had changed to joyful vivacity. She was fully relaxed as she looked lovingly at my father. She sat down and took me on her lap. I touched the white lace collar of her dress; she gently took my hand and held it. Her hair, combed back high, seemed darker, and from where I sat it looked like a crown on top of her head. She put me down and stood up, my father smiled, and together they crossed the study. My mother was stout, but tall and straight, and I loved to watch her walk. She had a way of collecting the folds of her skirt in her hand so that they would not interfere with her steps. I watched her now, holding the skirt of her blue dress in one hand and the tiny wooden egg with its mysterious message in the other, as she and my father left the room.

Whatever was written on that piece of paper, it must have had deep meaning for my mother, who kept the little wooden egg always among her most precious personal effects. It did not turn up, however, after her death, and will be a mystery forever. Did they write their expectations for the new century? Or their personal visions, wishes, hopes? Or was it some second sealing of happiness between husband and wife?

In our family the ritual of the birthday was never stinted. The Russians have a word for a birthday person—*imeninik* (birthday boy), or if it is a girl, *imeninitza*. He or she is to be king or queen for that day, and no one is to scold or punish or in any way cross the birthday person. My father extended the reign of this king or queen for two more days. One could hear such remarks as "Come here, tomorrow's birthday girl," or "Be careful, yesterday's birthday girl," or "How could you talk to her like that, she is the *imeninitza!*"

The birthday proper began early in the morning. On the dining-room table were spread the gifts from all the members of the family. Then, when everyone had gathered, the king or queen received from my father as many slaps on the bottom as the years he or she was old, with an extra hard one added as advance payment for the coming year. This was the coronation and brought much laughter. In the afternoon there was a children's party, and in the evening a party for the adult friends and relatives who came especially to celebrate the birthday.

My mother, busy as she was with her dental practice, with supervision of the household (made more difficult since Babushka was in actual charge), and with her involvement in my father's literary affairs, was always very careful to see that all birthdays were thoroughly celebrated. She bought all the presents herself, since she was the one who really knew what each child needed. But it was my father who stage-managed the affair, wrapping each gift in special paper with an inscription, sometimes even a drawing of a flower, and laying the presents out in the order in which they were to be given.

On the night before one of my birthdays, when I was still sleeping on the small bed in my parents' room, I remember being very excited and unable to go to sleep. I overheard my parents, who did not know I was awake, saying something about my birthday. Most of the conversation was indistinct, but I heard my father say quite clearly, "But, Olga, how could you buy her only one pencil box from everybody? Surely you must have something more for her?" Then the words became indistinct, and after a while I fell asleep.

The next morning I rushed to the dining room. The table was elaborately arranged, as on all birthdays, with many gifts, the individual packages finely wrapped and inscribed. I opened the first: it was a pen from my mother; the second was a pencil from my brother, the third an eraser from one sister, the fourth a penholder from another sister, and so on, to the last package containing the empty pencil box from my father. Papulia gave me my slaps and everyone laughed gaily. I was quite satisfied.

Another very different birthday comes back to me—my last in Russia. The times were terrifying—strikes, revolutions, pogroms, so that people avoided going out into the street. On that morning, the presents were on the table as usual, but no guests came to the party in the afternoon, not even my cousins, Natasha's children, who had come unfailingly for years to every birthday in the family, as we had gone to theirs. It was a sad and depressing afternoon, but the evening started out even worse. No one showed up, not even the close relatives and devoted friends. The lights were kept very low in order not to attract the attention of hoodlums lurking in the streets. We tried to cheer each other up by the thought that at least we were all safely indoors together, and were just resigning ourselves to no visits from anyone when there was a sudden ring at the door. Who could it be? we thought, alarmed, and then in came my mother's cousin, Avram Yampolsky, with his wife, Fanny. They even had a present for me—a book. "We remembered your birthday, dear," Avram said, "and we wouldn't miss it for anything in the world."

I have often hoped that the Yampolskys knew how happy they made me, dispelling the disappointment of the afternoon, and the sadness of the evening of my last birthday in Russia.

My father took an avid interest in all sorts of people—everyone was a possible subject and might later appear in a story. My mother was very sociable too, and loved to go out. I remember Babushka's disapproval when they went off to parties—she would withdraw to her room as if to say she refused to look after the household while her daughter went out to enjoy herself. My mother ignored these attempts at intimidation and told the nurse and maid what to do. No sooner were my parents out of the house than Babushka would emerge to take full command as usual.

There were also many parties and soirées at our house. Some of them were simple affairs, others elaborate, often with as many as seventy or eighty guests, and with celebrities to lend brilliance to the evening. There was vodka served in small crystal glasses, there were sardines and sprats from Riga, caviar in a large bowl, platters of smoked fish and meats, various cakes, and of course the inevitable samovar. We had two samovars, one made of copper for family use, and an enormous ornate silver one for special occasions.

A maid stood in the vestibule to admit the guests and take them to Mother's dental office, converted into a cloak room for the evening. The earliest soirée that I can remember was held in the cause of Zionism, then in its infancy, and distinguished by three important guests. Professor Max Emanuel Mandelshtam was a famous Russian ophthalmologist, a co-worker of Dr. Herzl's. He made a striking impression on me: his head seemed very narrow, and his face exceptionally long, an effect possibly created by his strange style of grooming. He combed his long black hair from the sides of his head to the back center, and down his neck to his shoulders, while his beard was shaved at the sides, but worn long and square from the chin. The second lion of the evening was Menahem Ousishkin, the strong man of the Zionist movement. Powerful, straight, square of stature and with a large, round, placid face, he looked to me like an immovable rock.

In a corner by himself sat a thin, spare young man with a whimsical smile and eyes that sparkled. This was Moshe Weizmann, the younger brother of the man destined to become the first president of the state of Israel.

We children were not supposed to mingle with the guests—it was not the custom then. We were to stay in our rooms, the older ones to do their homework, the younger children to go to bed. But with all the excitement we were neither sleepy nor studious. We kept our doors open so that we could hear when the program started, that is, when my father gave a resounding smack on his writing stand, brought out for the evening, and subdued the hubbub. Then came the voice of the chairman, "*Rabotai!*" ("Ladies and gentlemen" in Hebrew). This was the signal for us to sneak out of our rooms and filter quietly into the wings of the parlor.

The first speaker had started—both lectures and conversation were always in Russian. The seats were full, right to the back of the room. Little by little we advanced, to stand between the guests in the last row. Now and then one of them would pull our braids, to which we responded with suppressed laughter, attracting the attention of others nearby. My mother heard our giggling and motioned us back, but we pretended not to see her. After the speech was over, she came back and herded us to our rooms.

But we were too excited to be sleepy, and we stole into my mother's office and disarranged the rubber boots so that no two standing together matched. Then we tried to climb to the top of the heap of wraps without scattering them, which resulted in giggles and squeals of hilarity that could be heard in the parlor.

Now it was my father's turn to suppress us. But it was all he could do to keep from laughing when he saw what we were doing. He took a newspaper, folded it into the shape of a funnel, then made believe he was whipping us with it. Actually the paper barely touched us, but it made a magnificent noise. *Nafitscot,* as he called this punishment, was even more fun than the mischief that led up to it. Our laughter grew louder and louder as each of us clamored for a little more punishment. Then, without further ado, we went quietly to our rooms with no urging from my father. The symbol was much more effective than harsh treatment. We understood that we had misbehaved—but not seriously. And now enough was enough. We fell asleep to the strains of the Zionist hymn *Hatikvah,* played on the piano by composer Mark Markovich Warshavsky.

As far back as I can see along the corridor of my memory, one day stands out clear and undimmed. The year was 1896; the place was Kiev; the occasion the crowning of Nicholas II.

Though Alexander III had died two years before, and the crown prince had at once assumed the throne, the complicated ritual that would make him officially the "Absolute Ruler of all the Russias" was only now culminating in the ecclesiastical investiture of the crown at the Cathedral of St. Vladimir in the holy city of Kiev.

It was the first visit of Nicholas and his czarina to Kiev, and an occasion for much excitement and splendor. The ceremony was to take place on the exact spot on the cliff overhanging the Dnieper where Vladimir, Prince of Russia, had embraced the Christian faith and assumed imperial power. A monument to the saint still stands today, an oversized statue of a man in a cape, holding a cross as big as himself.

As I was to learn later in school—in fact, it was drummed into Jewish children in Kiev—Vladimir, in the year 998, considered many religions before deciding on Christianity. He turned down Islam, we were taught, because he would not go to the Arabs, and Roman Catholicism because this would have made Russia Latin. He rejected Judaism because he asked himself, "Why should I choose the religion of a people who are scattered all over the world, without a place of their own, a people hated everywhere they go?" But when he considered the Greek Orthodox faith, so the lesson went, "he did not know whether he was on earth or in heaven." The teacher invariably called upon a Jewish child to recite the section about why Vladimir did not embrace Judaism.

Eventually St. Petersburg (now Leningrad) became the seat of the czarist government and the hub of the ruling aristocracy. Moscow continued to harbor the feudal lords and the merchants. But Kiev remained the holy city, city of churches, and guardian of the Russian soul. Always patriotic, proud of its past, and imbued with the Slav mystique, it was aroused to heights of fervor on that day in 1896 as it waited for the arrival of its new, handsome rulers. The citizens had been agog for weeks; now, as the time drew near for the royal train to pull up at the station, they lined the streets, they crowded together on the sidewalks, they filled the balconies and rooftops.

The Jews of Kiev, too, were carried away by the general holiday spirit. I remember the Sabbath clothes, the festive atmosphere, though certainly they must have felt a little uneasy. Experience over the centuries had taught them never to beg for a new king—he might be worse than the old. They had not prayed for the end of Czar Alexander, in spite of his cruel persecution of his Jewish subjects. Fate had brought his son to the throne, and they could only hope that God had given the son a better heart.

Jews had lived in Kiev long before the Russians came there and had built it up into an important trading center. But now only a few Jews had a legal right to reside in the city proper—rich merchants who could afford the high residence fee, or professionals, necessarily few in number, since admission of Jews to academic institutions was highly restricted. All the rest had to live on the outskirts, in the ghettos of Podol and Dimiyevka. If a Jew without a residence right was caught spending the night in the city proper, he was taken to jail and then forced to walk under military convoy back to his native place, however far away.

Treated like stepchildren, limited to the outer fringes, to the poorest and most overpopulated provinces of Russia, excluded from civil service, forbidden to engage in agriculture, and with very few exceptions kept out of schools, harassed by officials both civil and religious, the Russian Jews still loved their fatherland, and the Czar of all the Russias was, for better or worse, their czar. On the day of the coronation they were out in full force to welcome Nicholas II and his czarina.

They had, furthermore, contributed large sums of money to a community project for refurbishing that part of the city along which the royal pair would ride. One of these wealthy Jews, a Mr. Margolin, had outdone everyone else. Entirely at his own expense he had decorated the streets with wreaths and bright paper lanterns of various colors, making a glamorous effect that had never been seen before in those parts. The illumination was very impressive; the story went that the czar asked the governor who was responsible for it. The governor answered, "the Jew Margolin," and the czar turned his face away.

I was only four, but I remember clearly standing with my family on the top step of the entrance to the First Imperial Gymnasium. My father lifted me above his head so that I could see everything. Over me were the paper lanterns of fantastic colors; below, the milling crowd of men, women and children. The lanterns were swirling in the wind. Occasionally one of the candles in the center would get thrown to one side and the paper would go up in flames, causing a great commotion among the people below. The wire frames of the burned lanterns went on swinging in the air, looking like naked men at a masquerade. I could see in the distance the vanguard of the parade. It seemed to be frozen in a haze, like a picture in a book.

But the real thrill was yet to come. My father had told me that when the royal carriage passed our steps, the czarina would throw kisses to me. The carriage came closer—now it was going by—and it was true! The czarina was throwing kisses to me, I saw it with my own eyes, it seemed to me that she was looking only at me. My father had told me that she would, and this placed it beyond any doubt.

I was happy to be singled out for such glory, and my happiness grew each time my father repeated the story to members of the family or to guests. "Well, Musa," he would say, "tell them how the czarina threw kisses at you." I believed it implicitly until I started to go to school, when it dawned on me that perhaps other girls had been told the same thing by their fathers.

But perhaps not. This was a special gift of my father's, part of the pattern he followed, first with his own children and then with his grandchildren. In the summertime, for instance, when we were in the country, he would take us for long walks, and on the way would endow us with ravishing gifts. To my oldest sister he gave one half of the pine forest. Another sister received the pond with all the rowboats in it. The meadow as far as the eye could see went to my older brother. "To you, Musa," he would say, "I give all the cherry trees. Every one you come upon is yours."

I do not know how the older children regarded their legacies—I did not hear them laugh. As for the younger ones, we definitely accepted the gifts in good faith, gleefully reporting our acquisitions to my mother, or more often to Babushka, since my mother was almost always preoccupied. Babushka would say nothing, although one could see she did not approve of such nonsense. But was there anything that she ever approved of?

I certainly knew then, as I know now, that my father was not poking fun at us, either with the kisses of the czarina or the beauties of the countryside. It was not in his nature to ridicule anyone he dealt with, much less his own children whom he loved as part of himself. These were fairy tales that he created and acted out for his own enjoyment as well as for ours.

II
The Worlds My Father
Came From

My FATHER never spoke directly to us about his childhood. His silence was significant, for usually he loved to tell his children stories, and we, who loved him and were absorbed by his tales, would have found the story of his childhood the most engrossing story of them all. It never occurred to us to ask him about his past; but, although we lacked direct information, even when we were small children the stray remarks and references overheard from the adults' conversations combined to form some definite impressions.

Then, too, when we were older, we would attend my father's regular readings of his freshly written stories to the entire family—that is, except for Babushka, who was consistently absent. A number of these stories dealt with children whose background was as unfamiliar to us then as it would be to children today. At the time we were too absorbed in the stories to relate some of the events and environments described to my father's own life, as we did later on.

It was only when he began writing his autobiography, *From the Fair,* which he dedicated to his children, that we first got a rounded view of his childhood and youth. Then half-forgotten remarks and bits of conversation began to take on meaning, and we asked our mother to tell us in greater detail whatever she knew about some of the episodes and incidents in *From the Fair.* So we came to see that his silence had concealed many unhappy memories. Perhaps he did not describe them because he preferred to show his children the brighter side of life—or perhaps because he himself wanted to forget and live in the happier present. But I think that his work draws much of its strength from his childhood.

In 1895, when he was only thirty-six, my father was already thinking about writing his autobiography. An autobiography, he believed, should present a panorama of the times in which a man lived and of the people around him, rather than a record of personal trivia. The best book was life itself, he wrote to a friend, and the best novel the real life of a man; and, since his own life had been rich in episodes and in people of all types, he had decided to write his story. He made several attempts that were frustrated by lack of financial and professional backing, and did not succeed finally until 1915—a year before he died—in New York, when he committed himself to write his autobiography in weekly installments for a daily newspaper. Some of these went to *The Day* and others, later, to *The Warheit*. Sadly, he only lived to record his early years.

To keep to his original idea of presenting a panorama of his times and to feel free to write objectively about himself, he framed his autobiography in the third person, with himself as a character in a novel. He chose the title *From the Fair* because, he said, people tend to compare their lives to whatever is closest to their immediate experience and in accordance with their own concepts. He gave the simile of the carpenter who observed that man was like a carpenter: a carpenter lives and lives and then dies—so also does a man. He himself considered that his life had been like a fair, full of sights and sounds and encounters with many different kinds of people and ideas and values. At the fair, so much is going on that a man is kept busy just absorbing everything—the buying, the selling, the conversations, the events. Only after one leaves can one sort out what has happened and try to find its meaning. So he called the story of his life *From the Fair*.

The world into which my father was born was the world of the proverbial poverty-stricken Jewish small town in Russia. Such a town was often called a *shtetl* (townlet) but my father coined a special word to describe life in such townlets. *Kasrilevka,* he named this world, from the word *kasriel,* meaning a man who is poor but proud, a man who can laugh at his own misfortunes and keep his self-respect. This was one level of Jewish life in Russia. But small-town life was not typical of the whole Russian-Jewish community. In big cities such as Kiev and Odessa there were middle-class Jews as well as poor Jews, and some Jews who were extremely rich and influential—like Margolin of coronation fame. My father concocted the name *Yehupetz* for this city world. Finally there was a third world, the world of the large estates, some owned as well as operated by Jews, others under lease to absentee landlords. Here, in small islands of affluence, Jews enjoyed the ease and comforts of the feudal age. Such sunny spots were soon to be blanked out by new czarist restrictions on the Jewish community, but in my father's youth they were still in existence.

Sholom Aleichem at one time or another lived in all three of these worlds. He spent his childhood in Kasrilevka, several happy years of early manhood on a landed estate, and finally he settled in Yehupetz. Later he lived in two additional worlds—continental Europe and the United States—but his earlier environments were the most formative.

My father was born Sholom Rabinowitz (Sholom Aleichem was a pen name) on March 2, 1859, in Pereyaslav, a town in the Ukraine. It was a medium, in-between sort of town, bigger than a Kasrilevka, much smaller than a Yehupetz, its economy and culture a mixture of both. But he did not live in Pereyaslav for long; his father, Nahum Rabinowitz, took the whole family to a very small town called Woronko when Sholom Aleichem was still an infant.

Woronko was the prototype of the Kasrilevka of my father's stories in every respect, materially and spiritually. The Jews of Woronko were poor because the general economy of the region, based on a primitive agriculture, was poor. Moreover, Jews could not, under czarist laws, seek opportunities elsewhere or hope to advance through education. Only very few escaped their rigidly circumscribed environment. The rest were left to ply petty trades: small shopkeeping, simple handicrafts and the like. Even these meager sources of livelihood were drying up with the decline of the economy and overpopulation. No one occupation provided an adequate living—many people engaged in several at once. Grandfather Nahum "acted as agent for land-lease properties, supplied sugar mills with beets, ran the rural post office, traded in wheat, handled freight on barges on the Dnieper River, cut lumber, fattened oxen for the market. But his real living was made in his dry-goods store. The term 'dry goods' meant also, in this case, groceries, hay, oats, home remedies, even hardware." The store, however, was run not by Grandfather Nahum, but by my father's mother, Haya Esther: "A very capable woman, quick at work and terribly strict with her children, of whom there were quite a few, over a dozen, all ages, sizes and complexions—dark-haired, flaxen-haired, and saffron yellow. . . ."

Even in Woronko, small as it was, there were gradations of poverty and of social status. Grandfather Nahum was on the top of the heap. His prestige was based not so much on his comparatively comfortable income as on his reputation for learning. As in other Kasrilevkas, it was erudition and not wealth that counted.

My father had happy memories of Woronko, where he lived until he was eleven or twelve, and he always spoke warmly of it. When a close friend, the Hebrew writer J. H. Ravnitzky, asked him in 1903 for some biographical data, my father wrote:

"In minuscule Woronko, I spent my best, my golden years, the good silly years of childhood. In that tiny place, my father was the aristocrat, the rich man, the first president of all communal organizations. He was Reb Nahum Vevik's." (The title "Reb" or "Rav" meant master in learning, and was used before the name as Mr. is now. "Vevik's" meant "son of Vevik." Vevik was the first name of Grandfather Nahum's father; in small towns they called a person by his first name and his father's first name, rather than by the family name.)

The letter continues: "And we, as Reb Nahum Vevik's children, were naturally no commoners, either. Saturday nights we had open house for the entire town for the observance of the Departure of the Sabbath. On the eve of every holy day, the people of Woronko came first to us for the blessing consecrating the festival. All the news of the world reached us first and spread to the rest of the town from our house. For a bit of socializing over a glass of wine, they came to us. For stories about the Rabbi (Hasidic), to our house. For political discussions, to our house. Virtually everything centered around our house. And we, Nahum Vevik's children, were regarded with due respect, and guided along the straight and narrow, and instructed in Judaism by the very best teacher; and we were truly devout."

Grandfather Nahum was a recognized Talmudic scholar. He was a pious, devout Jew, a devotee of the famous Hasidic Rabbi of Talna. Yet he had an open mind about worldly and scientific knowledge and about the secular literature that the growing enlightenment had brought to the larger cities but which was still anathema to the small-town Jewish communities. The first rays of light had begun to penetrate the walls of medievalism separating the small Jewish towns from the modern age. Reb Nahum Vevik's was ready for them. He delved, for instance, into the Scriptures, particularly the books of the Prophets, which were still regarded by the Talmudists as light reading, small challenge to one's intellect and less germane to the issues of the day than the Talmud. Unlike other scholars, he read the secular Hebrew literature just beginning to emerge, such as the first modern novel in Hebrew, Abraham Mapu's *Love of Zion*. He even read the rebel writers of the time, those who derided the supremacy of religion in Jewish life and demanded modernization of the culture. He was known to hobnob with the nonconformists and radicals of Woronko. His house was perhaps the only place where orthodox and modern met.

Unfortunately for Grandfather Nahum and his family, the grace and glory of living in Woronko had to come to an end. Sholom was barely twelve when their fortunes took a steep fall. The open-house Saturday nights were discontinued. Few guests other than relatives now turned up on the eve of holy days. Grandfather Nahum became taciturn and dispirited, keeping to himself or closeted with his brother Pinny. Woronko watched the sad transformation. Then the story was out: Grandfather Nahum had been victimized in several ways by his business partner and friend. It was a matter of real-estate enterprises, and the swindler had, among other things, renewed leases in his own name only, on property that he and his partner held in common, so that Grandfather Nahum lost an important source of income. All in all, he was financially ruined.

Woronko was outraged. Some declared that the malefactor should be brought before the Rabbi. But would such a rascal respond to the Rabbi's summons? Others urged Grandfather Nahum to take his partner to court: such a crook would rot in prison for twenty-five years for what he had done. But Grandfather Nahum shrugged off such talk. Prison . . . twenty-five years . . . he was not the man to do such a thing to anyone. He had been too trusting; he had been gulled. Now there was nothing else but to leave Woronko and return to Pereyaslav. Change your place, and you change your luck. The place was changed soon after, but the luck did not improve.

Grandfather Nahum with his wife, Haya Esther, and his mother, Minde, moved back to Pereyaslav to start a new life, leaving the children to board with a family in Woronko until sent for at the end of the school semester. When the children arrived in Pereyaslav they were shocked to find their parents running an inn. It was a disturbing sight to see their father taking in guests for money, their mother cooking for strangers, their Grandmother Minde serving them. They were further distressed by the general atmosphere of tension in the house.

There was no exuberant welcome; their mother and father seemed preoccupied and in low spirits. No sooner was the initial greeting over than their father examined the boys in their school subjects. Their mother returned hurriedly to the kitchen to prepare the skimpiest meal they had ever eaten: gruel and beans, with a portion of stale bread doled out to each as if bread were a precious delicacy. When the meal was over, what was left of the bread was locked in a closet. Such a miserable thing had never happened in Woronko.

What little they saw of their new home before being sent to bed was equally discouraging. There was a wide courtyard with a long row of stables for horses and wagons—all empty; a sprawling house with many large rooms, most of them with two or more beds for guests with limited means and a few with one bed for the more prosperous. But again—these rooms were all vacant. The furniture from their Woronko house was squeezed into one living room. The cabinet which had held so much silver and glass in Woronko was empty, except for the candlesticks and the menorah. The silverware had been pawned, never to be redeemed.

After this quick tour of their new home, they were told to say their prayers; then they all went to bed in one large, gloomy bare room on straw pallets on the floor.

Adjustment to the new circumstances was painful and arduous, but Grandfather Nahum accepted as fate his precarious position as innkeeper in competition with bigger, more elaborately furnished establishments and more experienced and aggressive managers. One of his main competitors was right across the road, Yasnogradsky's inn, which was always full—while his remained camparatively empty. Haya Esther carried without complaint the dual burden of a horde of children and the chores of running an inn, with only her mother-in-law to help her.

The children went to school and kept up their studies, particularly Sholom, the ablest of them, and in time they made new friends. Some of the local intellectuals found Nahum Rabinowitz a congenial soul, and made his inn their favorite meeting place. On a holy day, the relatives—and there were many in Pereyaslav—gathered there. When Sholom's bar mitzvah came around, it was celebrated on a scale befitting a son of Nahum Vevik's.

As he delivered his eloquent and learned sermon my father was able to notice the scene:

"Everyone seemed to be in high spirits, their faces gleeful. But most exhilarating of all was the expression on the face of Uncle Pinny, who sat in the place of honor next to the father of the bar mitzvah. Yet there was on his face an ironic smile, too, as if he were thinking, 'Yes, he knows a lot, the little devil, but does he say his daily prayers? Does he observe the Sabbath fully?' There were no reservations on the blissful face of the father of the bar mitzvah. He glowed with pleasure. One could see that no happier man lived. He held his head high, his lips moved as though repeating every word of his son's discourse, his proud glance swept over the other worshipers, then to his brother Pinny, then to his son's teacher, to the bar mitzvah himself, and rested on the mother of the bar mitzvah.

"And she, the mother, tiny Haya Esther, stood unnoticed, respectfully tucked aside among the other women in the gallery of the synagogue, her head covered with her silk Sabbath shawl, enraptured, silent, sighing softly, cracking her knuckles, and two glistening tears reflected in the sunlight like pearls rolling down her happy face—a face young and white but already lined with wrinkles. What were those tears? Joy? Pride? Happiness? Or hardship and weariness? Perhaps she already knew in her mother's heart that her young bar-mitzvah son, whose voice was now ringing so sonorously, would very soon be saying Kaddish for her soul. Who can tell why a mother weeps?"

In Pereyaslav that summer there was much weeping. An epidemic of cholera was taking young and old. Caught without any medical service to speak of (there was no hospital, nursing as a profession did not exist, and there were only a few doctors and some *feldshers*—practical healers who had picked up the rudiments of medical care by assisting doctors), the townspeople fought the plague as well as they could. They subdivided the town into districts, each district organizing its own group of volunteer "masseurs" (the accepted remedy in those days was to massage the cholera patient with ointment).

Grandfather Nahum joined these volunteers. Each evening after he returned from a long day of service, he told his family about who had been rubbed that day, who was improving, who had been consigned to the mercy of the Almighty. The family would listen, frightened. Grandmother Haya Esther would look from one child to the other as though she were counting them, then to her husband, and then said, as if thinking aloud, "If only he will not bring the cholera here!" Grandfather Nahum assured her that cholera was not the sort of disease one carried from place to place. It was a matter of fate. He who was doomed was smitten in his own house.

Whether he did bring it in or whether Haya Esther was doomed, the terrible disease struck her—and not without sending her an omen. One night she dreamed she had lighted candles for the Sabbath eve and that Sarah Fruma, a neighbor who had died of cholera the week before, appeared and blew out the candles. The next morning she told the dream to Minde, who laughed it off as meaning nothing. But both women had turned pale as ghosts. Later that day, Haya Esther took to her bed and asked for a mirror. She looked at herself in the mirror, then called to Minde to come and examine her nails. Minde assured her that her nails were normal, but quietly and immediately enlisted all possible forces to keep the angel of death from their door.

She sent some of the children to look for their father on his rounds of massaging. She put kettles of water to boil and sent for the best doctor in town, a Pole, and also for the *feldsher*. True, the latter did not know much, but he was a Jew and you could at least talk to him.

When Haya Esther's condition grew critical, Minde collected all the children—from the eldest, a married man growing a beard, to the littlest girl barely a year old—and lined them up in the hall outside the sickroom. When the doctor emerged from the room, Minde dropped on her knees, kissed his hand and cried, "Look my dear sir, please look, my dear doctor, at how many poor little worms, how many orphans my daughter-in-law would leave behind her if she were, God forbid, to die. Take pity on them, please, Doctor, take pity on these pitiful worms and save her life." The doctor was visibly moved. He threw up his arms in despair. What more could he do? He had already done everything possible. "Don't beg me," he said, pointing to the ceiling. "Beg Him."

Minde had already done that, arranging for old Jews in the synagogue to recite psalms day and night in vigil prayers for her daughter-in-law. She had been there herself, had opened the sacred ark, kissed the Torahs, crying out to God in heaven to spare Haya Esther's life. She had gone to the cemetery and prostrated herself across the graves of her forebears, alerting them to the dreadful danger, demanding their intercession with the All-merciful. Such a good wife, she told them, must not leave Nahum a widower and the children orphans; such a saintly woman as Haya Esther must not die. "No, dear God, you are a good God. You will not let her die."

As my father wrote, ". . . nothing helped. While God is truly a good God, the tiny Haya Esther did not rise from her bed. She died. It was on a Sabbath morning when the Jews were still praying . . ."

Grandfather Nahum wept. It was the first time the children had ever seen their father cry; they began to wail. Minde reproved God, asking Him why He had not taken her instead of a young twig, the mother of—may no evil eye harm them—so many pitiable little wretches.

Haya Esther had been a frail, slight woman, but she had held the structure of the family and the inn together. All collapsed when she died. Grandfather Nahum despaired of going on without her. During the seven days of mourning he sat most of the time on a low stool, in his stocking feet, reading the Book of Job and sighing, "What will I do now? What can I do?"

After a week of this, his brother Pinny made a sharp reply: "What can you do? You will do as other Jews do in such circumstances. You will—God willing—remarry."

Grandfather Nahum was deeply hurt. Remarry? After Haya Esther, get married again? And his own brother telling him to do this? Who knew her better than Pinny? His voice broke and tears flowed again.

Yet it was not long before Grandfather Nahum did remarry, and he could not have done worse.

The new wife, brought from Berditchev, the large town near Pereyaslav, was a combination of the proverbial shrew and the wicked stepmother. A perennial scold, she never stopped complaining about her lot and finding fault with her stepchildren, especially after she began having her own—she was to have five. She abused her stepchildren, cursed them, beat them, begrudged them food, meager as their portions were. They were forced into chores at all hours of the day and night. She even resented the "waste" of kerosene in the lamps when they did their homework after dark. My father's description of the life they led as soon as she came into the house makes it seem like one long, dreadful nightmare. It was all the more distressing because they were totally defenseless—while their father winced at his new wife's treatment of them, he did nothing to protect them.

My father never mentioned to us, as children, details of the torment he and his brothers and sisters suffered at the hands of the stepmother. We all knew, however, that there had been a stepmother and that there had been mistreatment. Something came through to us, however indirectly, to make us even more frightened than most children of the wicked stepmother figure prominent in Russian fairy tales and folk myths, tied in with witches, the evil eye, and curses. Our story books in which a stepmother appeared were all smeared with crayon marks in violent colors. There was nothing that frightened us more than the thought that our mother might die and we would then have a step-mother. Perhaps the fact that my father never mentioned this scourge of his young years made the subject even more fearsome.

I was nine or ten years old when a package arrived from America containing a photograph of a young man with a walrus mustache. My father merely told us it was his youngest brother, Berl. But Babushka told us how and why Berl, whom she called the Redhead because of his hair, went to America. The Redhead was only sixteen years old at the time, and his sister Sophia a year or so younger, when they determined to bear the torture of their stepmother no longer. She let them go hungry, pinched Sophia black and blue, and, getting a grip on Berl's head, she beat it against the wall. Berl wanted to go to America and take his sister Sophia along. My father provided the passage and additional money to sustain them in New York until they found work and could support themselves. (Berl, Bernard Roberts in this country, became a luggage manufacturer, and his son Nathan, named for Grandfather Nahum, is now a U.S. Brigadier General, Re-tired.)

The full story of the misery of our father's childhood we learned much later, from his writing, when he read to us the installments of his autobiography before sending these off for publication in the news-paper, in the last year of his life. I was long haunted by a scene he described, when he attended school only half days; the other half, and much of the evening, he was a "puller-in" for the inn, calling upon the passing coaches and wagons to put up at their inn. He told it in the third person, as he wrote the story of his life.

"The hero of these stories remembers the days when he sat for hours on the bench at the gate, broiling in the sun in the hottest spell of summer; freezing, like a dog, in the bitter cold of winter. Wrapped in a tattered coat, wearing boots that begged to be taken to a cobbler, he rubbed one foot against the other and peered into the distance to catch sight of a covered wagon or a coach with passengers. When one finally approached, he would jump up on the bench and shout, 'Here, sirs, stop over here! Put up over here!' But as though in spite, the vehicle would rush past and stop at the other, richer inn of Reuben Yasnogradsky across the road. There, it was known, the rooms were very spacious, furnished with soft chairs and mirrors and many other things the Rabinowitz inn did not possess. That was why Yasnogradsky's inn was always jammed with 'fat' guests (those who could afford a whole room all to themselves) while Rabinowitz's inn was nearly always vacant, so deserted you might as well convert it into a doghouse. And Sholom felt terribly aggrieved. Against whom? Against God! Why had God not arranged things so that Sholom was the son of Reuben Yasnogradsky instead of a son of Nahum Rabinowitz?"

Frozen to the bone, young Sholom would creep into the house to warm up for a minute, only to be struck by a torrent of abuse and curses from the stepmother. No guests had showed up, she would scream. What the devil should she do with all the bread she had baked? And all the fish she had cooked! She might as well throw it all to the dogs. Or—she turned to the children—did they think perhaps they would be getting all that good food? The poor dears, too delicate to eat stale bread! Let them choke on it! The whole delicate brood— no evil eye, so dainty!

Then her eternal cry: "You couldn't be left, could you, with your grandfather and grandmother to sicken and waste away. No! You had to be sent here, may the devil send for you, to eat us out of house and home, may the worms eat you and gnaw away your living flesh. A contamination upon you, a dilapidation, a degeneration. . . ."

Sholom, sick and weary of the unending invective and accusations, would immediately go back outside, preferring the biting wind to the stepmother's tongue-lashing. Here he could at least have peace, here Sholom the dreamer could forget the cold and dream that perhaps God would send some guests, fine guests in fur coats and with yellow leather luggage, like the ones that stopped at the inn across the road. If God willed it, He could make it happen.

The stepmother possessed an inexhaustible supply of colorful curses which she delivered without great vehemence. They rolled off her tongue as naturally as breathing and in many interesting and diverse ways—by word or idea association, or by alliteration, or by rhyme. For example, if she were giving a child something to eat, she would say, "Eat, may the worms eat you," or serving a drink, it would be, "Drink, may leeches drink your blood." Or if shushing them, "Silence, may you be silenced forever!" There might be a rush of rhymes: ague-plague, sicken-stricken, peak-pine-and-break-your-spine.

The young Sholom conceived the idea of collecting and arranging these gems in a sort of lexicon of abuse. Here are some of the entries in his dictionary:

"Ass, alley cat; bedbug, bellyache, broomstick; diddler, dogcatcher; *fonfatch* (nasal speech); *golem;* Haman, hempseed; *kishke*-no-end (glutton); lammer, leech, licorice; *pempik* (pot belly); *pupik* (navel); *shmendrik* (worthless one); *smarkatch* (runny nose); Turkish pepper, toad, ulcer, yelper.

He entitled his lexicon "The Glib Tongue of a Stepmother." Unfamiliar with lexicography and inexperienced as a writer, the young man labored hard on the manuscript, writing and rewriting it, sometimes far into the night, especially after a day that had been fruitful in curses. One day his father saw him deeply engrossed in writing and came up behind him to see what it was. He read a few lines and then lifted a few sheets from the stack and took them to read to the stepmother. Sholom was horrified, expecting a new gust of accusations from her and a sharp rebuke, at least, from his father. Instead they both seemed to enjoy the whole thing immensely, his stepmother's laughter rising even louder than his father's. She was especially amused by an entry under *p: pupik.*

Ironically, this was my father's first literary effort. His memories of his second effort also had associations with his stepmother. In his early teens he happened to read his father's copy of *The Love of Zion.* Reading it surreptitiously—he was not supposed to read such an adult love story—he was deeply moved by it. He dissolved into tears over the suffering of the hero and fell passionately in love with the heroine, seeing her in his dreams, talking to her in the romantic words of the Song of Songs, pressing her to his heart, kissing her. Now he began writing his own novel, patterned after this one, also in Hebrew, to be called *Daughter of Zion.* He could do his writing only at night, since one half of the day he was at school and the other half he spent doing his chore at the inn. After everyone had gone to sleep he would write away for hours, using up precious kerosene.

One night, either the scratching of Sholom's pen in the stillness of the night or the beam of light escaping from under his door awakened the stepmother. She got out of bed, and in her bare feet burst into Sholom's room. Her shrieks and screams filled the house. Everyone woke up in fright; the place must be on fire. But soon her voice resounded over the house: "Kerosene oil he's burning! May he burn and roast, dear God! An ague, a plague, a cholera, a conflagration, a suffocation upon him."

When Grandfather Nahum arrived on the scene, he said nothing, only took away Sholom's manuscript and the Mapu novel. The next day, while Sholom waited for a reprimand, Grandfather Nahum showed the manuscript to one of his friends, an avid reader of Hebrew literature. The friend extolled the fine handwriting and the rhetorical Hebrew, and after he had finished it, he said, "I told you, Reb Nahum, you don't know what you've got in this boy. He'll grow up to be something, you'll see. Come here, you little devil, let me pinch your cheek!"

The reprimand never came.

A third effort at writing finally liberated Sholom from the harassment and torture of the stepmother. He was about fifteen then, and had just read a Hebrew translation of Daniel Defoe's *Robinson Crusoe*. He wrote his own version, "The Jewish Robinson Crusoe," and rather than keep it a secret he showed it to his father. Grandfather Nahum liked it so much that he showed it to his guests at the inn, and all marveled at it. "Since then," Sholom Aleichem wrote to his friend Ravnitzky, "my father looked upon me as something precious, released me from the stepmother's authority, did not permit her to beat me, to have me rock her children in their cradle, or chop raisins for wine (when we had a wine cellar), and forbade me to shine the shoes of guests, carry samovars, run errands, and other chores I used to do till then."

This change came about not without a dramatic moment. One morning, not long after the *Robinson Crusoe* incident, Grandfather Nahum was standing in prayer shawl and phylacteries, reciting his morning prayers. In the same room the stepmother was chattering away, chiding, complaining of the children's ravenous appetites, Grandfather Nahum stood at the wall unperturbed, ignoring her nagging and continuing with his prayers. Suddenly she turned on Sholom who was pacing the floor trying to learn a poem by heart for class:

"He thinks, this fine scholar, excuse the expression, that he's something special, a privileged character, too high class to do anything but eat in this house. Oh, yes, with the huge crew of servants and maids I have around to help me! Never mind, it's still not beneath the dignity of your highness, fine scholar in worn boots, to carry the samovar to a guest. Don't worry, you won't lose a single hair, not even your appetite, and it certainly won't handicap you in making a good marriage. . . ."

The "fine scholar" was ready to drop his book and go to the kitchen for the samovar, when Nahum suddenly turned from the wall, rushed toward his son, grasped his hand, and in a loud voice cried, "No, never! No! I won't have it. It must stop." For perhaps the first time, he angrily gave his wife a command: never again to order Sholom around. The other children, if she must, but not Sholom. He was not like the others. He must be allowed to study. "Once and for all," he finished, "this is the way I want it, and this is the way it's going to be."

The stepmother said nothing. And, strangely, she obeyed her husband's command without a word of protest. She did, of course, continue to make remarks about the "scholar" and to calculate out loud (but not too loud) that he was using at least a ton of paper a week and three bottles of ink a night for his fine writings. Often she forgot to fill his lamp or to prepare his breakfast, but she never again forced him to do a chore.

In all fairness to the stepmother it should be said that her life with Grandfather Nahum had turned out to be much harder than he had given her reason to expect. She had neither expected the poverty nor the number of children: six of his children had been sent off to their maternal grandparents in Boguslav when Grandfather Nahum had gone in search of a wife, and he had misrepresented himself to her as a widower with only half as many children as he actually had. He may have indeed hoped that some of the older ones would soon be on their own and that perhaps two of the girls would remain in Boguslav. But the fact was that the stepmother had hardly established herself at the inn in an already difficult routine when a covered wagon drew up to the door and delivered the other six children.

To her credit, too, she showed respect for her husband, however much she mistreated his children. She complained and she reminded him of his deceit, but she never abused or cursed him and did not interfere with his intellectual life, his studying, his conversations with his friends. In return, with the one exception of his gifted son, he gave her complete sway over the children and the household.

The stepmother looms large in my father's autobiography; her shadow lay heavily over his teens. Yet he never mentions her by name—she is simply "the stepmother"—and he never gives a hint of her personal appearance. He was to face new and more important problems as he grew older, but none as unrelievedly oppressive as those connected with her.

One day in 1909 I chanced to see this woman who had become for us children a witch. I was in Warsaw, preparing for my entrance examinations for the university. I occasionally met my father's half-brother (one of the stepmother's sons, Shloyme Rabinowitz) for lunch. On that particular noon we were strolling in the heart of the Jewish section when he stopped suddenly and pointed out a woman. "That's my mother," he said. "Your father's stepmother. Let's go over and you can meet her." We crossed the street, but before she had recognized her son I quietly slipped away. Somehow, I could not go through with it. I never mentioned this incident to my father, not even to my sister Tissa, who was living in Warsaw then. Today I have a vague image left of a nondescript little woman wrapped in shawls, with a whitish cataract on one eye.

All through the years Grandfather Nahum showed concern for his second wife. In his last letter to my father, written shortly before his death in 1888, he refers to her "crimes" against her stepchildren and implores his son to forgive her and aid her when he would be gone. The letter was written in flowery Hebrew, with Biblical allusions, particularly to Jacob commanding his son Joseph to forgive his brothers who had sold him into slavery in Egypt. He had just reached his fifty-eighth year, Grandfather Nahum wrote, the life span of his father, and he, too, would soon be gathered unto his people, though he did not know how soon. He exhorted his son to hold fast to his enlightened Jewishness, as he conceived it, and to have the faith of his fathers "engraved on the walls of his heart." Then he added:

"Our father, Jacob, may he rest in peace, before his death *commanded* his younger son, who possessed the means. But I will not, God forbid, command you, for how can a man command in a matter that is not his? But in supplication, I beg you, my dear son . . .

"A poor family will remain like foam upon the waters. For whom does it have here and what does it have? Therefore, my dear son, if your heart is so inclined, may the memory of your father be dear to you so as not to turn away your protective eye from the unfortunate family, but extend your helping hand, more or less. I know, my son, I know full well her crimes against you in the days of old, but let the love for the memory of your father cover all her sins. All this I do not command you, God forbid, but if you will be so inclined you will do it out of the kindness of your heart, and you will be deserving to raise your daughters in gladness and ease, in affluence and happiness.

"These are the last words of your father."

Sholom Aleichem kept faith with his father's request. He had always had a deep attachment to him, not only because Grandfather Nahum had been especially considerate of him, but also because he was a kindred spirit and had been the first person to recognize his son's literary inclinations and to give him encouragement in early boyhood. In the family archives there is a small leaf from a Russian calendar dated January 31, 1888, with a notation in my father's handwriting, "To be remembered," and then a note in Hebrew dated according to the Jewish calendar for that day. As is customary, the date is not written in Arabic numerals but in letters of the Hebrew alphabet, each letter possessing a numerical value. The year was 5648, given in Hebrew letters, and my father had turned the letters around so that they spelled out "Thou shalt take pity," and a parenthesis was added: "on the widow and children." The note reads:

"On Sunday, Torah Portion Truma, first day of Adar, 5648, between three and four in the morning, my father died, the crown of my glory, Menahem Nahum, son of Vevik, Rabinowitz, and was buried that same Sunday between two and three in the afternoon, here in Kiev. His pure soul ascended into the heights of heaven. His remains rest in peace in the eternal place of burial in Israel. And his memory will not pass from my heart until my last day. These are the words of his young son, who is writing this with a sorrowful soul and a broken heart. Sholom."

III
Visions and Reality

WHEN MY FATHER was fourteen years old, Grandfather Nahum registered him at the Russian district school of Pereyaslav. In those days this was not considered the right thing for a good, pious, learned Jew to do. Some of the relatives protested. While it was right and proper for a Jewish boy to learn the Russian language, arithmetic, and such subjects, since they would be needed in later life, these things could be learned at home between the periods of real study devoted to the Talmud. It was considered dangerous to expose a boy to the Christian atmosphere of cross and crucifix and Greek Orthodox priest who came to teach the pupils the catechism. Besides, what could this possibly lead to? Beyond lay the gymnasium and the university, which were closed to Jews except for a mere handful. At best, such exposure turned a young man away from Jewishness; at worst, it brought him to actual betrayal of the faith of his fathers.

But Grandfather Nahum was a firm believer in the new enlightenment and in education. Also, he knew that Sholom was in a different category from that of most Jewish boys; he needed a thorough education to realize his gifts. As to where all this exposure might lead, knowledge never handicapped anyone, and besides, there was always the Jewish Teachers' Institute at Zhitomir. There a graduate of a district school could prepare for the profession of Licensed Russian-Jewish Teacher, or for that of Certified Rabbi, called a Royal Rabbin.

The district school of Pereyaslav had a three-year course. My father did so well his first year that he was awarded a scholarship—

or at least a fragment of one. The Russian director of the school said that Sholom qualified by law to receive a full grant for excellence in his studies, but since he was a Jewish boy he could only award him a stipend of one hundred and twenty rubles. In those days, even that was a great distinction for a Jewish student. Sholom graduated at seventeen with the highest honors.

The early teens were my father's important formative years. In this period, his native gifts and inner stirrings found direction and channels. His reactions to all he had suffered, the crises and economic straits the family had known—and there had been many since his birth—shaped his views and his values, determined his attitudes toward people. Those early trials grounded to reality my father's rich fertile imagination, which was always related to details of real-life situations, rather than lost in the mists of fantasy. His tales provided for him, and later for his readers, both a momentary escape from pain and the sustaining force to survive. He was gifted with a keen, observing eye, ever on the alert for the idiosyncrasies of human appearance and manners, particularly their humorous aspects. He had the ability to mimic both speech and action. Above all, he had from his earliest years a drive toward self-expression and communication of his thoughts and feelings.

My father once wrote in a letter to the writer Ravnitzky that in his childhood his imagination was "easily fired and reached fantastic heights; houses appeared [to him] to be cities, courtyards became countries; trees were people, girls were princesses, rich men princes; grass, armies; and thorns and nettles turned into Philistines, Edom and Moab."

It is significant that of all the characters described in my father's autobiography, none is sketched with greater tenderness or admiration than his childhood playmate in Woronko, Shmoulik the Orphan, who was raised by the local Rabbi. Writing about Shmoulik half a century later in *From the Fair,* my father still marveled at that small boy's inexhaustible imagination, which, he said, enriched his own mind and widened his horizon . . . "Elements of Shmoulik's dreams" were "carried in his heart, perhaps in a different form, to this very day."

Yet from the start there was a marked difference between the two boys in their attitude toward the dream world they created. Shmoulik let his imagination fly away, losing all contact with reality, while my father's was like a kite that soars up but is always attached to something on the earth below. Shmoulik's stories ran the gamut from a strange adventure of the Rabbi and his wife to a princess in a crystal palace, to twelve robbers in the woods, to witches and ghosts and creatures that were half human, half beast.

When Sholom asked him how he knew of these things, the boy replied, "Why, silly, that's nothing! Why, I know how to pump wine from walls and draw olive oil from the ceiling."

Asked how, Shmoulik replied that these gifts, too, were nothing special, for he could also turn sand into gold, and bits of glass and pottery into diamonds and jewels. But Sholom insisted on knowing just how Shmoulik could perform these miracles.

"With cabala!" Shmoulik answered. "The Rabbi (with whom he lived) is a cabalist. Everybody knows that. He never sleeps." Cabala was the esoteric medieval Jewish cult.

"What does the Rabbi do?" Sholom asked.

"At night, when everybody's asleep, he's awake. He sits all by himself and practices cabala."

"And you see everything he does at night?"

"How could I, silly? I'm asleep."

"So how do you know he practices cabala?"

"Who doesn't know that? Even little kids know that. The Rabbi can do things nobody else can do. At his word, all the twelve wells of quicksilver open to him, and all the thirteen gardens of pure saffron, and gold and silver and diamonds and jewels appear before him, as much as there is sand on the shore, so much you almost don't want any."

"So why," Sholom asked, "do you always go hungry? Why can't the Rabbi provide a decent meal, at least for the Sabbath?"

For while Sholom accepted the dream as fact—that the Rabbi had access to riches—he wondered, logically, why the Rabbi didn't use his powers for food, at least. The question halted Shmoulik. For a moment his fantasy came down to earth, but his inventive mind quickly found the answer.

"Because," he cried, "because he *wants* to be poor! He would rather suffer in this life. He's doing penance. But you can be sure that if he wanted to, he could be richer than Korah in the Bible. He could put a thousand Rothschilds in his vest pocket. He knows how to become rich, he knows all secrets. He even knows where the treasure is hidden."

The "treasure" referred to a local legend of a Jew-hating general who had lived centuries before. This villain amassed an enormous fortune by robbing the Jews of the region of all their gold, silver and precious stones which he buried temporarily in some hillock somewhere in the countryside and never came back to reclaim.

Sometimes Shmoulik combined the treasure story with another legend—that of the two magic stones with which every wish came true. After rubbing one of them on your lapel and making your wish, whatever you wanted would appear at once, right before your eyes. This treasure motif recurs again and again in my father's works. In 1888 he wrote a little story about an entire town engaged in a frenzied search for a treasure large enough to make all the townspeople rich, and buried somewhere within reach. But as the people dug, they quarreled and the treasure eluded them by sinking deeper and deeper into the earth because, so the legend went, it could only be reached if the whole community lived in peace and accord. Twenty years later, my father wrote a four-act play, *The Treasure,* on the same theme.

When Shmoulik talked of the treasure, Sholom, realistic as always, asked where it was. Shmoulik did not know, but he was sure that the cabalists held the key to the secret—a certain magic phrase and a certain verse from the Book of Psalms, which had to be repeated forty times forty times. Which verse was it? asked Sholom, and Shmoulik answered, "If I only knew! But even if I did know which verse, it wouldn't be easy to find the treasure. First you have to know the magic phrase, then you have to fast forty days and recite forty chapters of the Book of Psalms on each fast day, and on the forty-first day, as soon as the sun sets, you have to sneak out of the house so cleverly that not a living soul sees you, for if someone does, God forbid, you have to begin the forty days' fast all over again. If all goes well and nobody sees you—it must be a dark night, by the way, at the beginning of the month—you have to go downhill, beyond the synagogue and stand there forty minutes on one foot while you count forty times forty, and then, if you have made no mistake in the counting, the treasure will show itself to you in the form of a fire, a little fire. As soon as you see it, go over to it. It cannot hurt you, for it does not burn, it only lights. And all you have to do then is cup your hands over the flame and gather up the gold and silver and diamonds and other precious stones, and also the two magic wishing stones. . . ."

According to Shmoulik, a rub of one of these stones, and the words "Let there come, let there appear a real good breakfast" would produce a silver tray with fried pigeons and hot buns. For dinner you could order a golden tray full of delicacies fit for a king, "Braised tongue and stuffed goose necks, their savory aroma penetrating your entire being, and fresh crisp shortbreads and wines of all the best kinds, and nuts and carobs and heaps of candy—all from nowhere, and so much you almost don't want any. . . ."

Sholom was fascinated by the story, yet he noticed Shmoulik's "dry lips, pale face, and dreamy eyes," and knew that his friend would not refuse right then and there a piece of braised tongue, some stuffed goose neck, or even a bite of a bun. Sholom swore to himself that the next morning, God willing, he would steal some nuts, a couple of carobs and some cakes from his mother's store for Shmoulik. For all his absorption in the story of the magic wishing stones, he had not failed to notice the reality of his friend's hunger.

The friendship between the two boys was of short duration. Sholom was heartbroken when Shmoulik's mother appeared suddenly out of nowhere and took him away. Sholom was never to see or hear from him again.

Half a century later, he wrote:

"What do you think? Is he still living, this strange Shmoulik, with his dreamy eyes and his beautiful, charming speech that flowed like the purest oil, gliding like good honey? Where is he and what is he today? A preacher? A Rabbi? A teacher? A merchant? A broker? Or a poor man, a beggar perhaps? Possibly fate brought him to America, the Golden Land. . . . Or is he already in that place where we shall all be in a hundred years, where the worms will be feasting on us. If there is anyone who knows anything about Shmoulik the Orphan, let him tell me." No one ever did.

Shmoulik was a strong influence for some time after the boys were separated. On that first sad night in Pereyaslav when the children joined their parents in the desolate inn after having left Woronko forever, my father, seeking solace for his unhappiness, dreamed that Shmoulik came to him with the magic wishing stones and asked him to choose which hand they were in. But while he was painfully wondering which to choose, another little boy from Woronko, Gergele the Thief, ran up and snatched the magic stones and disappeared.

Shmoulik's stories helped the young Sholom endure the bitter cold as he sat on the bench outside the inn, waiting in vain for a coach to stop at their gate. He would dream of the treasure. But in those days the treasure takes the form of a magnificent coach with most desirable, rich guests who drive without any urging from him right up to the courtyard. Each orders a room for himself alone, with a samovar all to himself. Sholom's father appears, "in skullcap, all smiles, to greet them, and asks them if they intend to stay for the Sabbath. They reply, 'Of course, but why only for one Sabbath? Why not for the next three Sabbaths?' The guests turn out to be merchants who have come to purchase grain, which means that Grandfather Nahum, who sells grain, will earn a fine commission on the deal. Then the stepmother appears, in her Sabbath shawl in honor of the guests, her face shining with joy. She looks at the guests and asks the children. 'Who brought them?,' and Sholom answers proudly, 'I did. I called them and they came.' "

Such a daydream was characteristic of my father. Often during the distressing years that followed his graduation from the district school, and also later in life, he found comfort and the strength to go on by letting his imagination play with dreams of happier times and situations.

It was no wonder he became dedicated early in his life to literature and to writing. His imagination needed an outlet. When he had only just begun to go to *heder* and was studying the Hebrew text of the Pentateuch with commentary by the eleventh-century scholar Rashi, he was inspired to write his own commentary. A desire to be a writer came even earlier, one Saturday evening in the Woronko home. The leading citizens had come as usual to celebrate the departure of the Sabbath. Grandfather Nahum was reading to his guests from a book printed in Yiddish, a small thin volume with yellow leaves, soiled and torn at the corners. The guests were enjoying the book with gusto, frequently bursting into laughter and expressing their appreciation for the author with delighted cries of "What a wag, what a rogue, the devil take him!" Even Sholom's father could not repress his laughter —it was a very gay and happy scene. Sholom was too young to understand what the book was about, and he never learned the title or the name of the author, but, as he put it later, "he envied that man who had written that book, and his greatest wish was that, with God's help he, too, when he grew up, would write a book like that, a little book which people would read and laugh at, and for which they would curse out the author so good-naturedly. . . ."

The desire to amuse people was a part of my father's nature and showed itself long before he could have seriously thought of becoming a writer. In his letter to Ravnitzky he wrote: "To notice and point up the ludicrous in everything and everyone—this was almost a sickness with me. Unthinkingly I used to mimic everybody, my teacher Reb Zorach, his wife, the other pupils, their fathers and mothers, even Baruch Ber, the drunkard, and the Gentile janitor with his crooked legs. I used to get many slaps for this. At the *heder* I was the comic. Everyone used to laugh, laugh until they cried, except me. At home, Mother noticed these 'tricks' and tried to root them out of me. . . ."

As the boy grew older his comic talents ripened into a healthy sense of humor. His ability to mimic served him well in the creation of character, but rather than laugh *at* people, he learned to accept them and laugh instead at the situations in which they found themselves.

With his graduation from the district school my father faced the pressing problem of what to do next. During his last year at school, life had been easier for the family and particularly for Sholom. With the aid of a non-Jewish friend in town, Grandfather Nahum had given up the unprofitable inn and had acquired a tobacco store with an adjoining wine business in the cellar below. This brought in a comfortable living. When he was sixteen, my father began to give private lessons in Russian and other school subjects; he was so successful that he could afford, with his father's permission, to move out of the parental home into rented quarters. This gave him peace and quiet and allowed him to study late at night without disturbing anyone.

The next logical step was to seek admission to the Jewish Teachers' Institute at Zhitomir, for which he had the highest qualifications in both Hebrew and Russian subjects. After four years there he could become a licensed teacher. His acceptance at the Institute seemed assured, but the reply was slow in coming, and devastating when it did arrive. Since the applicant would be eighteen years old on admission, the letter read, and thus subject to military service at the end of his junior year, he would be unable to complete the course. They therefore could not admit him. The road to advancement, to a promising future, closed against Sholom.

This left my father, after graduation, at loose ends. His coterie of friends had dwindled; his closest companion, a year younger than he, had been admitted to the Institute, which added a touch of envy to his frustration. The prospect of continuing indefinitely as a private tutor in Pereyaslav was shattering. He began to seek for some chance to get away—for a position, any position anywhere that would open the door to opportunity. It did not help him that he was and always had been too trusting of people—inclined to take everyone at his word, embellishing prospects with hopes of his own, and often ending up misled and misused.

Take, for example, the incident of the tanner. This man, who lived in a nearby town, used to stay at the Rabinowitz inn whenever he came to Pereyaslav to purchase hides for his tannery. One day he visited Grandfather Nahum with what seemed an excellent proposal for Sholom. His town desperately needed a Russian teacher. The people would take Sholom to their hearts and he would prosper there. Moreover, he himself would give Sholom free accommodation and receive him as a member of the family. When Sholom protested that he could not accept this generosity, the tanner reluctantly suggested that Sholom, if he wanted to do something in exchange, could teach his children. Grandfather Nahum gratefully accepted the tanner's offer, and before long he and Sholom visited the town.

The tanner had described his house as luxurious, and in Sholom's imagination it had become a palace. In reality it was an ordinary small-town dwelling. They found their host, coatless and in bare feet, bent over a heap of smelly hides. He was obviously embarrassed as he pulled on his boots, put on his coat and shouted for a samovar for the guests. With the samovar was a choice of tea, coffee, and chicory, and a variety of cakes. Dinner that evening was elaborate with filled, fried and baked fish, several kinds of soup, different meats and side dishes, desserts and preserves. For supper there was an array of dairy dishes, along with a samovar and a variety of pastries. At night they were put up in the living room on two comfortable sofas with soft bedding and pure linen sheets. In the morning Grandfather Nahum left, sure that he had placed his son in a most comfortable situation.

The next day, however, things were different. For dinner there was plain soup and a bite of meat. For supper, only bread and cheese. At bedtime Sholom found himself not on a comfortable sofa in the living room but in a back room on an iron chest that gave him a backache. The next day dinner was a dish of herring with potatoes, which gave him heartburn; for supper there was just bread and butter and tea; and at bedtime he had no bed at all, just a heap of hides on the floor. The odor was terrible and, moreover, in the same room was a howling baby. When Sholom got up in the middle of the night to rock the crib, a cat jumped out. Sholom decided to leave at once.

From then on, the job of finding suitable quarters turned into a "series of angry landladies, persistent cockroaches, sticking bedbugs, malodorous mice and rats and other pests."

Furthermore, the town showed no awareness of its need of a Russian teacher. The teachers in the Hebrew schools felt themselves perfectly able to teach Russian and resented the intrusion of a new teacher. Only in the house of Stempenyu, the *klesmer* (*klesmer* is the specific term for a musician who plays at weddings), did Sholom feel at home. The family were virtually social outcasts and always in need of money—which the young tutor readily loaned, knowing it would never be returned—but it was a happy, jolly place, full of children, a home after Sholom's heart. Despite this haven, Sholom could hardly wait for the end of the semester, when he left, determined never again to be a teacher in a small town or seek his life's career in such a place.

It must have been a sad homecoming for him. He was returning a failure, his economic independence lost. He was back under his father's roof, facing the I-told-you-so derision in the stepmother's eyes. She had never thought much of those "special gifts" his father saw in him, nor had she seen any point in so much schooling. What was the fine scholar going to do now?

Not so long after, a friend of the family told Grandfather Nahum that a very rich Jew, a "magnate" who lived in a distant village, was searching high and low for a Russian-Hebrew teacher for his children. He wanted someone from a good family. Grandfather Nahum recalled that the man had often stopped at the inn in the days before he became a "magnate." Sholom immediately left for the village, armed with a letter from his father—in Hebrew, of course, and loaded with flowery praise for his excellency, the "magnate."

Most of the money which Sholom had saved from his teaching went into clothes and haberdashery befitting a young man about to accept a tutor's position in the home of a "magnate." What was left after the purchase of his railway ticket melted away at each train stop, as Sholom joined the other gentlemanly passengers rushing to the buffet for refreshments. Why think about money? In a matter of hours he would be in the rich gentleman's home, with all his needs provided for.

The "magnate," however, was neither as accessible nor as susceptible to the charms of a letter written in Hebrew as they had thought in Pereyaslav. There were three hurdles to overcome: first, a guard at the gate, a dullard of a peasant on bow legs; then, a vicious dog, kept on a chain, to be sure, but far too close to the path; and finally, a slick, self-important Jewish lackey at the door.

"The guard," my father wrote, "does not open the gate before you tell him who you are and what business brings you there, but a five-kopek piece saves all this nonsense, and there goes the last coin in Sholom's pocket. The dog is silenced by the guard, but the lackey is more difficult to overcome. First he tries to exact information as to who the visitor is and what is the substance of the letter he, the man-servant, is to deliver to his master. Then he tries to disabuse the young visitor of any illusions he might have about his visit. If it is a position in the administration he wants, there are no vacancies; if it's the teaching position he's here for, there have already been count-less applicants. There is one right there on the lawn, in fact—a big fool, but at least he has a beard and the spoiled brats might have a little respect for him. Finally the lackey puts the letter on a silver tray and disappears for some minutes, only to return with the report that the magnate has opened the letter, looked at it, but has not read it. Sholom, trying to put the best face on it, suggests that perhaps the magnate is too busy right now. Yet, he thinks to himself, the letter is from Nahum Rabinowitz! He will call again the next day. He is determined to make the magnate read his father's letter."

It was getting dark when Sholom walked back to the village where he put up for the night at the only inn, a ramshackle building run by a poorly dressed, highly inquisitive innkeeper. Learning that his new guest was a son of Nahum Rabinowitz of Pereyaslav, he was over-joyed to welcome him, since he had once stayed at the Rabinowitz inn. Now he was more anxious than ever to learn what had brought Sholom to the village, and if there was any way he could help him. He invited Sholom to take the evening meal with his family, but Sholom did not respond to the innkeeper's obsequiousness. He re-sented the intrusion on his privacy of this uncouth person and, even more, was afraid of being the object of pity. He suspected that the innkeeper knew all too well why he was there, especially as the innkeeper claimed to be a relative of the "magnate's" and had said that all sorts of people were flocking to try for the teaching position. "Jews need to find a livelihood," he said, "a piece of bread." Then he added, as if to rub it in, "They often go hungry."

It seemed to Sholom that the innkeeper knew he was hungry and, in his pride, told him he had already eaten; he hurried to bed, his stomach empty. The next morning he rose and left the inn early so that nobody would notice that he had had no breakfast. Again he called at the "magnate's," but the lackey reported that the letter was still unread. The same thing was repeated the next day. Meanwhile Sholom was completely penniless. In desperation he hit on the idea of selling his watch, which he believed—because the man who had sold it to him said so—to be gold. But the village watchmaker laughed out loud. Gold? This watch was made of some metal he called "tombac," which he did not deign to explain to the ignorant young man. No, he would not exchange it even for a nickel watch. No, he would not buy it, not even for a single ruble. He was busy, and would the young man go away and bother him no longer?

Sholom could, of course, still borrow a postage stamp from the innkeeper and write to his father for money to pay the inn bill and the fare back home. But he could not face the humiliation and the failure, at least not while there was some hope that the letter might be read. Again he went to bed hungry.

The next morning Sholom woke to the tantalizing smell of freshly baked bread and boiling milk. He dressed quickly and hurried to the "magnate's" place only to be told that he still had not read the letter. Back in his room that evening, having sidetracked the innkeeper's questions, he stretched out on his bed, holding his nose to ward off the tempting odors of marinated herring and fried onions that "excited the sense of smell and aroused the appetite.

"And to drive away the tempter, Sholom closes his eyes and concentrates on thoughts and meditations that carry him on the wings of a radiant fantasy into the wonderful world . . . of golden dreams. That is where he loves to retire whenever he is alone. No one can disturb him there, not even his closest friends. This is the magic that . . . Shmoulik had left within him, the world of the two magic stones—rub one and say, Let there come, let there appear, and you have a breakfast before you, fresh savory rolls and shortbreads that melt in your mouth, and the aroma of hot coffee and milk pervades the air. Even before you get to the coffee, there appears a fat soup with noodles and a quarter of a chicken, and fried duck with carrots, and a pudding of matzo flour baked in goose fat, and two kinds of wine, a red one and a white one, the kinds that his father keeps for Passover for his gourmet friends.

"Through with his excellent breakfast, Sholom feels like taking a nice rest. A rub with the other magic stone . . . he finds himself in a crystal palace of twelve rooms. The walls are papered with hundred-ruble bills. The floor is carpeted with silver coins, decorated with gold pieces. The furniture is of pure white ivory, fitted in velvet. At every turn, there is gold and silver and precious stones. It is all enclosed by an orchard of the finest fruits. A stream rushes through the garden, and it is full of goldfish. Divine music is playing—the best violinists in the world. And he, the hero, does nothing else but distribute alms generously, handfuls of gold to some, silver to others, precious stones to others—coins, food, clothing. He does not skip over anyone, not even his worst enemy. On the contrary, to his enemies he gives even more than to his friends; let them feel. . . ."

The next day, dazzled and famished, the dreamer awakened with gnawing pangs of hunger. Once more he went to the "magnate," and once again the answer was the same: his letter had not been read. In that impossible and incomprehensible situation my father turned to the synagogue; it was after the services and he was alone. As he wrote:

"It had been a long time since the hero had prayed so feelingly and so reverently. He was by then far from the piety of his childhood. These were the days of the enlightenment, when to be pious was considered disgraceful and to be religious was to be thought of as a fanatic, and to be a fanatic was worse than to be a convert today. But now the desire to pray came from within. A sort of religious ecstasy came over him, and he let himself go, praying aloud, chanting like a cantor. During the Eighteen Benedictions, he burst into tears and wept long and bitterly, with heaviness of heart. After he had had a long cry, he felt relieved, as though a stone had rolled off his heart. What the crying meant he could not explain rationally. It came as of itself, from deep inside, a purification of the soul. Perhaps it was a result of weakened nerves, or of the extended fasting? He decided to end the fasting that day, come what may. Enough of starvation. . . ."

As though in answer to his prayers, Sholom's dreams began to come true soon after he left the synagogue. The innkeeper met him with the exciting news that a rich young man, a fabulously rich young man, who had arrived that morning, was a relative of Sholom's. He immediately conducted him to the special room reserved for very select guests and introduced him to a young man who was sitting at a samovar and drinking tea. He was a pleasant-looking person with blue eyes and a small round beard; he introduced himself as Yeshia Loyeff and invited Sholom to join him at his breakfast—as if my father needed any urging! He remembered that breakfast always:

"Never in his life, before or since, was a glass of tea more appreciated; and no item of food in the world ever had or would have again so wonderful a taste as the fresh small bagels, the biscuits, the shortbreads, the preserves, which disappeared all too soon, not a crumb of it left, not even for the sake of good manners. The guest had swallowed it all, like a hungry goose, and before he realized the impropriety of his behavior, it was all gone. . . ."

The family relationship between the two young men was not very close. The first wife of the father-in-law of one of Nahum's children was a sister of Yeshia Loyeff's late mother. But even so, Yeshia wanted to know all about his newfound relative, and on learning that Sholom had come to apply for a teaching position with the so-called magnate, he asked Sholom if he especially wanted that position—or would he consider going with him to his father's estate as teacher for his little sister? Yeshia assured Sholom that his father was in a position to pay well, just as well as the rich man in this village, if not more.

Sholom was too astounded to say a word. He did not believe his own ears—it must be a dream, a hallucination, or else this young man Yeshia must be an angel from God in the image of a man.

When he was finally able to speak, he tried to sound as cool and collected as possible. The proposition was, to be sure, quite attractive, but he had a recommendation, that is, a letter from his father to the "magnate," and what would he do in case the "magnate" . . . The innkeeper, who had never left Sholom's side, interrupted to ask what language the letter was written in.

Hebrew, of course, Sholom told him. The innkeeper shouted, "In Hebrew!" and burst into raucous laughter. "Young man," he said to Sholom, "you'll have to wait a long time before that one learns to read a letter in Hebrew, a very, very long time."

Yeshia joined the innkeeper in uproarious laughter. Sholom understood.

He found in Yeshia Loyeff a kindred spirit. He was well versed in ancient Jewish lore, in the Bible, the Talmud, the philosophical works of Maimonides, and he was also well read in modern literature. He could recite portions of Mapu's novel by heart, and was generally a most amiable young man. The two soon became fast friends; and within hours they were in Yeshia's phaeton on the way to the Loyeff estate, Yeshia having settled the bill at the inn.

They stopped at a town called Boguslav, where Yeshia was to meet his father, Elimelech Loyeff, at the inn and continue the journey home with him. The latter was waiting when they arrived, and Yeshia told his father who Sholom was and how they had met. Elimelech Loyeff "saddled his pince-nez on his nose and unceremoniously scrutinized the young man the way, for example, one inspects fish at the market. . . . His inspection over, he extended a warm hand, and in as friendly a manner as was possible for such a formidable-looking man, he greeted the young stranger, again unceremoniously, in the familiar 'thou' instead of the formal, polite 'you.'" But Sholom was left in suspense as to whether he could have the position, for father and son had some private business to discuss. He left them alone and moved into another room.

Here Sholom found himself in the social center of the inn. In a corner, surrounded by a group of suitors, sat the innkeeper's young and pretty daughter, with a Russian book in her hand—a Russian book being a sign of intellectuality—discoursing on this and that for the benefit of the young men around her. Sholom was introduced. The young lady wanted to know if he had read *Sand Dunes* by Friedrich Spielhagen, a popular German novelist of the day. Sholom answered, Yes, of course he had read it, as well as all the other novels by Spielhagen. Then someone mentioned Berthold Auerbach, and Sholom at once referred to some of the heroes in that author's novels. Bogrov's *Memoirs of a Jew,* when it came up, Sholom knew almost by heart. And so on. . . . The cultural marathon continued, and as the road became more and more difficult, the other young men dropped out of the race, so that only Sholom was left to counter the young lady's thrusts with such heavyweights as Buckle's *History of Civilization in England* and John Stuart Mill's *Essay on Liberty*.

The Loyeffs had emerged from their private talk during the heat of this literary contest. Father and son exchanged glances and followed Sholom's discourse with marked delight. Finally, Elimelech Loyeff turned to Sholom and said, "Tell me something, young fellow —my son informs me that you are as knowledgeable in our sacred writings as in secular books. I would like to know if you still remember what Rashi wanted of the daughters of Zelophehad?" The reference was to the eleventh-century commentator on the Bible passage Numbers, 27, in which the daughters of a man named Zelophehad baffled Moses with their claim to their deceased father's property, and Moses had to turn to God himself for a decision. Sholom remembered the passage very well and answered the question fully. This led to further discussion about the Scriptures, the Talmud, and even modern

Hebrew literature. Everyone in the room was amazed.

Elimelech Loyeff put his hand on Sholom's shoulder and said, "Yes, but with all the learning, knowledge, erudition in the world, one may still not be able to fill out a receipt! Here's a pen and ink, let's see you write a letter in Russian to the director of a sugar factory, advising him that he will not be receiving any sugar beets unless he sends a certain sum of money." This was a test that was easy for Sholom. His letter went from hand to hand and all admired the penmanship no less than the style. But Elimelech Loyeff had one more hurdle for Sholom.

"Now, please," he said, "I would like you to write the same letter in Hebrew, for the director of the factory happens to be a Jew. . . ."

Sholom quickly translated the letter into an ornate Hebrew which he executed in his excellent calligraphy, all the lines of equal length, each letter standing out clearly, like a pearl.

"In short," my father writes about this important moment in his life, "the young teacher passes the improvised examination brilliantly. He is dizzy with his own success. He feels his ears burning. His fancy lifts him up on its wings and carries him into the world of dreams and magic reveries. He is happy and radiant. Shmoulik's old dream of the treasure is beginning to come true for him—and in a completely natural way. He comes, in his fantasy, to a rich estate, and becomes acquainted with old Loyeff's daughter. They fall in love and disclose their secret to the old man. He places his hands on their heads and blesses them. 'Be happy, dear children,' he says. The young man writes a letter to his father in Pereyaslav, 'I'm getting married. Come.' Old Loyeff sends a phaeton with spirited horses for the father. . . . But Sholom is interrupted in the midst of his dream. They are still at the inn, and old Loyeff is calling him aside to discuss practical matters, such as his remuneration. 'Or shall we,' suggests old Loyeff, 'leave it for later?' 'Of course, leave it for later.' And Sholom feels like a man who has dozed off and is just getting involved in a pleasant dream when he is awakened. . . . The fantasy lifts like a veil. And the magic of the treasure and all the good and sweet reveries vanish into thin air."

Late that night my father arrived in Sofievka—the idyllic place, the place of light, where the reality was so extraordinarily pleasant that one had no need to dream.

IV
Paradise

THE HAMLET of Sofievka and the gracious, well-ordered life on the huge Loyeff estate nearby would have seemed a desirable place to any poor boy from Woronko and Pereyaslav. To the sensitive young Sholom, with his innate aversion to drabness and want and his boundless imagination, Sofievka was a veritable paradise, more especially after his recent experiences.

He came there in the darkest hour of his youth, and he found a world of sunshine and beauty, of kindness and of love. He wrote of this period:

"He was brought there as an employee to serve for a short time as a teacher, but he remained permanently. There he found his second home. There, as we shall presently see, his fate was sealed, his bliss, his life, forever. For the time being, as a teacher, he spent nearly three years there. Those three years may be regarded as the best, the most beautiful, and the happiest of all his years. It may be said that this time was truly the spring of his life—in every respect."

To reach the Loyeff estate they passed first between the two rows of low log cabins with thatched roofs making up the peasant village, then past a long, broad pasture and another field where the mounds of hay and stacks of straw stood ready for threshing. Next, the gate of the estate, guarded by a peasant who doffed his hat and bowed low—almost, indeed, knelt—before opening up. Finally, the long turf track led back to the broad manor house with its whitewashed walls, thatched roof and two porched wings.

Inside, the walls, too, were whitewashed; the floors were hardwood, spotless and polished. Many rooms, all with several windows, opened on a large hall. The furniture was simple, old and in good taste. There were a number of well-trained men and women servants, and meals were served in an elaborate dining room by a servant in livery and white gloves. The table was set with silver and fine china and glass. All this lived up to and surpassed the extravagant fantasies of wealth that Sholom had conjured up.

Old Loyeff, as my father calls him in his autobiography, was a tall, powerful man with the figure of a field marshal and a booming voice. Photographs show him wearing a dressy jacket and a fashionable cravat. He is hatless, without even a skullcap; his wavy hair is neatly combed. Above his small, square trimmed beard is a short straight nose, and small eyes which seem to be looking far into the distance. My father read kindness into his expression, but my mother said simply, in her outspoken way, that her father was a "tyrant."

Indeed he must have been. When old Loyeff was home, everyone else was silent; the servants wore soft padded shoes and moved about like shadows. Only his voice could be heard resounding throughout the house.

Grandfather Elimelech owned and operated a large landed estate near Sofievka, in the province of Kiev. He had a Jewish overseer named Duddy, who supervised the work of the peasants living on the estate or in the village nearby. He was in charge of all operations, from planting and harvesting to shipping the produce to market. It went by horse-drawn wagons either to the railroad station or to a ferryboat on the riverbank of the estate, and from there to wherever it was to be sold. But even with Duddy there, my grandfather was too active a man to stay away from where the work was done. At sunrise, in shiny jackboots and velvet smock reaching to his knees, he was in the fields with his peasants or on the riverbank or at the animal stalls, directing, lending a hand, teaching them how to do a job with less effort and greater results. The estate was noted for its high yield and efficient management. The Christian gentry of the neighborhood admitted that one could learn from the Jew how to manage an estate, how to make the soil more productive and keep the peasants both hard-working and satisfied.

My father said that Grandfather's peasants would all, without exception, have given their lives for their "*Pan* Loyeff." They feared and respected him, but they also loved him—loved him for his kindness and his fatherlike concern for them. One must keep in mind that the older peasants still remembered the days of serfdom, abolished only fifteen years before, and that many of them still bore the marks of the floggings and clubbings they had received from former masters. Until 1860 Russia was feudal, with landowners, whose serfs, bound to the large estates, worked for their masters most of the week, and in return were lent strips of land to work for themselves. The "emancipation" meant that the peasants, no longer serfs, could own outright these small strips of land, paying the landlord for them over a period of many years. Under this so-called emancipation, the cruel beatings had given way to slaps and curses. But on the Loyeff estate the peasants were treated like human beings.

When cholera hit the village, for instance, Grandfather Elimelech went from hut to hut and administered whatever medical aid was available, even massaging the afflicted with his own hands. The peasants trusted him with their money, too, as well as with their lives. Few of them could add two and two, so that they had to depend on the honesty of their employer in all their accounts with the estate. They did so with easy minds, sure that old Loyeff would not do them out of a single kopek.

My grandfather had married my mother's mother, Rakhil Yampolsky (whom I have referred to earlier as Babushka) in 1863. She was then twenty-three and divorced. She never spoke of her life before she married Elimelech Loyeff, but we knew that her father had married her off to a man she did not like, and that before the year was out she was back home, determined never to return to her husband. Her father had no choice but to get her divorced and look for a better match. He found that in Grandfather Elimelech, a widower of substance, admittedly some twenty years her senior with two growing sons, but a very handsome, interesting man with considerable wealth.

As I remember Babushka, she was a good-looking woman, tall and straight, perhaps a little too slim for the fashion of the time, when plumpness was still a feature of feminine pulchritude. There was a charcoal sketch of her by a well-known artist, which hung on the wall of our dining room, depicting her with a round face and a double chin. Often she would point to this picture and say with a sigh, "See? That's how I used to look!" Babushka was convinced that adverse circumstances (financial, of course) and not age had changed her appearance. Judging from the sketch, she must have been beautiful indeed; even at sixty she was still attractive with her proud carriage, her sparkling brown eyes, her small, chiseled features, and her fine head, elegantly oval, covered by the neat reddish wig.

Babushka was not an intellectual like her husband, and she had had no formal education. Her learning was limited to knowing her way in the prayerbook and reading and writing Yiddish. Grandfather Elimelech, on the other hand, was a scholar, much given to study and reading. Babushka showed no antagonism to cultural pursuits; she was simply indifferent to matters outside her domain, and sat silent and unconcerned through her husband's intellectual discussions with his friends. She may not have been an ideal intellectual companion, but she was no hindrance to him.

In other areas they must have had much in common. Both were wholeheartedly committed to the punctilious observance of the proprieties, strict decorum, and firm discipline of peasants, servants and children. And, just as Grandfather Elimelech had taken up his position of country squire as though born to it, Babushka had easily assumed the manners and learned the habits of an aristocratic lady accustomed to opulence.

Old Loyeff possessed a large and interesting library and spared no expense on new publications. The books were fiction and nonfiction, in original Hebrew or in translation from French, German or Russian. After returning from the fields, covered from head to foot with dust, grain, blossoms and straw, he would change his clothes, wash, brush his hair, and sit down at his writing table to read his mail, brought by a messenger on horseback from the village post office. His correspondence was dealt with industriously and efficiently while dinner was being prepared; after dinner he would turn to his bookshelves for the latest acquisition and read until bedtime.

Old Loyeff knew much of the substance of his books by heart and loved to retell a story in his own words. It was rare to find a person with such an excellent memory, my father said, and with so articulate a tongue. "I might say that he was an orator with a sense of humor, particularly when he told tall stories. He had a story, parable or proverb for every topic of conversation, for every occasion. A man of wide experience of life, he had much to tell, and told it most interestingly, with impersonations and mimicry. He would not just tell, he would compose, create, poetize, paint pictures in all colors. And wherever he went, no matter how many others were present, he was the only one everyone would be listening to."

My father recalled an amusing incident between old Loyeff and Duddy.

Duddy was a short, solid man "with shoulders of steel, an iron chest, and a hand like a hammer." He had arrived on the estate as a youngster and had remained there ever since. Here, in the cottage Grandfather Elimelech had given him, with its garden plot and couple of cows, he had married and raised a family. As overseer of the estate he was a stern taskmaster, but the peasants respected him: he drove them hard and stood for no nonsense, but they knew he drove himself harder. Word had only to pass along the fields that Duddy was coming and all hands redoubled their efforts at fever pitch.

But this terror of the peasantry became, my father wrote, "smaller than a child, quieter than a lamb, his arms drooping, his breath held, when he stood before old Loyeff." No soldier ever "stood before his general or field marshal with greater respect and more fear than Duddy before his master." He never approached my grandfather except when he was called or was expected to present his report. In old Loyeff's presence he would stand straight, never daring to sit down, never speaking unless spoken to. Their interview over, he would wait patiently to be dismissed.

One winter evening, Duddy came to present his report on the estate. As usual, at the end of his speech, he stood at attention and waited for his dismissal. But Grandfather Elimelech was in a genial, talkative mood. There were some others present, and old Loyeff began to speak of neighbors of his who were Polish gentry. This led him to hold forth on Poland and the Polish insurrections against Russia, the second of which had taken place only a little over a decade earlier. This, in turn, led to a discourse on the Russians and Russian history prior to Peter the Great. A book of Russian history happened to be lying on the table before him, and he picked it up and began to read a chapter on Peter the Great. Since the book was printed in Hebrew, he translated, as he went along, into Yiddish, and explained some of it for Duddy's benefit. Duddy was still standing at attention and Grandfather Elimelech told him to sit down on a nearby chair. Duddy did not feel sufficiently at ease to do so and remained standing. Old Loyeff again told him to sit down. Bashfully Duddy went to the back of the room and sat down on a chair which was under the pendulum clock, an ancient timepiece that always made a steady creaking noise before it struck and then boomed the hour with a terrific clang.

Duddy was not used to lectures, nor was he in the habit of sitting inactively in one position for any length of time. He became drowsy and had to struggle to keep his eyes open. But little by little, under the steady flow of my grandfather's voice and the ticking of the pendulum, he fell asleep. Suddenly the clock creaked, then boomed, as it started to strike the hour of ten. Duddy jumped straight up from his chair and, thinking that it was the fire bell, shouted, "Water, water!" For a moment, Grandfather Elimelech was confused; then he sized up the situation. He put the book down and glowered at Duddy through his spectacles. "That look on *Pan* Loyeff's face," Duddy later told my father, "I'll remember on my deathbed."

Grandfather Elimelech and Babushka had only one child, my mother, who was born in 1864 and whose Jewish name was Hudl, but she was never called by that name; in the family she went by her nickname, Bibi, and her older half brother renamed her Olga. She was approaching her thirteenth birthday when Sholom, eighteen and a half, came to Sofievka to be her teacher. There were also two other girls growing up on the Loyeff estate, daughters of Grandfather Elimelech's two sons by his first marriage: Manya, nine years old, the daughter of Israel Loyeff, and Natasha, five, daughter of Yeshia Loyeff, who had first brought Sholom to the estate. Both girls had been given up by their mothers after their parents were divorced. Natasha had been completely abandoned; her mother had not once made any contact with the family. It was said that she had remarried and moved to some distant town, but nothing definite was known, and the Loyeffs were unable to find any trace of her. Similarly, both girls became orphans when their fathers died within a few years of each other. Babushka raised them as if they were her own daughters, and my mother regarded them as sisters. Natasha and Manya became attached to Sholom, who often made them laugh, and who guided them in their reading. Upon the death of Grandfather Elimelech in 1885, when my father was twenty-six years old, they became his wards.

At Sofievka my father first tasted the delights of luxurious living. He was given a large, bright room with windows opening on a garden and orchard. The smell of flowers and fruit pervaded the air. When he arose in the morning, no matter how early, Grandfather Elimelech would already be at work somewhere on the estate, and Babushka busy with household affairs. As Sholom ate his solitary breakfast, served by the manservant, he basked in beauty and serenity.

After breakfast he would spend an hour or two with his pupil in a formal lesson and then they would walk in the garden or through the orchard. Describing these morning walks, when tutor and pupil examined at leisure the growing plants, the shrubs and trees, and tasted the ripening currants, the cherries and the grapes, my father wrote:

"While it is true that these fruits could be had in the city just as well as in the country, city fruit does not have the taste and fragrance of fruit freshly picked off a tree. And, of course, fruit is especially sweet when you eat it, not alone, but with a girl who is dear to you and beloved; with a girl to whom you are dear and beloved, as one of her own, as a brother. . . ."

And he continued, "How could she feel toward him any other way? Her father and mother treated him as though he were their own son. . . ." As were Olga and Manya and Natasha, so was the teacher floating in affluence, knowing not a single want nor being concerned about anything involving money. "As a matter of fact, money in that house did not exist as such. There was money, to be sure, much, very much money, but nobody except old Loyeff knew the value of it or ever worried about the possible lack of it. Every need was readily provided for, and most generously. Food, drink, clothing, comforts, driving about at will, in style; a servant at every turn; lackeys and horses—as many as you wanted and when you wanted them. When you went to the village, all the peasants would bow and remove their hats. Natural-born counts could not feel themselves better off, freer, or more respected."

In the afternoon the young tutor would perform his other duty— the handling of old Loyeff's correspondence. After reading the mail, old Loyeff would instruct Sholom how to reply. He did not waste time or words, and this process went at a fast clip. Sholom was soon familiar with my grandfather's business and could anticipate his directives. Then dinner—always a ceremonious affair, with several guests present: friends, neighbors, brokers, agents who had come to buy grain.

Winters at Sofievka had their own advantages and charms. There were the longer hours for reading and, more importantly, for writing. My father said that in the three years that he spent at Sofievka he wrote more than in any ten years after he became the professional writer known as Sholom Aleichem. Writing never came more easily than on the estate. "Sholom wrote all through the night—long, heart-rending novels, melodramatic plays, complicated tragedies and comedies. Thoughts came pouring like wine from a barrel; his fantasy gushed like a fountain. Why he was writing he never bothered to question. As soon as he finished a piece, he would read it to his pupil, and both would become enraptured, convinced it was a masterpiece. But the conviction was short-lived. No sooner did he finish a new piece than the preceding one seemed pale, colorless, by comparison. The best place for it was the oven. And so to the fire went scores of novels, dozens of plays."

None of the feverish writing from the Sofievka days is extant.

While the three years my father spent in Sofievka were formative and decisive for him, they were much more so for my mother. She had been a girl of not quite thirteen when her teacher arrived; she was a full-grown young lady of sixteen when he was forced to leave.

She reported her first impression of her teacher in the fragment of the memoirs she never completed:

"On that evening in September 1877 when he came into our house, my fate was sealed. He entered with my father and brother, looking very young, his blond hair long and wavy, one lock occasionally drooping over his forehead. He was smiling; his eyes were blue with green streaks. His skin was very fair; his head large, his neck short and fairly thick. He wasn't exactly handsome, but he was different from any young men I had seen before. I had known boys with black, burning eyes, and some youths of the titled landowners about us, like young Count Wolkonsky, who was very handsome and well-mannered. I looked at our guest and compared him to all the others, and he enchanted me. . . . He turned to me and talked to me as if I were grown up, telling me about some of the girls he had met at Boguslav whom I knew, and at once we had something in common to talk about. . . ."

My father accompanied her, so to speak, into her womanhood at the same time that he led her into the world of knowledge and thought.

He himself, though past eighteen when he came to Sofievka, had had few encounters with the opposite sex, and these had been slight and of an entirely romantic nature. At fourteen he had suffered the classic first love—Rose Berner was her name. She was the belle of the town, the only one who could play the piano and speak French. She talked loudly and freely, and was never seen without a crowd of suitors, the richest boys around. Sometimes she was even seen with non-Jews—military officers. No other girl could have carried that off, but she was Rose, from the best family in town. To Sholom she was the Shulamite, the Rose of the Song of Songs. After one glance from her beautiful eyes he had fallen desperately in love.

He would watch her parading with her admirers, especially with a boy named Chaim who was not much to look at but who spoke French. What's more, he played the violin and had a rich father. Many a time Sholom stood outside her window listening to her piano and Chaim's violin, wishing it were he who was in there with Rose. He blessed the hands that plucked such heavenly music from dead instruments and cursed the day he had been born into poverty. He swore he would learn to speak French and to play the violin far better than Chaim, so that one day he could go to Rose and say, "Return, O return, Shulamite, turn your face to me, Rose, and just listen how I play the violin." Then Chaim would come in with his French conversation and Sholom would say, "Be careful, I understand every word," and Rose would cry in surprise, "You speak French too?" and then he, Sholom, would be the one walking with Rose, with the whole town talking of how they were to be married. . . . At that point in the dream Sholom's brother, sleeping in the same bed, would wake him up, complaining that he was kicking in his sleep.

The second love came about two years later, when he was going to the district school, where the pupils enjoyed a levity of behavior regarded as unbecoming among the orthodox *heder* boys. They talked to girls and met them not in private, God forbid, but in public places such as the promenade on the town bridge. It was probably there that Sholom met the girl who caused him such anguish. She is never referred to by name, she is "the Cantor's daughter."

"Without the slightest exaggeration," my father wrote, "the relationship between angels could not be purer, more innocent than the one that had developed between the Cantor's daughter and the hero of this autobiography."

After several weeks of glancing, smiling, formal greetings, it seems that the Cantor's daughter took the initiative and suggested that Sholom come to her synagogue instead of his father's on the night of Simchas Torah (Feast of the Torah). This was a challenge to his maturity and he took it up, although he knew his father would disapprove. He told her that he wanted to meet her alone, without the girl friend who was always with her; she said that her parents forbade it, but that her friend was a quiet, honest girl who also had a young man she wanted to talk to. In fact, the Cantor's daughter declared, her friend was also in love.

Also! This could mean only one thing to Sholom—the Cantor's daughter was in love, and with him. He believed it all the more when he looked at her glowing face, her gleaming eyes. She seemed strangely familiar; the white skin, the wavy blond hair, the long thin fingers. He had seen all these before, in a dream. He could not wait for Simchas Torah, so he wrote her a long letter that took him a day and a half to compose, the words flowing forth like a fountain. He sent it through her friend's suitor. She did not answer at once, but finally a letter came—she was sorry she could not write as beautifully as he, but that if she had wings she would fly to him . . . she could not sleep waiting for the Simchas Torah. After such a letter, how could Sholom doubt that she loved him?

On the night of the joyful holiday, Simchas Torah, the women, particularly the young ones, come down from the gallery of the synagogue to join in the jubilation. The Torahs are removed from the ark by the men and paraded in a circle to be kissed. Sholom, because he was Nahum's son, was given the honor of parading with a Torah. He kept his eyes on the womenfolk, but the Cantor's daughter was not among them. He kept looking and looking; then, suddenly, he felt warm lips kissing, not the mantle over the Torah, but his fingers! He looked down, and it was she, the Cantor's daughter, with her companion beside her. "All the heavens opened, and all the angels descended to sing praise, praising the world that is ruled by God in heaven—what a good, sweet, dear world! . . ."

He was so stunned that he almost dropped the Torah, which would have been a calamity. He wanted to stop a moment and look longer into the eyes that were smiling at him, but those behind him pressed him forward. When the circling with the Torahs was finished, he hurried back. But she was gone. She had disappeared as quickly as she had come. She was not in the synagogue, not in the yard. He would have thought it all a dream, but he could still feel the warmth of her lips on his fingers.

He never saw her again. Soon after that night, she ran off with a gentile boy, a store clerk with whom she had, apparently, been in love all along, and converted to the Christian faith in order to marry him.

This was a tragedy for the Cantor and for the Jewish community. But for Sholom it was disaster—not only a disappointment in love, but in human nature itself. The Cantor's daughter had tricked and cheated him. All through his life my father was to suffer such disillusionments, such betrayal of his trust in people. He wrote in the end that this was what had shortened his life.

Heartbroken, mortified, and shocked, he came down with a high fever, and went into a delirium shot with visions of his childhood. When he recovered, he saw that his face was thinner, his eyes bigger, his whole body longer. He seemed to himself to be a different person. He had changed from inside out; the boy had become a young man.

The innocence and romanticism that in some ways never left my father's nature he brought to his relationship with his young pupil, Olga, during the three years in which they were never separated for even a single day. In the morning, as I said, there was their study period; in the afternoons the strolls in the garden and orchard. After dinner they would retire again for study and reading. They read without any rigid or specific plan, selecting freely—mostly fiction, the classics of world literature, such as Shakespeare, Dickens, Tolstoy, Goethe, Schiller, Gogol. They also read the less worthwhile of the contemporary popular novels, the so-called French Boulevard writings—books by Eugène Sue, Xavier de Montépin, Von Born, Aschar. In between the lessons and the reading, they diverted themselves by watching the threshing machine at work, or by strolling in the fields where the peasants were harvesting. The teacher would try his hand at reaping, gathering and binding, and he learned that it is much easier to watch the process than to do it. "Observing does not make one sweat or develop calluses on one's hand," he wrote. But it did give one an appetite. So, back they went to the house for black bread and sour milk. . . .

As the day was long, teacher and pupil would take another stroll in the garden or be driven in the phaeton to visit neighboring estates, or to call on Postmaster Malinovsky—who was later to play an ugly role in their lives. Everywhere they were received with great cordiality. There would be a samovar and refreshments of all sorts at one place; cool drinks at another. The postmaster would produce a bottle of vodka, which, however, he emptied all by himself. If they dropped in on the Duddys at their little cottage, where it was always jollier than in the big house, they were welcomed with the most delicious dishes, which were regarded as beneath the dignity of the big house—sour dill pickles right from the barrel, hot potatoes in their jackets, *schav* (sorrel) with garlic bulbs, apple cider instead of tea . . .

My father describes, almost *en passant,* the feelings of young teacher and pupil toward one another:

"That the young man was born to be a writer neither had the least doubt. Teacher and pupil spoke of it, daydreamed about it, built beautiful castles in the air on it. In planning his future books they forgot their own plans for themselves. It never occurred to them, either, to give expression to their feelings, or even to think of their own romance as such. The very word 'romance' was apparently too hackneyed, the word 'love' too banal for what had developed and grown between them. They were so naturally for each other that they could not have been anything but unselfconscious about how they felt about each other. Would it ever occur to a brother to declare his love for his sister? However, I am afraid we shall not be far from the truth to say that outsiders knew more and talked more about the romance of the two young people than they did themselves. They were too young, too naive, too happy. There was not a spot on their sun. They never saw, or thought about, any opposition or resistance from any source. They never suspected for one moment that they might some day have to part. Yet the day for parting came, though not for a while."

The time had come for Sholom to present himself, as required by law, at the recruiting office for military service. He was twenty-one. This step was regarded as a crisis in a young man's life. Throughout the czarist regimes, military service was despised by the people and avoided whenever possible. The czars' wars had never been defensive, thus had never aroused patriotic feelings. Russian soldiers had always suffered cruel treatment from their petty officers—abuse, curses, beatings—not to mention the horrible conditions and rotten food. Furthermore, it was only five years since the new system of universal individual draft had been established, and the dreadful memories of the preceding system were still fresh in people's minds.

Under the earlier system, quotas of recruits had to be supplied by the local authorities. In practice this meant that only the poorer and lower classes were drafted, which lowered both the social status of the army and its morale. Moreover, under Nicholas I, conscription was for a period of twenty-five years after a six-year training period, which meant that virtually half a lifetime could be spent in military service.

It can be imagined what an even more baneful tragedy military service was for Jews. The Jewish soldier was singled out for special cruelty by the anti-Semitic officers. He could not live up to the tenets of his faith; he could not eat kosher food, pray properly, or keep the Sabbath. Moreover, since he was drafted at a tender age, he was likely in time to forget the little Jewishness he knew—in many cases, even his Jewish language. Therefore, especially since married men were exempt, parents tried to marry their sons off as early as possible, for it was not uncommon for the official "catchers," as they were called, to round up prospective recruits among children as young as twelve years of age; if they looked somewhat older, they could pass them off as being fourteen, which was the minimum age for the long service.

Alexander Hertzen, a famous Russian liberal writer, once described meeting a large unit of Jewish youngsters on the road. Many of them were no more than eight or nine years old. They were being marched by officers to their military camp a long distance away. The officer in charge told Hertzen that half of the children would not live to reach their destination. "These Jewish boys are puny and delicate," he said. "They can't stand trotting in mud ten hours a day with only dry bread to live on. Then, of course, they see only strangers, no father, no mother, no comforting. Well, you hear a cough, and the youngster is dead. . . ."

No wonder, when the law which exempted married men was rescinded, some parents adopted extreme measures, even going so far as to maim their boys by amputating a finger of the right hand or inducing some ailment that would disqualify them. Grandfather Elimelech had lived a good part of his life under this cruel system, and his dread of military service remained with him long after the juvenile draft was abolished in the late 1850s, the period of service shortened, and recruiting individualized in 1874. He spent a fortune to obtain for his son Yeshia an "honorary release" from actual service and have him enlisted in the reserve. But then came the Crimean War, with the prospect of the reserves also being called for active duty. Again he moved heaven and earth. He had Yeshia reexamined and rejected on physical grounds. This involved not only making deals with the military officials but also engaging physicians to induce symptoms of heart ailment, which, tragically, proved all too real. Yeshia was rejected after all, but continued to ail. He was sent abroad for treatment, but he succumbed to a heart attack at an early age, leaving his daughter Natasha, an orphan.

When it came to Sholom, no natural father could have been more concerned over a son's threatened induction into the army, or made a greater effort to prevent it, than Grandfather Elimelech did on behalf of his daughter's teacher. He had Sholom's registration transferred from Pereyaslav to the little town of Kaniev, where he had influence. He sent word to his friends there to spare neither effort nor money in Sholom's case. For all that, he was worried and nervous when the young man went to report at Kaniev. My father, with his romantic dreams of adventure, was for the moment not altogether unhappy at the prospect of military service. He bought himself big boots and a soldier's hood: he was confident that he would be liked in the army, find favor with the officers, and soon become a corporal or a first sergeant, which was as high as a Jew might expect to rise in the service.

Still, when the time for his departure arrived, Sholom's boldness left him. He has to confess, he writes, to the shame and disgrace of hiding in his room when he was about to take leave of the Loyeff family, perhaps forever. He buried his face in his pillow and wept bitter tears. But his pupil, in her room, was weeping even harder. Her eyes were so swollen from crying that she would not come to the table for the last meal. Pretending that she had a headache, she stayed in her room and refused to see anyone all day.

"Sad, very sad, was the parting. Mourning in the house, anguish and grief eating away at the heart. In the phaeton, as the driver Andrey raised the whip, our young hero took a last look up at the window of his pupil's room. There, he saw two weeping eyes, saying wordlessly but quite clearly, 'Godspeed, dearest, my dearest, but come back very soon, for I cannot live without you.' The young man heard these words with all his senses, and his eyes answered, 'Fare you well, dearest, my dearest. I am coming back soon, for I cannot live without you.' And only then did he realize how closely he was bound to that house. No power on earth could tear him permanently away from it, save death. . . ."

As the phaeton trundled along the dirt road, Sholom found comfort in dreams of a happier situation. He saw himself back from Kaniev, released from the service. He proposes to his beloved, turns to her father and says, "I love your daughter, do with me as you will." Old Loyeff throws his arms around him and says, "I'm glad you

have told me this at last—I have been waiting for it for a long time."
And the pair are married in grand style. . . .

As it turned out, Grandfather Elimelech's influence worked and my
father was exempted from service. But he did not speak to old Loyeff
of his love for his daughter, and this was a grievous mistake. Whether
the old man would have embraced Sholom it is hard to say—but he
might have done so, for he was not the man to seek a rich husband
for his daughter. He did, after all, like Sholom very much, and he
appreciated his knowledge and abilities. Certainly a direct approach
would not have evoked the violent reaction that ensued when he
learned of his daughter's "romance" from Aunt Toibe.

Although Aunt Toibe was not really an aunt, but Grandfather
Elimelech's cousin, who lived in Berditchev and who visited him
only on rare occasions, for a few days at a time, she behaved like his
stern older sister. She addressed him by the familiar "thou" and
lectured him freely on incidents and behavior of which she disapproved. A woman with a sharp, all-seeing eye and a lively curiosity,
she had no inhibitions about speaking her mind. She was glad, for
example, to find her cousin living like a lord, in riches and comfort,
with the beauties of nature all around him, but this did not justify
his putting on airs, as though, she said, he really were a lord. Such
behavior was unbecoming in a Jew. It was God who had given him
all this wealth. And it behooved him to go to town on every holiday
for services in the synagogue, instead of staying at home. Strangely
enough, Grandfather took this from her without protest.

My father learned many years later, probably from my mother,
who heard it from Babushka, that Aunt Toibe had found something
to say about the young teacher, Sholom. He was a very nice young
man, well educated, and from a good family. But "where was it written," she wanted to know, "that a teacher and his pupil must be so
close?" She had noticed it from the very first day she arrived. It was
enough to watch their eyes as they sat at the dinner table to know
that something was between them. She had been observing them ever
since. She had even seen them going together to Duddy's. What
business did the two have there? And what did they do there? She
saw them through the window with her own eyes. They were sitting
close together, eating from the same plate and laughing. Now, if
this were a *shidach,* a prearranged match, well and good, but the
girl's parents seemed unaware of it. On the other hand, if this was a
love affair, the parents most certainly should know, for wasn't it better

to give your daughter in marriage even to a poor teacher with only two shirts to his name than to wait until they eloped in the dark of night?

Aunt Toibe brought all this up with old Loyeff one day when he was taking her to the train for her return trip to Berditchev. But she had not meant to break up whatever was between the daughter and her teacher; she wished only to point out to her cousin that it was wrong of him to be so busy with the affairs of the manor that he did not even notice what was going on in his family.

As she saw her cousin's rage mount, she tried to reason with him. What was so terrible about this? What was there to flare up over? Was it the fault of the young man that he was poor? Poverty was no disgrace; fortune was in the hands of the Lord, as was happiness.

Grandfather Elimelech retorted that personally he had nothing against the young man, but how dare they have a romance in his house without his knowledge? He was not against his daughter's marrying a poor fellow, but for her to decide to do so on her own without consulting him, why, that was . . .

When old Loyeff returned from the railway station, my father sensed his ugly mood, but he had no idea of the cause. There was no family dinner that day, each person eating alone at different times. The pupil wanted to go for a walk with her teacher as usual, but was told she was not to go out of the house. In the evening, Yeshia arrived to stay overnight. The minute he came, he and his father went off together to talk privately, their faces grave. There was a deadly silence in the house, the oppressive silence before a storm.

Like innocent lambs, my father wrote, teacher and pupil had no inkling of what was going on. They only felt that something important must be brewing. What it was, they were to learn in the morning. In my father's own words, here is what happened:

"And when morning came, and our hero came out of his room, he found no one in the house, not the old man, nor his wife, nor their son, nor their daughter. Where were they all? Had they gone somewhere? None of the domestics knew. On the table there was an envelope marked for him. He opened it, hoping to find a note, but there was no writing, not a word, only money—all his pay that had accumulated during his entire stay. Outside, there was a sleigh (it was winter), with a sheepskin rug to keep the feet warm, waiting with its driver for Sholom's departure. He could not get a word out of anyone on the estate. Even Duddy, who would have cut off his arm for the

75

teacher and his pupil, replied to all of Sholom's questions with a mere shrug of his shoulders and a sigh. His fear of old Loyeff had overwhelmed him. This infuriated the indignant young man. He lost his head. He did not know what to do. He made an effort to write a letter to old Loyeff, another to the enlightened Yeshia, his friend, another to the pupil herself, but the writing would not come. The catastrophe was enormous, but he had not expected such an insult. He could not write one word. So, without further hesitation, he got into the sleigh and told the driver to take him to the railway station. He was going—where? That he did not know himself. Wherever the train would take him . . ."

My father made one stop on his way to the station, at Postmaster Malinovsky's house in the nearby village. Malinovsky had always been very friendly when the teacher and pupil had visited him on their outings in the countryside, and would drink toasts to his honored guests. The teacher, therefore, turned in his difficult hour to Postmaster Malinovsky for assistance in keeping contact with his pupil. He asked the postmaster to see that his letters were delivered to his pupil, privately, without her father's knowledge.

Malinovsky was most sympathetic to the plight of the two young lovers, crossed his heart and swore to God that he would follow Sholom's instructions faithfully. This covenant called for a drink, and Malinovsky produced a bottle of vodka and a plate of herring. As the bottle became empty and Malinovsky full, he embraced the teacher and kissed him ardently, and swore again that every one of the teacher's letters addressed to his pupil would be delivered privately into her own hands. He crossed his heart again—Malinovsky's word was sacred.

The first love letters that my father sent to my mother were indeed delivered promptly by Malinovsky—to old Loyeff himself! My father continued to write for some time, but naturally, when he received no reply, he stopped.

V
Into the World

AT THE END of the chapter dealing with his tragic departure from Sofievka, Sholom Aleichem added two lines of dots, then wrote:

"What do these dots mean? They indicate a long dark night. All is enveloped in a thick fog. The lonely wanderer is groping his way. Repeatedly, he stubs his toe against a stone, or falls into a pit. He falls again, rises, tries to proceed, and again he stubs his toe against a stone, and again falls into a pit. In this darkness, he acted foolishly, made mistakes, one worse than the other. . . ."

As the dots indicate, my father did not intend to tell about these mistakes and pitfalls which presumably took place in the period between his forced departure from Sofievka in the winter of 1879 and his reunion with his beloved pupil, who married him without her father's blessing in May 1883. What he did tell about his life during that period consisted of one dismal failure that reduced him to just as miserable a state as when Yeshia Loyeff appeared like an angel from heaven, and one success that left him spiritually only a shade less desolate.

He arrived in Kiev in 1879 with illusions about the great good intellectuals of the new age and with a considerable amount of money in his pocket—and he was to lose both.

His first move was to visit an outstanding Hebrew writer named Yohalel. It was meant primarily as the courtesy call of an admirer, but Sholom vaguely hoped that the master would offer some fatherly advice to a fledgling writer. He found an insignificant homely little man, cross-eyed and sour, who held down a petty bookkeeping job in a sugar plant where he was not even known to be a writer. Yohalel was in a pensive mood, pacing the floor of his dingy room, his hands folded on his chest. He acknowledged his young visitor by one slanting glance from his cross-eyes, but did not say a word, did not motion him to take a chair. The young admirer remained standing at the door for a while, then turned and left.

He then went to see another representative of the more enlightened sector of the Jewish community. This was the Certified Rabbi, an official imposed by the czarist government upon the local Jewish community who elected and paid him a salary to represent them with the authorities. His duties were primarily to keep a record of births and deaths, to issue marriage licenses, and other formalities. The Jews, especially the older generation, did not respect the Certified Rabbi. He was despised because, for all his official title of Rabbi, he had little knowledge of Judaism, and because of his ambiguous position between the helpless, oppressed Jews and their hated oppressors. Moreover, his election was often rigged by the ruling hierarchy, which made him beholden to the rich. However, his range of contacts and the secular education necessary for the post insured that the Certified Rabbi was more worldly and enlightened than many other Jews. Moreover, he was an influential member of the community.

However, the Kiev Certified Rabbi, whom Sholom after much difficulty finally saw, was, although pleasant, unable to do anything more for the young man than refer him to another czarist-Jewish functionary. This was the Learned Jew, the official censor of all books published in Hebrew and Yiddish. He was a queer, irascible character who, when my father presented himself, became greatly agitated, shouting, "What do they all want of me? Why are they sending everybody to me? What can I do for anybody?"

My father politely apologized and retreated. When he was halfway down the stairs, the irritable Learned Jew called him back and gave him a note to a prominent barrister of Kiev by the name of Copernik.

It took several days and much running about before my father learned that Mr. Copernik could best be approached at the courthouse. The courthouse was a maddening place, crowded and noisy with people in formal cutaways—the proper costume for court. Sholom was too nervous to stop one of these personages and ask for Mr. Copernik, but he finally gathered enough courage to inquire from a man with a friendly face carrying a legal briefcase outside the courtroom where he might find Mr. Copernik. The man did not reply directly, but asked Sholom why he wanted to see Mr. Copernik, so my father showed him the note. When the man told my father to wait—he had to step into the court for a while and then he would talk with him—my father assumed this was Mr. Copernik himself.

On his return the man questioned Sholom about his qualifications and took him to his hotel room to discuss the possibilities of hiring him as a legal secretary. This man, however, was not Copernik, but another barrister, Appelbaum, from the nearby town of Belaya Tserkov (literally, White Church). He was so friendly and offered such generous terms that my father readily agreed. They were to leave for that town in the late afternoon.

Before leaving, Appelbaum asked my father to wait while he made a few personal calls: there was his good friend the governor general of the province to see; if he failed to drop in on the lieutenant governor that jealous man would resent it; and he should have a word too with the chief of police, but he would not bother—that small fry could come to see him instead. He returned after a short while loaded with packages of fruit and other food. These were the gifts, he said, of the wives of the governor general and the lieutenant governor, and the chief of police's mistress—whose lawyer he was in a case involving millions.

In Appelbaum's home in Belaya Tserkov, where the relationship between man and wife seemed rather strained, the "barrister" gave Sholom some lessons in legal practice. In effect, he told him, you must never let anyone think you consider him greater than yourself; you should keep your tongue busier than your head and barrage the other fellow with so many words that he doesn't know what he's doing—even the judge won't know you are citing law decisions that never existed; clients are sheep to be shorn, cows to be milked, horses to be ridden; nobody respects a moralist; a scamp is more popular than a professor stuffed with law. Never be seen in the street without a bulging briefcase, even if it is merely full of dirty laundry. Never be caught in your office without your head in a thick book, though you never read it; never let a client go until he is sucked dry.

"After such a lecture," my father later wrote, "the author of this autobiography might have understood what sort of a barrister Appelbaum was, but Appelbaum had such a wise sympathetic face, charming you with his eyes and enticing you with his speech, that unwittingly you became devoted to him. . . ."

After dinner, Appelbaum took his briefcase and said he was going to the club for half an hour; he had to see a man there. His wife protested that the half hour would stretch to a day and a half, and she knew whom he was to see—not a man, but kings and queens and jacks. He interrupted her. "Don't forget the aces, what kind of game would it be without aces?" The wife gave him a look, my father wrote, that another man would rather die than bear. Then Appelbaum turned to his newly appointed secretary and asked him how much money he had on him. The secretary obligingly took his money out of his pocket and showed him exactly how much. Appelbaum stretched out his hand. "Could you lend me the money for only a short time? I'll give it back to you when I return from the club."

"With pleasure," said Sholom, and turned all his money over to him.

Appelbaum did not get home in half an hour—not in many hours. At noon the next day, his wife sent their son to bring his father home for dinner. The boy came back with the news that his father had left the club in the morning for Kiev. In Belaya Tserkov Sholom soon discovered that Appelbaum was no barrister, but a shyster without a license to practice who preyed on the ignorant and did not have a kopek to his name.

Once again stranded in a small town, without money, Sholom had to write home for funds in order to return to Pereyaslav. The letter was written, he said, in flowery Hebrew, "the language that permits you to say so much without telling anything." And once again he had to face an ignominious homecoming and the problem of earning his livelihood.

Time passed—weeks, months—without any prospect of a position. Sholom read and wrote. He published his first work (on the need for reform in Jewish education) in a Hebrew periodical, and wrote other articles that appeared a year later. He always belittled these first literary efforts, referring to them as "articles without content" and "silly correspondence"; yet today they still stand up as better written and more pertinent than most of the material published at that time.

Finally an opportunity opened up. The term of the Certified Rabbi in the nearby town of Louben had expired, and some people wanted a change. Applicants were invited, each candidate to deliver an oration to prove his knowledge and talents. Above all, each candidate, to be elected, needed "influence" in town, an indirect sponsor. My father's "influence" was a relative of the family by marriage, a leading citizen of Louben. My father presented himself, made an excellent oration, and was elected.

As to the quality of these orations, my father reported a story he heard in Louben which one of the townspeople considered relevant. It concerned a novice minister who went to the bishop for advice as to what to tell his congregation in his first sermon. The bishop advised him to tell them about the miracle of the forty saints who got lost in the wilderness with nothing to eat for days and days. Then one loaf of bread appeared before them, and though they all ate, and ate, there was still bread left. The novice, in the excitement of his first sermon, told the story backwards—he had one saint wandering in the wilderness, famished, and coming upon forty loaves of bread, and eating and eating, and still bread left. . . . When the service was over, the bishop reproached the young minister for such a stupid mistake. He replied, "Your excellency, for these peasants, even this was miracle enough!"

How my father felt about his election he did not spell out, but there are indications that he was not too happy. In the small towns, the attitude of the people toward the Certified Rabbi was even more negative than in the larger cities. One of Sholom's best friends attacked him for choosing such an office; no decent man, he said, could shake his hand, since a Certified Rabbi was nothing but a hypocrite, a bootlicker, a Tartuffe, a tool of the rich and a henchman of czarist bureaucracy. Moreover, he accused, an honest man does not take away another man's daily bread, like a dog snatching a bone from the teeth of another dog.

Sholom was hurt by these words from a friend, all the more since they were partially justified. Running against an incumbent *was* socially acceptable and proper, yet it went against his personal ethic. He had accidentally met the incumbent on the street a day before the election. How pale the man had become, his eyes full of fright, his glance saying, my father wrote, "What have I ever done to you?" "Just as tragically," he wrote, "as a dog looks when it is attacked and bitten by other dogs and driven off to the ends of the world." Sholom was so overcome by compassion and guilt that "if this state had lasted another minute he would have fallen on the neck of the incumbent, asking forgiveness, and withdrawn from Louben . . . its fine citizens, and the candidacy for Certified Rabbi. This would have been human, all too human. But that sentiment lasted only a minute; soon the egoist, the *I* came to the fore, and *I* prevailed."

My father went through with the election but, borrowing a phrase from Chekhov, he said that after his friend's severe criticism, "he felt like one who had eaten soap."

But his natural optimism seems to have reasserted itself. Why, he wonders, must a Certified Rabbi necessarily be such a dishonest person? Why must he be a hypocrite? Why not pious and devout? Why merely an accessory to the Jew-hating czarist officials? No, he would not be the typical Certified Rabbi. "Humane, that is what he will be! A humane man, that is what he wishes to be!"

These were the last lines that my father wrote in his autobiography.

He held the position for two and a half years, and during that time he contributed to Hebrew publications, particularly to *Ha-Melitz*. Although these pieces may not have added much to the shaping of my father's literary career, they proved crucial to his life and destiny. For it was through them that the teacher and pupil of Sofievka days were able to contact each other again.

My mother, then nineteen, had resisted all parental efforts to marry her off, and had not forgotten her former tutor. There was only one person in whom she could confide freely, her cousin Avram Marko-vich Yampolsky, who lived in the nearby town of Boguslav. He was only a little older than my mother, well educated, and sympathetic to her plight. He may have first discovered that a Sholom Rabinowitz was writing for *Ha-Melitz*. Or my mother may have herself discovered it, since the publication came regularly to the house. In any case, at my mother's request, Avram Markovich wrote to find out whether it was her Sholom Rabinowitz who was the author of the articles: the magazine gave him my father's address in Louben.

It was thus that they were able to write to each other and revive the love that had grown so strongly between them during the idyllic three years. Avram Markovich was their intermediary, and through his aid it was arranged for my mother to go to Kiev and be married privately to my father without her father's consent or knowledge. The ceremony was performed by a Rabbi Zukerman on May 12, 1883.

This was not an easy thing for my mother to do, as she was deeply attached to her father. The young couple returned to Louben to live, but my grandfather, having accepted the marriage in good grace, persuaded Sholom to give up the Rabbinical office and come to So-fievka to live. Perhaps he regarded the position of Certified Rabbi as beneath the dignity of a son-in-law of his. Whatever the reason, Sholom resigned the post and with his young bride spent the summer on the Loyeff estate. But in November of that year they moved to Belaya Tserkov, where they lived for three years.

Here my father made another stab at economic independence. He took a position with the Kiev Jewish millionaire Brodsky, as inspector of his sugar estates in Southern Russia. Again, Grandfather Elimelech insisted that his son-in-law give up the position. He may have reasoned that the post would mean long separations from my mother, or again it may have been pride—Loyeff's son-in-law did not have to be in the service of anyone. Most likely, in the back of his mind lay the wish to induct my father eventually into the management of the Sofievka estate. For the present my father should forget about earning a livelihood; he would be provided for by his father-in-law. (It was not uncommon in the Jewish middle class for a man to support a new son-in-law for some years to allow him to round out his Talmudic studies or his general education before launching him in a self-supporting enterprise.)

With my mother at his side, my father happily devoted himself to his writing as productively as during the early Sofievka years. Up to this time he had written only in Hebrew, but now he turned to Yiddish. This was a strange and daring departure for an intellectual. Serious books, books of literary merit, were always written in Hebrew —by the elite, for the elite. Stories in Yiddish were as a rule written only "for women," that is, for the barely literate. On the occasion of the celebration in 1909 of the twenty-fifth anniversary of his literary debut, my father was asked by the Russian newspaper *Kievskaya Misl* why he, an intellectual, had turned to Yiddish. He answered, in Russian, of course, that when, in 1883, the Hebrew magazine *Ha-Melitz* began to publish a supplement in Yiddish—the first journal in that language to appear in Russia—he had been amazed at "the simplicity of the novelty." Here was a publication in a language that all Jews—even women—could read! He was struck by the realization that Hebrew, with its difficult vocabulary, its flowery style, and the scholarship needed for its mastery, was serving only the special few who had had the opportunity to acquire such a learned tongue. Why should the others, who might be equally intelligent readers, be left out? Besides, a Jewish author *thought* in Yiddish even if he wrote in Hebrew, so why not write directly in the language of his thinking? Why not write in Yiddish?

On the other hand, how could anyone who wished to be considered a serious literary writer use a language which was at that time so denigrated, a language in which only prayers for women were being published? What would his father say?

He invented the pen name Sholom Aleichem, which means "Peace unto you," a greeting among Jews, so that neither relatives nor friends would know that he was writing works in Yiddish. The pseudonym became even more useful in subsequent years when he was in business and associating with influential citizens of Kiev to whom even being a writer at all was declassé, let alone a writer in Yiddish.

After my parents had been in Belaya Tserkov two years, a tragedy hit our family which gradually changed their way of life and their entire future. This was the sudden death of Grandfather Elimelech. According to Babushka, these were the circumstances:

My mother had given birth to her first child, my late sister Tissa, in April of 1884. Nine months later she was ill for a while, which greatly worried Grandfather Elimelech. In recent years he had lost both of his sons within a few years of each other. In both cases death had come unexpectedly, and each time the sad news had reached him by telegraph. As a result, he had formed a strong psychological association between telegrams and death; moreover, my mother was now the only child left to him and he must have subconsciously feared for her life.

One day he and Babushka were sitting in their living room talking about my mother's illness. The butler came into the room with a telegram on a tray. As soon as he saw it, Grandfather Elimelech clasped his hands and cried "Bibi, too!" Then he collapsed. When Babushka touched him, he was dead. The telegram was from a broker and had to do with a shipment of grain. My mother was at that very moment well on her way to recovery.

My grandfather died on his own land, the land he had loved so much and had tilled with his own hands. As there was no son to take his place, it fell to my father to step in and take charge. He was not the man to run such an estate; he was a writer, not an administrator. The estate had to be liquidated.

Even the funeral presented a tremendous complication. In those days there were no professional undertakers or private cemeteries, and only one cemetery in the town in which Jews could be buried. It belonged to the Jewish community, and the burial service was performed by unpaid volunteers from among a group known as the Sacred Society. There were no fees, but those who could were asked to make a contribution toward the upkeep of the cemetery and the overhead expenses of the Sacred Society. Upon my grandfather's death, the Sacred Society of the local community demanded a contribution of 30,000 rubles, an unheard of, exorbitant sum, without which they refused to handle the burial.

Under Jewish religious custom, interment had to follow as soon after death as possible. It would have been an indignity to the dead to move the body elsewhere for burial—the "contribution" had to be made. This holdup, as it were, became a public scandal of such magnitude that it was headlined in Kiev's Russian newspaper, and my father wrote to the paper to clarify the matter for its non-Jewish readers.

The next complication was the liquidation of the Loyeff estate, a very complex affair requiring much time, effort and legal work. According to the surrogate court record in our family archives, the final value of the estate was 220,000 rubles ($110,000), which was a vast sum of money in Russia in the 1880s—perhaps over a million in purchasing power today. Under the czarist law, the wife's property belonged to her husband, so my mother's share went to my father. Babushka, Natasha and Manya also shared in the estate, but gradually all of it came into my father's hands to manage.

For about two years the family continued to live in Belaya Tserkov, but in 1888 they moved to Kiev. My father had already engaged in some trading on the Kiev stock exchange, and when they moved there, he made this his vocation, trading in produce, grain and sugar, as well as in stocks. For a time he did rather well, increasing the fortune my mother's share of the estate had brought. But in the fall of 1890 he lost it all.

This was a crushing disaster. The family moved to Odessa, and my father went abroad for a while, a desolate traveler in Paris, Vienna and Czernowitz, while Babushka paid off his creditors from her portion of the estate. My father returned to his family and struggled to eke out a livelihood from brokerage and trading on the exchange with money from the estate that the other heirs offered him. Natasha was the first to offer her share; in fact, she begged him to take it. The Odessa sojourn lasted for two and a half years, and it was during that time that I was born.

Just how my father lost the fortune in 1890 will remain a mystery;

the people who were directly involved have all passed away. In our family the calamity was never mentioned except for the veiled allusions Babushka occasionally made to us children. It may have been mostly due to the market crash of 1890. But considering my father's prodigious literary output during his first three years in Kiev and his time-consuming efforts on behalf of Yiddish letters, not to speak of the social life of the period, it would have been a miracle if in addition he had had much time and energy left for business. (He once told Berkowitz that his novel *Yosele Solovey* had cost him 30,000 rubles. He had been so absorbed in its writing that he had completely neglected the stock exchange.)

A letter which my father wrote to a close friend at that time expresses his involvement in his literary activities and his frustration at having to suspend them for affairs of business. "I am pregnant with so many thoughts," he wrote, "so much imagery, that I must be made of iron that I do not come apart at the seams, and ah me, I have to run after a ruble! The *birzha* be damned! The ruble be damned! That a Jewish writer should not be able to live on his writing alone, but have to run in search of a ruble! Those who know me, who see me every day, ask me when do I write? Truly, I do not know myself. This is how I write—walking, running, sitting in someone's office, riding on the trolley; and just when they bother my head about timberland, a plantation, a plant somewhere—just then the most beautiful imagery emerges and the best thoughts come to mind, and I can't wait a minute, a second, to put it down on paper. Damn the business! Damn the world!" It would not be fanciful to surmise from this letter alone that my father's literary success must have been achieved in some measure at the expense of his business career.

From 1887 to 1890 Sholom Aleichem wrote three of his major novels, *Sender Blank, Stempenyu* and *Yosele Solovey*, which were dramatized and produced on the stage years later; a score of short stories, including some of the most popular ones like "The Knife," still a favorite of youngsters in many lands; several one-act plays; and many articles and book reviews in Hebrew as well as in Yiddish. He also edited and revised a volume of Yiddish folk songs (and financed the publication) by Mark Markovich Warshavsky, whose songs (such as *Aufn Pripetchik*) are still loved by Jewish audiences everywhere although they may not know the composer's name.

And he took two bold steps that changed the whole literary climate of the Yiddish world.

The first step was a short fiery book that came like a bolt from the blue, startling the literary community with its daring and originality. Written in legal format, like the record of a court trial, it put the most popular Yiddish writer of the time, N. M. Shykevich, whose pen name was Shomer, before the bar as the accused. A prosecuting attorney and a defense lawyer argued the charge that Shomer was debasing the language of his people and defiling the minds of his readers. Shomer was an old-fashioned writer even in his own day, Germanizing his Yiddish to make it "high class," telling romantic, heartrending stories of princes who married chambermaids, of warring brothers—one an angel and the other a devil, of a wicked stepmother starving, beating and torturing her kind and beautiful stepdaughter. Every story ended happily and virtue always received its reward: the stepdaughter married the richest, handsomest and most generous boy in town, and the stepmother, at last widowed and poor, had to beg and be granted assistance by the warmhearted heroine. All this may sound harmless, but "the trial" established that such writing corrupted the good taste of the reader, blinded him to the realities, and was a major obstacle to the advancement of Yiddish literature and culture. Shomer stood condemned by the court.

The impact of *Shomer's Mishpot* (*The Trial of Shomer*) on the Yiddish reading public and on Jewish intellectuals was far-reaching, and it swayed many of Shomer's more intelligent readers against his writing. Shomer published a reply which with its coarse insults and vehemence further injured his literary standing and social prestige. He angrily left Russia with his family and settled in New York.

Twenty-four years later my father was given a reception at Carnegie Hall, and in the crowd that pressed forward at the end of the reception was Shomer's widow. She introduced herself and they chatted amicably. When she said, "It was on account of you that we went to America," my father grinned and replied, "You lost nothing by it, did you?" Indeed, Shomer was even more successful in America; his novels ran as serials in the Yiddish newspapers and a number of his plays were produced in Yiddish theaters. His children were able to receive an education and a social position that would have been beyond their reach in Russia, and one of his sons became a playwright on Broadway.

The second step was the founding of *Di Yidishe Folks Bibliothek* (The Jewish Folk Library). Along with ruthless exposure of the evils of Shomer's kind of writing, my father was determined to publish examples of what he regarded as *good* Yiddish writing. To this end he started a literary annual, which was to equal in form, content and make-up the best of such publications in Russian. He planned to select the best contributions of the foremost Yiddish writers, as well as to persuade celebrated Hebrew writers to write pieces in Yiddish for his publication. Actually all Jewish writers were bilingual at that time. They knew Yiddish as their mother tongue, but chose to write in Hebrew for social and cultural reasons. Sholom Aleichem set out to change this attitude; he wanted to make it natural, dignified and remunerative to write in Yiddish.

With his personal prestige—"Kiev banker turned Maecenas with a passion for Yiddish"—and the fantastic royalties he offered, which were high even for a Russian literary magazine, he obtained novels, short stories, poems, essays and articles both from established Hebrew writers whose works had already become classics and from the younger group—and, of course, from the most able Yiddish writers of the day. The famous I. L. Peretz, who with Sholom Aleichem and Mendele Mocher Sforim is now considered one of the fathers of modern Yiddish literature, had been writing only in Hebrew before the annual was founded. In 1888 Sholom Aleichem paid him 300 rubles for his first Yiddish writing, a poem called "Monish." No Yiddish poem has made such a sum for its author before or since. No wonder the devotees of literature in Hebrew complained that a crazy Kiev millionaire was inveigling Hebrew writers to turn to Yiddish by offering fantastic prices.

For his *Yidishe Folks Bibliothek* my father became a demanding editor and a severe critic. In this area he was no respecter of persons or reputations. He edited every piece that he accepted; some he practically rewrote. He carried on a lengthy correspondence with any author whose work needed revision; if the author did not co-operate, he made the revision anyway. He edited the poem by Peretz, though that writer was then older and better known than he was, and even rewrote a few verses entirely—something for which Peretz never quite forgave him, although he did not restore the original in subsequent editions. My father even dared to ask Mendele Mocher Sforim to revise a section of the novel he had contributed. Mendele had become a literary celebrity in both Hebrew and Yiddish before Sholom Aleichem was born. My father called him *Zayde* (grandfather), a nickname that stuck from then on. All his life he regarded Mendele as the giant of Jewish letters and stood in awe of him, yet in connection with the *Folks Bibliothek* he dared suggest that a certain portion of the novel in question was not worthy of its author—that it was burlesque rather than true satire. My father justified his editorial boldness by declaring that he was not functioning in a personal capacity but as his readers' deputy.

Much of the content of the two editions of the annual that my father managed to publish before the financial crisis has become part of classic Yiddish literature. The annual contained roughly three hundred and fifty pages and entailed much time and effort, not to speak of money.

There was a strong driving force behind Sholom Aleichem's pre-occupation with establishing a genuine Yiddish literature at the expense of his own creative work and his financial security. He was doing battle against almost all the Jewish intellectuals of the time, who regarded Yiddish as an uncouth vernacular unfit for aesthetic experience or serious thought. In fact, some 80 per cent of the Jews in the world spoke Yiddish then, and there had been some form of Yiddish literature for at least eight hundred years. But respectable Jewish writing had been religious in nature, and consequently in Hebrew—the historical language of the Scriptures and other sacred books. When at last secular literature appeared, it was still written mostly by learned men, Hebrew scholars, who wrote in that language.

But with the secular, democratic trend in Jewish life that started about the middle of the nineteenth century, Yiddish began to come into its own. The process was not unlike the emergence of the other modern European languages several centuries earlier when great writers, like Dante, for instance, appeared, and raised the vernacular to a position equal to that of the sanctified Latin. Thus, although there had been a Yiddish newspaper (in Amsterdam) in the early seventeenth century, it was a novel by Mendele Mocher Sforim in 1865 that opened the channels for a genuine modern Yiddish literature. It remained for my father to activate this revolution, which he did dramatically and decisively.

This phase of my father's life is not too well known today, or fully appreciated, because he did not continue his activity for long and was not at the front when the battle was won. But the seeds he planted were scattered by the winds of the social turmoil that began to shake the czarist regime at the turn of the century, and soon they germinated and bore fruit. Within a decade it was Hebrew that was on the defensive, needing to justify its existence as a modern form of expression. A new generation of Yiddish writers grew up, forming literary centers in Warsaw, Vilno, Odessa. By that time Sholom Aleichem had little contact with these writers, living as he did in a distant, non-Jewish city. Yet by his own literary contributions he realized the vision that he had held onto so tenaciously—no one was above or below reading a story by Sholom Aleichem.

Back in the late eighties and early nineties, however, the situation was still tentative, still pioneering. Not a single writer in either Yiddish or Hebrew lived on the income from his works. Mendele was the director of the Community Talmud Torah (Hebrew school) in Odessa. Peretz, a lawyer, was secretary of the Jewish community in Warsaw. My father was the only businessman in the literary "troika," as he called it, and certainly the only big businessman in the entire literary profession. But his failure in the financial world late in 1890 ended that distinction.

VI
After the Crash

LEAVING KIEV was a tragic, disastrous event for my father and his family. It was humiliating to admit failure; it was mortifying not to be able to face the creditors. Odessa, where the family waited for my father to return from abroad, was close to Kiev, and had the advantage of containing a literary community, with Grandfather Mendele as its leading light. My father's first months abroad were trying. Aimlessly wandering through the cities of Europe, he was in no mood to enjoy their attractions, and wished only to pass the time while his mother-in-law settled with the creditors. His state of mind was such that at the hotel in Czernowitz he registered merely as Solomon (his legal and Russified name), instead of Solomon Rabinowitz, and became a victim of mistaken identity. The local police were looking for a swindler named Solomon, and my father was arrested. Not until the police at Odessa were contacted could his identity be proved and his release obtained.

In the spring of 1891, he returned from abroad to start anew in Odessa. With some of the securities salvaged from the crash, and possibly with additional money from Babushka, he went back into the market. There were ups and downs, but he managed to keep afloat. Soon he was again engaged in literary activities and social life along the same lines as in Kiev.

Now he made plans for a third issue of *Folks Bibliothek*. As these would necessarily take time to materialize, he prepared a sort of prospectus, which he called *The Harbinger of the Folks Bibliothek*, a literary journal in itself, composed of poems, short stories, book reviews, etc.—all done by himself under different names. He was short of money at the time this publication was due from the printer, and my mother sold a piece of jewelry to pay the printer.

He wrote both fiction and nonfiction in Russian for the local newspaper and in Hebrew for *Ha-Melitz.* In a prosperous moment he gave a gala dinner in honor of Mendele—the first literary banquet in the history of Yiddish letters. As in the case of the *Folks Bibliothek,* this dinner had to be on a grand scale, comparable to the finest Russian literary affairs. It was held at the most fashionable hotel in the city at my father's expense. All the Hebrew and Yiddish writers, as well as the leading intellectuals of the community, were gathered together on that festive evening. Odessa was noted for its *bons vivants* and, as always, there was plenty of good food and fine wine. The party continued into the early hours of the morning until one of the guests, M. L. Lilienbloom, brought to mind the stark realities. He was a famous and older Hebrew writer, a controversial figure in his early days as a fighter for enlightenment. At that time he was serving as Secretary of the Jewish Burial Society of the city. "My friends," he said, "it's broad daylight, time for me to go to the office and bury Jews. . . ."

This literary gathering was the high point of my father's life in Odessa.

At first the literary colony, especially Mendele, tempted my father to stay in Odessa permanently, but then doubts developed; Kiev was a metropolis, a great Russian cultural center, and the heart of big business. My father was, after all, still a businessman.

The inevitable letdown came not long after: an adverse turn on the market proved ruinous. The capital with which he had started, everything he had gained since his arrival in Odessa, all was irretrievably lost. There was nothing he could do in Odessa now, so the family moved back to Kiev, where there were opportunities around the bourse as well as inside it.

I recall an ironic incident connected with the Odessa move. It concerned our furniture, which seemed to present an insoluble problem. Over the years of affluence the family had acquired many luxurious pieces, as well as valuable furnishings—art, Gobelin-tapestries, Chinese porcelains, Irish linens. When we first decided to move to Odessa—since there were no storage facilities in Kiev—we had to choose between selling our furniture or taking it all to Odessa. Neither alternative seemed desirable or practical. Selling in a hurry would mean a great monetary loss, and who could say when the family would be able to buy anything as good as these possessions in the foreseeable future? The money from their sale would soon melt away, and anything my parents could afford to buy in their place would be an additional comedown—psychologically as depressing as the loss of the fortune. This was exactly the moment when the moral lift a sumptuous home can give was needed, not the reverse.

But taking all the family belongings to Odessa was out of the question. An apartment still had to be found there, and who could tell what sort of place it might be? Moreover, no one knew how long we might stay.

One day, not too long before the move, my father came home with a great idea. He had met a man named Schorr at the house of a mutual friend. Mr. Schorr was a very rich man, a merchant who paid the residence fee and thus could live anywhere in Kiev. He had taken an apartment about the size of ours but had not yet furnished it. He was therefore willing to take our furniture and effects and care for them until we came back, in the meantime using them, of course. This seemed a suitable way out of the dilemma; even Babushka could see no flaw. So the family left almost all of their furniture with Schorr, taking only the most necessary or precious articles, like the Gobelins.

When the family returned from Odessa, my father called on Mr. Schorr to arrange for the return of our furniture.

At first Mr. Schorr was very courteous; he invited my father to sit down and offered him a cigar. But when my father asked when it would be convenient for the movers to come for the furniture, Schorr blandly said, "What furniture?"

The conversation went something like this:

My father, thinking that Schorr was joking, said, with a broad sweep of his arms, "All this furniture!"

"Why should you send movers for this furniture?" asked Schorr, his face hardening.

Amazed, my father replied, "To take it back, as we arranged."

Schorr looked him straight in the face. "How do you mean, 'take it back'?"

Still thinking it must be a practical joke, however inept, my father said, "Come, come, Mr. Schorr, this is no time for jests. We have an apartment and need our furniture, so I want to set a time for the movers to take it back, as we arranged."

"Arranged? Who arranged? What furniture? What are you talking about?"

"Now, Mr. Schorr, you know this furniture is ours; we lent it to you on the basis that we could get it back any time we needed it."

Then Schorr let the cat out of the bag. "*Do you have a receipt? Can you prove you lent it to me?*"

"A receipt?" My father was flabbergasted. "Why a receipt? Couldn't I trust you? Would you not have been offended if I'd asked for a receipt?"

Schorr ignored the question. "So, you have no receipt, and you can't prove that you lent me this furniture with this arrangement to take it back, as you say?"

"Why prove? *You* know it's true."

But Schorr's only reply was, "This furniture is here, and here it stays."

"But people in town know I lent it to you, even your friends!"

"Who cares?" answered Schorr.

"I'll call you to a court of honor."

Schorr shrugged off the threat.

My father returned to the hotel where we were staying, crushed and ashen. It might have been possible to take Mr. Schorr to court. Witnesses could prove that the furniture had originally belonged to us; others could testify that they had heard the arrangement made with Mr. Schorr, while he would be unable to produce a bill of sale or record of buying the furniture anywhere else. But neither of my parents could go to court, since they had lived in Kiev illegally before the move, and had no right of residence now. The first thing the court would do would be to banish the entire family, on foot under convoy, to Pereyaslav.

We bought new furniture of fairly good quality, but not to be compared with the old. The mishap was a taboo subject in our house; the name Schorr was never to be mentioned. But my brother and sisters spoke of it a lot among themselves. It was as if they had lost a part of the family. The wish grew to see the furniture again, like the nostalgia for one's native place. One summer, having learned that the Schorrs were away on vacation, they contrived to be admitted to the apartment. They walked through the rooms quietly, as if in a funeral parlor in the presence of the coffin, looking at the familiar pieces and touching them. Then they left and came home morose and silent. Now, even for them, the matter was closed and to be forgotten.

The only time my father ever referred to this incident in our presence, he sounded more saddened by his disappointment in human nature than by the loss of the furniture.

A few years after our return to Kiev, my mother decided to learn a profession. Since medicine was beyond her reach, she chose dentistry. A Jewish dentist named Lev Semyonovich Blank had just opened in Kiev one of the first, if not the very first, school of dentistry for women in Russia. He had taken great pains to obtain the necessary permit and accreditation. The course ran for two years, the students receiving a diploma on graduation. My mother's, when she brought it home at last for us to admire, read:

"The Blank School of Dentistry gives the right to practice dentistry to Olga Mikhailovna Rabinowitz by permission of his Imperial Majesty, Czar of all Russia, Finland . . . etc. Nicholas II."

One of the ostensible reasons for my mother's decision to learn a profession was that it would give her a residence right in Kiev. This would make it possible for her children, within the limited quota for Jews, to be admitted to the Gymnasium. For Misha this might mean the official First or Second Gymnasium, opening the door to an academic education. The residence right would also protect Babushka, but would not extend to my father.

Another reason that must have been at the back of my mother's mind was the desire to supplement my father's earnings.

The rest of the family money had been lost on the stock exchanges of Odessa and Kiev. My father now depended entirely on his brokerage, which made greater demands on his time and energy than he could give, absorbed as he was in his writing. In fact, the dental practice made a substantial contribution to the family income all through those seven years in Kiev, as well as after our departure from Russia. For several winters in Nervi, Italy, my mother had an arrangement with a local dentist to treat patients in his office under his license.

Babushka, naturally, was against the idea. Whoever heard of a mother of five going to school? She would be taxing herself too much, and if she, God forbid, broke down, what would become of the children? My mother paid no heed. Poor Babushka! She could not understand the modern ways of her wayward daughter, so she ascribed everything to my mother's being her father's daughter—unpredictable, unconforming, stubborn.

My father looked upon his wife's decision with the eyes of a parent viewing a new feat of his child prodigy. He always had an unbounded admiration for my mother. All through the years he was fascinated by her practical sense, her limitless energy, boldness, wisdom, and her way with people. He never took these qualities for granted but continually rediscovered them. Her new profession was a romantic adventure for him, and he participated vicariously every step of the way. While my mother was still in her first year at the dental school, he was already planning her office. It would be in our apartment, of course—office buildings were almost nonexistent—but which room would be best, both for patients and to preserve family privacy? How should the shingle read? What should the office hours be? And so forth.

Babushka was not entirely wrong. It was not easy for my mother to go through the course, with the responsibility of five children, particularly in the winter months when one or the other of them was nearly always in bed with some childhood disease.

I recall being laid up with the mumps, and Mother, early in the morning before rushing to school, bending over me, checking my temperature with her lips on my forehead, promising in a warm whisper to return very early that day, meanwhile Babushka would take care of me and I should be good and obey her. There were times when three of us were sick at once, but my mother did not miss her classes.

The happy day of graduation arrived, and we were overjoyed to have our mother home again with us all day. Our next excitement was the arrival of the office equipment. On the day that delivery was to be made my father did not leave the house. At every ring of the bell, we children rushed into the corridor, and my father emerged to see if it was the delivery man. A long day passed; toward evening two huge men appeared at the door carrying immense crates. My father became completely involved, discussing the best way to open the crates and how to extricate the various pieces, and pointing out where each should go.

The equipment was surprisingly similar to that in dental offices today, except, of course, that there was no electricity. The chair was of red velvet, raised and lowered by a foot pedal. The drill was operated in the same way. The instruments, wrapped in silver paper, were kept in a special cabinet. My mother brought them with her to America in 1914 and years later showed them to a young relative

studying dentistry in New York. He said they were the same as those
he used in school.

As soon as all was in place, my mother put on her white coat and
stood beside the chair to get the feel of her new profession. We looked
lovingly at her, an impressive, beautiful presence; her dark hair coiled
on top of her head made her look even taller, and her eyes were
brighter against the whiteness of the coat.

The shingle for her office was riveted to the stone wall of the
apartment house—a massive plate of bright metal reading:

DENTIST
Olga Mikhailovna Rabinowitz
VISITING HOURS:
From 9 A.M. to I P.M. and from 3 to 6 P.M.

When I visited Kiev in 1966, I could still see the rivet holes of my
mother's shingle on the wall of the apartment house.

The shingle was up, but patients were slow in coming. People were
not accustomed to lady dentists. Friends, knowing that my mother
had just started her practice, may not have had confidence in her.
Those who did come were the poorer people—low-paid petty officials
and soldiers. There were days without a single patient, days with
perhaps one or two. Once we overheard my mother saying that patients like to come to a doctor who has people in the waiting room.
This gave my brother Misha an idea: all of us, Babushka too, and
perhaps a couple of relatives, should dress up like patients in coats
and hats and sit in the waiting room. The idea amused my father, and
he elaborated on it: one of us should puff out a cheek to make it
look swollen; another tie a shawl around the jaw, etc.—it was a
source of laughter for some time.

I remember a dramatic moment in my mother's professional career
when she was late in her ninth month of pregnancy with her sixth
child, my brother Numa. The doorbell rang with unusual persistence;
the maid opened the door and a big strapping soldier came in, his
cheek swollen into a mound, his eyes wild with pain. When the horrified maid ran to my mother, she only said, "Tell him I'll be right
there."

Babushka, who had seen the patient at the door, could hardly control her anger and fright. "Bibi, you won't do anything of the sort!
You must send him to another dentist. In your condition, pulling a

97

tooth is dangerous. You may hurt yourself. At least, think of your children—what will become of them?"

Babushka's pleading made me cry, and I, too, begged my mother to send the soldier away. But she got up from her chair, saying to me, "Go play with your dolls, nothing will happen to me."

Nothing did happen. A short while later, both dentist and patient emerged from the office, the soldier moaning but obviously relieved, and my mother looking triumphantly at Babushka: "What a tooth, what a tooth!"

When my father related this story to friends, with details added, one might have thought that the tooth was as big as a horn, and the pulling as hard as dragging a rock uphill. But he did in truth regard as heroic this act of my mother's. What if Numa had wanted to come out into the world just then?

When Numa actually was born—this was 1901—the family's financial condition was very precarious. There was an unforgettable incident connected with his birth. I knew some of the details at the time, but at the birth of my own first son, my mother told me the whole story.

She had given birth to Numa in her own bedroom, of course, and in the early morning. In spite of a sleepless night, my father felt wide awake and full of energy. He washed, shaved, dressed and told my mother that he was going for a walk and would be back in an hour. She was too exhausted from the delivery to ask or even wonder why he was going for a walk in the cold, damp March morning. All she cared about was that he would be back soon.

Hour after hour passed; he did not return. Concern began to develop into commotion. Babushka ran in and out of my mother's room. Terrifying words like "arrest," "on foot under convoy," hung in the air, since my father had no residence right in Kiev. My mother, only a few hours after childbirth, flushed and excited, sat up in bed, to Babushka's great horror. It would be the death of her daughter! Finally the maid was sent over to the Mazors' to inform Natasha of the misfortune.

Natasha was now married to Moyssei Savelevich Mazor, a lawyer with the full title of barrister, which only a few Jews attained. (He became a prominent jurist in Kiev, and after the Revolution, was appointed Professor of Law at the University.) He had a very clear, cold and logical mind, treating everything, however minor or trivial, very thoroughly, and never jumping to conclusions. He could not stand a breach in routine. If it were a legal matter, he had fixed office hours; if a family matter, he was the last person to get excited or alarmed. He regarded his wife's spirited temperament with the same logic. Excitement and exaggeration were women's privileges; his wife was a woman; therefore it was logical for her to be that way. Natasha had learned not to bother her husband with trivia, and it was only on rare occasions that she ever entered his study during the day.

When our doorbell rang on that memorable day of Numa's birth and Natasha and Moyssei Savelevich came through the door, Babushka broke down for the first time. My mother would certainly be so shocked by the unexpected visit of Moyssei Savelevich at this unusual hour that it would bring on post-natal fever. Therefore Moyssei Savelevich had better remain in the parlor, while Natasha went in to see my mother and to find out all the details of my father's departure; she would then report to her husband, who would decide what to do next. But after hearing Natasha's report, Moyssei Savelevich decided he must talk to my mother himself—an indication that it was a very serious matter indeed.

Entering the bedroom, he evidently thought that under the present circumstances it was unbecoming to congratulate my mother on the birth of her son; after the conventional greeting he pulled up a chair and proceeded to question her as if she were a witness in court, or at least a client. What kind of identification papers did Solomon have on him? Did he have a permit to reside temporarily in Kiev? Was it in good order or expired? By that time my mother was indeed running a fever, and her face was fiery red. Natasha's face was red too; she kept turning her head away from the bed to hide her tears. Babushka was whispering fiercely to Natasha, "Imagine, going out for a walk on a day like this! Now what will become of her six children? O God, God!" The infant was forgotten. The midwife was upset and scolded me: "Stop biting your nails! Go play with your dolls!"

At this point the maid brought in a lighted kerosene lamp, and my mother suddenly realized how late it was. Couldn't Moyssei Savelevich somehow check with the police? Moyssei Savelevich shook his head. If Solomon had *not* been arrested, checking with the police would only cause them to learn all about him for the first time, and they would be sure to pick him up on his return. If, on the other hand, he *were* arrested, wouldn't he have let his family know—or at least contacted Moyssei Savelevich as his lawyer? No, he did not believe that my father was under arrest.

At this point the door quietly opened, and there, peering round it, was my father's embarrassed face. Babushka rushed to her room without a word. But Natasha ran to meet him, threw her arms around him, crying *Dyada! Dyada!* (Uncle). Even Moyssei Savelevich's always sombre face showed some joy and relief.

And, of course, there was no limit to my mother's happiness. All that she had gone through on this terrible day evaporated in the joy of seeing my father back, free and well at her side. She relaxed in a daze of bliss.

No one seemed anxious to probe into the details of my father's absence. He himself tried to introduce a lighter note into the strained, heavy atmosphere. When the midwife was ready to give the newborn its first bath, in Mother's room, he called all of us to witness the ritual. The midwife protested—it would be too much excitement for her patient. And accusingly to my father, she said, "I don't have to tell you what a day she had after you got lost. . . ."

But he won her over, and lined up the children for the ceremony. It was the first time I had ever seen a newborn baby; when I saw the tiny body with its dangling limbs, I screamed at the top of my voice, "It's not human, it's not human!" My outburst seemed to amuse my father immensely. For years to come he would laughingly tease me about it, especially on my brother's birthday.

What really did happen to my father that day?

There were three versions of the story. One, simple and bare of details, was told to my mother that night at her bedside; another, in greater detail, was told to Natasha and Moyssei Savelevich in the parlor. This one must have been humorous, judging from the laughter. The third, told to my mother later, was the one she recounted to me.

Like many dramatic moments in the life of our family, my father's disappearance had to do with lack of money. He was not the man to worry, as Babushka did, about how the birth of a second son might complicate the military service problem of his first son ten years hence (an only son was exempt). He was happy to have another child, and especially another son. His immediate problem was financial: the doctor had to be paid, and also the midwife who was to stay on with my mother for a while; and there were other expenses connected with the confinement. For all this, there simply was no money in the house. The only possible source was a loan from a friend or a business acquaintance. When my father went out for a walk on that cold day in March, he was actually going in search of a loan.

He had a few people in mind. One lived close by and he could walk there: the maid half-opened the door and said the *Barin* (Master) was not in, and not expected until late. The second choice was a man who also lived close by, but in the opposite direction. My father hailed a droshky and went to see him. The man received my father politely, listened to him patiently, and even encouraged him to go into details about his plight; but when my father came right out with his request, the man slowly shook his head. He regretted that he could do nothing; he had just suffered a reverse himself. The third prospect lived quite a distance away. My father hesitated for a moment, thinking he had better return home—after all, he had promised to be back in an hour, and besides he was beginning to feel very tired. But the thought of the need at home impelled him to make another effort. He took a droshky to the third place.

The ride was long and tedious. His eyes felt heavy. He kept wondering how to approach the man in order to avoid another failure. Suppose he refused? He banished that thought—it was more pleasant to think how he would divide the sum he was going to receive among the doctor, the midwife, and other pressing creditors. Arriving at his destination, he ran up the flight of stairs and rang the bell. A pleasant, hospitable servant helped him off with his coat, showed him to the living room, and informed him that the *Barin* was not at home just now, but she was sure that he would be soon.

"How soon?"

"Oh, very very soon," she said, directing him to a comfortable chair. Then she left the room, closing the door behind her.

He stretched out in the chair, which was large and soft and cushioned, and relaxed. Everything became misty, indistinct. His eyes closed, and he fell asleep.

He slept long and soundly. The daughter of the house came in, with a lighted candle, to practice on the piano, which stood in a corner of the room. She did not notice Sholom Aleichem in the chair, and he did not hear her playing. It was only when she stopped that he woke up, confused, wondering where he was and why. After an embarrassing moment, he asked the girl where her father was. She was surprised at the question. Her father? Why, both her parents were out of the city, visiting Uncle Sasha in Kharkov!

"In Kharkov?" my father asked in amazement. "Why did the servant say the *Barin* would be here very soon?"

"Oh," the girl replied, "Mashka calls my big brother *Barin* also."
He rushed back home.

All was well after he returned, except for the money problem, of
course. This remained hovering, as usual, over his head.

The Kiev bourse was the third largest in Russia, after those in St.
Petersburg and Moscow. It conducted its transactions in an imposing
building at Number 1 Institutskaya. But very few of the Jews operating on the *birzha* were ever inside the bourse proper. The more substantial brokers among them traded with agents of firms on the stock
exchange in a nearby café, which was operated by an Italian, Semodenni. For perhaps 99 per cent of the Jewish brokers, Semodenni's
was the *birzha*. There were also many would-be brokers and traders
who did not even get into Semodenni's but manipulated outside in
the street, working through intermediaries with brokers in the café,
who were in touch, through more intermediaries, with brokers close
to the firms on the exchange. One of my father's major characters,
Menachem Mendel, belonged to this lowest category, trading out on
the street.

The Yiddish term for this sort of trading, characteristically self-
derogatory, was *dreyen,* going in circles. What was a trader, a *birzhevik,* doing on the *birzha?* He was *dreying,* circling around another
birzhevik, who was circling around a third, who was circling about a
fourth, who was connected with the bourse.

I am sure that my father must have been at some time inside the
bourse, although he never had a seat on the exchange. He himself
never fell below Semodenni's, but out of personal interest, which was
of course literary, he consorted with the hopeful traders in the street.
He wanted to know them, to learn all about them. Some of them
called on him at home, and I remember these strange visitors. They
were not dressed like city people—their frock coats were longer, their
hats wider: some had long scarves around their necks; a few affected
city dress, but their small-town manners showed through.

They were a restless lot, nervous, fidgety, with a furtive look in
their eyes; they sat on the edge of their seats as if they might have
to jump up suddenly. They were hurried in their speech, not wasting
time to complete sentences or to listen to the end once they had
guessed the speaker's drift. They liked to handle something, twist

some object in their hands, trying to steady their nerves, just as some people smoke. As soon as one of these *birzheviks* sat down facing my father at his desk, he would unconsciously look for something to pick up and twiddle. There were many objects on the desk—pens, pencils, clips, inkwells, glue, scissors, as well as a few odd playthings, one of which was a perfect miniature bicycle with rubber tires and a bell that rang at the slightest pressure. Invariably the visitor would reach for the tiny bicycle, turning its wheels as he talked or listened. My father came to know their characteristics so well that one day when a *birzhevik* came to see him he handed him the bicycle before the conversation had even begun. His visitor was startled: smilingly my father said (using the word *dreyen* to make a pun), "You'll have to twist something, so twist this."

These men came to see my father primarily to listen to him, hoping to learn something about trends on the market or pick up a tip on a stock. But my father preferred to hear them talk, prompting them with such questions as why had they come to Kiev, where were they from, whom had they left behind? Had they permission to stay overnight or were they planning to take the long tedious ride by trolley at the end of the day to Podol, the suburb where Jews were permitted to live, and then take the same trek the next morning to Semodenni's? What was the last trade they had made, did they lose or gain? What prospects did they have? What were they aiming for?

My father soon realized that these people did not have the slightest conception of the intricacies of the stock market. Nor did they understand the produce exchange. They expected to operate on the *birzha* just as they traded with the peasants on market day in their small towns—buying and selling, living by their wits, that was all there was to it. On the *birzha* they were involving themselves in a game which they did not even know that they did not understand. They were carried along like driftwood on the surge of trade. Occasionally a few crumbs from a windfall dropped down to them; they would lose these soon, and try again, only to end up with a further loss.

One of the visitors had a heartrending story of unmitigated failure. Whatever he touched went up in smoke. When my father asked him why under these circumstances he didn't pull out, his answer was, "How, then, would I make my living?"

It was from such people that my father created Menachem Mendel. The first part of the work was written in 1892; the rest appeared sporadically during the next eighteen years. Menachem Mendel is a composite type of symbolic proportions, the personification of the *luftmentsh*, the man "living on air," always hoping, always on the verge of making a great fortune, or at least a comfortable living, and inevitably coming to grief at the end. Bad luck is blamed for the disaster, what Menachem Mendel calls *shlim-shlim-mazl*.

This hero is not individualized, like the other characters in my father's works, by personal description or biographical background. We are not told how he looks, or how he happens to be in his present situation. All we have are letters between a husband, Menachem Mendel, and his wife, Shayneh Shayndel, who is constantly quoting her mother's words of wisdom. From a few lines in the first letter we learn about the poor situation in which he left his wife and children in Kasrilevka for the middle-sized city of Kishinev, to collect the dowry promised to his wife at the time of their marriage by an uncle living there. As the uncle had no cash, he gave Menachem Mendel a letter of credit to a broker, Barbash, in Odessa. In Odessa, Barbash tells him there is no coverage for the credit; if and when that uncle of his in Kishinev will send in the wheat, he will honor the letter of credit, but not before. After urgent appeals to the uncle, Menachem Mendel receives from him one hundred rubles in cash and a note for two hundred more. This is the capital with which he emerges into the arena of big business.

While waiting for this money, Menachem Mendel is fascinated by the big city. When he writes to his wife, the first thing he talks of after the traditional honorific and lengthy greeting, is Odessa: "How big it is and how beautiful, and the kind people here, and the golden business you can do here!"

He goes on: "Just imagine, I come out, cane in hand, on the Gretsk, that's the name of the street where Jews trade, and I can have twenty thousand deals. If I want wheat, it's wheat; oats, it's oats; cotton, it's cotton, flour, salt, feathers, raisins, sacks, herring—in short, you name it and Odessa has it. At first I smelled out two businesses, but they weren't to my liking. So, I circled about on the Gretsk for a time till I came upon something real good. I trade in 'London' [British pounds] and make good profit. You pick up sometimes twenty-five rubles, another time fifty, if you strike it right it's a hundred. In short, 'London' is a business in which one can become rich in one day. Just a little while ago a fellow came here, some beadle of a synagogue, and in one shot cleaned up thirty thousand rubles, and now he laughs at the rest of them. I'm telling you, my precious spouse, gold is rolling in the streets here. . . ."

But Shayneh Shayndel is not impressed. In her reply she asks, "Why don't you tell exactly what you're trading in? How much is it a yard? Or is it sold by weight? . . . You say you just bought it and there's already a profit. What sort of material is it that its price swells in your hand? Even mushrooms, Mother says, need rain. And if there's a profit, why don't you sell it? What are you waiting for?" She complains that he does not say a word about his life in Odessa, and quotes her mother again to the effect that when a cow joins the herd in the pasture, it forgets to return home, concluding, "If you would listen to me, you would sell whatever it is and come home with what little money you clear. You'll find better and nicer business here."

Menachem Mendel ignores her repeated calls to come home. He neglects to respond to her reports of trouble in the family, such as the sickness of the children—not to speak of the local town gossip. He is obsessed with the chase; he will catch fortune by its tail. His letters are aglow with the excitement of projects; he talks about bears, bulls, calls, puts, straddles—terms which naturally puzzle his wife, and which he tries to explain to her according to his own primitive understanding of them.

Generally, he barely manages to keep afloat. For a moment or two the sun may shine and he makes a little money. He can even spare some to buy jewelry for his wife. Now he is in high finance, trading in rubles, as well as in pounds, no less. "When the newspapers talk of war," he writes, "the ruble takes a dip and 'London' moves up, up. Only last week there was a rumor that the English queen was not feeling well and calls jumped overs the rooftops. Now the papers say the queen is feeling better, and the ruble picked up a little; you can get all the calls you may want."

In this expansive mood, he tells Shayneh Shayndel that he is a big operator, buying or selling ten thousand English pounds, and even twenty thousand on one deal—on margin of course. Only the other day he could have sold a few calls and several puts and cleared a considerable profit, but his broker would not let him. "I'll break your neck if you let such excellent pieces out of your hand," said his broker, and assured him that a call of fifty rubles would later be worth two hundred, three hundred, five hundred, a thousand rubles. And why not two thousand? If only half of what the broker said would

come true, Menachem Mendel would soon be a very rich man. All
he was waiting for was the ultimo, the monthly clearance. He would
cash in all his "differences" and then go on a bearish track. He would
buy rubles and knock the stuffing out of the pounds. Then he would
come for his wife and children in Kasrilevka and take them to Odessa,
rent an apartment on the finest street of the city, buy good furniture,
and live, as they say there, the life of Odessa. But again his wife is
not impressed. She would not think of moving to Odessa, she hates
the city, and advises her husband to spit in the face of that broker,
and sell, sell out as best he can and return home. He simply must
come home now—and she gives him a list of things to bring from
the city.

Menachem Mendel does leave Odessa, but his last letter from there
reveals that things did not turn out as he had hoped. The ultimo had
arrived, with disastrous results: Bismarck caught a cold, the political
situation become confused, and nobody knew what was going on.
"London" was as high as gold, the ruble had dropped to the lowest
depths. "If you ask me about my puts and straddles, there are no puts
and straddles. Nobody gives, nobody takes. As if for spite, I was stuck
with my goods with small people who choked on the first squeeze. If
I only had changed over the day before! But can one be a prophet? I
tell you, it's a conflagration, a plague. You wouldn't know the place.
They are running about like poisoned mice, addled and muddled.
Everybody shouting, 'London—where's my London? Give me my
London!' In short, my precious spouse, it's bleak, black night. All the
profits I made, all the initial capital I had, the jewelry I bought for you,
my Sabbath coat off my back—all down the drain. My situation is
miserable beyond words. I am longing, pining for home, my heart
goes out. I curse myself a hundred times a day for coming to this. I
wish I had broken a leg before I stepped forth in this Odessa, where
a human being doesn't have the least value, one could die in the
middle of the street and no one would even stop to look. . . . I tell
you, my precious spouse, I am so disgusted with this Odessa, with the
birzha here, with the café, with all the creatures here, I would run
to the end of the world!"

One would think that after this harrowing experience Menachem
Mendel would forswear chasing rainbows and go home to Kasrilevka
to settle down like the rest of the Jews there, at least for a while.
But no—in that last letter there was a postscript about the Lombard,

the pawnshop in Odessa where people get loans on their valuables. The pawnbroker gives very low valuations but charges a high interest, so the interest soon exceeds the value and the objects in pawn are sold at auction. People buy up the bargains and make a profit. If he had money he would do a little trading at auctions, recoup all his losses, and make a heap more. But what could he do? "Without money one had better not be born, and if born, he had better die." Obviously he had not yet lost his illusions.

Menachem Mendel did not return to Kasrilevka. From his next letter his wife learns he is in Yehupetz (Kiev). He is no longer trading in wind, in empty air, he writes; now he has a decent solid business. He deals in papers. He swears he had meant to go home, in fact he was on the train to Kasrilevka when a fellow passenger, going on to Yehupetz, told him he was dealing in papers there. It's not "London," which depends on Bismarck and the English queen and you never set your eyes on it, but papers, which depend only on St. Petersburg and Warsaw, and you can feel them, hold them in your hands. . . . In short, he's in stocks. So he is back on the *birzha,* this time in Yehupetz, in the street outside the exchange.

He fares no better there, of course. After a preliminary lucky break he is wiped out as devastatingly as in Odessa. Menachem Mendel swears to forsake speculation for good. Disgusted with trade, and deriding his former colleagues, he moves into another area, though not actually too far off. He becomes a broker. So many things are bought and sold in Yehupetz, each one going through the broker who specializes in a particular brand of goods on the market. Menachem Mendel deals with all goods irrespectively, each time believing that at last fortune has come his way. Every trade, after all, has to have a broker, every broker must deal with another broker, around whom there may be others helping and sharing in the commission. Menachem Mendel begins with sugar and immediately earns fifty rubles—he does not know himself how it happened. But that's all he earns. He tries hard, even inquiring of his wife whether there were ample rains and not too many bugs in the countryside, for beets like rain and dislike bugs. But he soon realizes that sugar is not for him. The big brokers hold the monopoly on the trade.

He does no better as a discount man. Now this was real money. You buy up uncollected debts at a very good discount and go out to collect them. But he cannot collect them. The same pattern runs through his essays in timber, house building, farms, factories, mines and oils. In oil he almost has a real break. He hears from a broker, who has it from another, about an oil field in the Caucasus, the oil belt of Russia, where Rothschild has properties. Menachem Mendel knows a broker who knows a broker from Yehupetz who went to Paris, and is said to know a broker close to the Rothschilds. The ex-Yehupetz broker is persuaded to come back to Yehupetz—he had other reasons for coming, to be sure—to look into the oil-field matter. He expresses his willingness to handle it, and wants to know the location of the property. But none of the brokers connected with the deal seem to know it. One of them knows the name of a town nearby, but the Parisian broker says there is no such town in the Caucasus.

So Menachem Mendel gives up his brokerage too. Now he wants an honorable trade, and he takes to writing. He has met a writer, a man who sits in his hotel room and writes things down and sends them to the newspaper; he is paid one kopek per word. Our hero figures that he can write at least a thousand words a day, which would make it ten rubles—not a fortune to be sure, but a fair income, and honorable. He tells his own story, counts the lines, sends it off to the newspaper, and actually sees his name in print—Menachem Mendel printed out. In the editor's correspondence column a reply appears to the effect that the writing is not bad, but much too long-winded. The editor would like to see more; it must not be fantasies, however, but descriptions of actual life situations in Yehupetz. So Menachem Mendel sends the editor reams upon reams of paper, borrowing from his landlady to pay for paper and postage. But neither money nor a letter comes in return. He writes again and again, begging for some word, good or bad, but to no avail. He writes Shayneh Shayndel now that his situation is "the water reaching up to his neck." She sends him just enough to pay the hotel bill and return home.

Once again he is actually on the train back to Kasrilevka; once again something turns up to make him change his mind. This time it's a package of papers a matchmaker had left behind at the hotel as a pledge that he would return to pay his bill. When he did not return, the landlady, just as Menachem Mendel was leaving, gave him the package of papers—it was of no use to her and Menachem Mendel might meet the man somewhere. On the train, Menachem

Mendel inspects the package and finds it a veritable gold mine—lists of families with marriageable daughters or sons, the social and financial status of the families, the dowry offered or requested, and the specific requirements in each case. All you needed to do was match up a couple by means of this book, and then get the parties together. You could easily figure out the commission to the matchmaker.

Naturally, he could not pass up this golden opportunity just to return to Kasrilevka. He at once turned matchmaker and actually arranged a match, and a very profitble one—that is, almost. He represented one of the parties, and another matchmaker represented the other. Both were so involved in the material negotiations between the parties that they neglected to ascertain the sexes of the two young people they were matching up. In the final negotiations it turned out they were trying to marry off two girls!

I have dwelt at such length on this tragicomic hero not only because he looms so large in my father's works, but also, and more important, because the world of Menachem Mendel was so much like the world my father lived in for the first eighteen of his thirty years of literary creativity. Menachem Mendel took in his stride the agonizing wrestle with luck and fate. The *birzha* was the staff of his spirit as well as the mechanics of his life. But my father, with his heart in creative writing, found such a life exasperating, mortifying. Not until he became a famous author did he completely abandon his business life. Even after the initial disaster in 1890, he continued to dabble in the stock market; this went on until 1903, when all the family funds had disappeared. But by this time the prestige of Yiddish literature had grown sufficiently to support a Yiddish author—at least one as popular as Sholom Aleichem.

In his introduction to the second edition of *Menachem Mendel,* my father wrote:

"Menachem Mendel is not a hero of a novel, and not at all a fictitious character. He is, poor fellow, a plain Jew, with whom the author is personally closely acquainted. We passed through, together, a stretch of life of nearly twenty years. Having first met in 1892 on the "small *birzha*" of Odessa, we went through, side by side, all the seven pits of purgatory, the *birzha* in Yehupetz, walked together to St. Petersburg and Warsaw, passed through many a crisis, shifted from one possible source of livelihood to another, and, alas, found happiness in none, and were compelled finally to do what all Jews do—emigrate to America. There, they say, Jews are doing well—that, however, we shall see in his subsequent letters from America. . . ."

Apparently my father hoped to bring Menachem Mendel to the United States and relate his vicissitudes here.

Menachem Mendel is symbolic on several levels. He is the Russian Jew under the czarist regime, deprived of human rights, divorced from agriculture, excluded from industry, barred from education, who perforce must function in mid-air—the *luftmentsh*. He is also modern man who has lost his roots, adrift in the modern city, not yet adjusted to the intricacies of the new urban civilization. Or he might be considered the Don Quixote of the capitalist society. Deeper yet, he represents the eternally restless human soul, reaching out for goals beyond the horizon, seeking to break through the narrowing confines of human association.

VII
Daily Life in Kiev

IN 1966, sixty-one years after we left Russia, I returned to Kiev and found our old apartment house still standing and in fair condition, though now without a doorman. On the outside wall, near the entrance, a plaque inscribed in Ukrainian read, "Sholom Aleichem, the writer, lived here, 1898–1903." Our old apartment was now subdivided into six single units, each occupied by one tenant. These tenants had read many of Sholom Aleichem's works in translation, but they looked upon his daughter from America as a relic not only of a different world but of a different century as well.

I can remember well our apartment in Kiev with its elegant furnishings—the living-room pieces which had been imported from Vienna, the large black concert grand on which my father loved to improvise sad melodies, the vast lamp that hung over a massive dining table. For servants we had two live-in domestics, a cook and a nurse-maid for my baby brother, and also a woman who came in to do the laundry. The children who were old enough went to school, which in Russia at that time called for money.

We could hardly, then, be called "poor" by any standards, except perhaps those of Babushka, who had lived with Grandfather Elimelech on his estate. My father had no definite steady income; money came in at irregular intervals, in unpredictable amounts, rarely as much as anticipated. Babushka, used to the ultimate security, never recognized any relation between the needs of the family and its income.

With a dozen people in one apartment, there was always something happening. The day was begun early and turbulently by Babushka, who rose long before the rest of us; she made her appearance properly dressed, with a thick bunch of keys suspended from the belt around her waist. The multitude of keys was necessary because she kept so many things locked up—the sugar, the silver, linens, the big trunk in her room. Her trunk, which always fascinated me, contained her personal treasures. It was enormous, with thick wooden walls reinforced with iron straps, and a curved top. Inside it everything was laid out in perfect order, as Babushka was not only cautious and suspicious of the servants, but incredibly neat.

The servants, among her main concerns, were her bête noir. Her first act in the morning was to go to their quarters to make sure that they were up and working. They always were, of course, but how were they doing their chores? They never pleased her, and she scolded and shouted at them so that sometimes her voice reached as far as our bedrooms.

My parents could not bear her treatment of the servants. My father was dismayed, but since he could do nothing about her behavior he preferred to hear and know nothing about the servants. He felt uncomfortable, anyway, in the presence of servility. One custom he disliked was that, in the winter months, the maid would kneel down at his feet as he was about to leave in order to pull his boots over his shoes, or to remove them on his return. When a new maid automatically dropped on her knees as my father appeared at the door, in order to remove his boots, he would raise his hand in refusal, preferring to take them off himself. The maid did not understand, but she would never do it again. In his presence Babushka refrained from speaking harshly to the servants.

My mother expected the servants to do their work but regarded them as members of the household. She protested and pleaded with Babushka about her overbearing treatment, but in the end, as in most household matters, resigned herself to the inevitable. Housekeeping did not really interest my mother, while for Babushka it was second nature—and she was very efficient. Still, my mother wanted to have some part in the running of her own household, and sometimes she would leave the house for a while just to avoid another battle with Babushka, who loved her only child dearly but did not realize how she was frustrating her.

Babushka was in charge of the marketing, making out the order for the servant to take to the stores or stalls. But she would not let the servant go by herself, as she was sure that she would cheat. So my mother did the buying, while the servant carried the basket. Coming home, my mother, ill at ease because she was carrying nothing while the maid, one step behind her, was burdened down with a heavy load, would order one of the tramps hanging around the market to carry the basket back to the house for five kopeks. Babushka, of course, objected—not to the spending of five kopeks, but to the servants' being spoiled. They were already so indulged, she said, they didn't do a stitch of work.

The worst ordeal for my mother was engaging a new maid, with Babushka doing the interrogating and making the final decision. Unfortunately this took place quite often, for, with Babushka in charge, the turnover of servants was pretty constant.

From the employment office would arrive a young woman carrying a slip of paper with her name on it, her home town, and a stipulation that she was to get "sugar and tea from the table." This meant that she could have tea and sugar whenever the family was having it, in contrast to the older system of doling out a certain amount to last for a specified period. The pay was seven rubles a month. After the interview the slip of paper was marked "accepted" or "not accepted," as the case might be.

Standing between the two formidable figures of my mother and Babushka, who were seated at the table, the maid would be questioned. Sometimes the unpleasantness would come immediately. If the girl looked too citified, perhaps because she had been in Kiev for several years, with the manner and dress of girls one saw on the street, Babushka would shake her head and tell my mother in a low voice, but loud enough for the girl to hear, "Look, a veritable *panyenka* (ladyship), I wouldn't know how to address her." Red in the face, my mother would have to tell the girl she was not accepted and write it down on the slip of paper.

If the girl looked like a typical peasant fresh from the village, Babushka would feel at home with her and start the questions. Did she have a boy friend? Invariably, the answer was no. Sometimes the no was qualified—she did have a *coum*. (In the Greek Orthodox Church, the godmother and godfather at a christening were usually young people, who were known as *coum* and *couma*. They had a special, formalized relationship, in which it was taboo to marry each other.) Did her *coum* ever visit her? God forbid, never. Did she have any other relatives? No, none; on holidays she went only to church.

Before long the girl would be caught with a man in her room; taken to task for it, she would declare that it was only her *coum*. But she had said that he never visited her! This was the first time, she would say, she couldn't imagine how he had found out where she lived. My mother was inclined to be tolerant, but Babushka would have none of it. She would discharge the girl and begin the search for a new one, again faced with the whole process of interrogation.

Even without the *coum* complication, Babushka usually found something to berate the maid for. Occasionally she suffered a setback. Once, after a severe tongue-lashing, one girl lifted her head and said, "Ma'am, I'm not a serf. Serfdom was abolished a long time ago. If I do not please you, I can go." Babushka was stunned and speechless. The words "serf" and "serfdom" struck a nostalgic chord in her heart. She had been born and had grown up under that system, and though she saw it officially abolished, serfdom had remained in spirit for the better part of her life. The peasants on the Loyeff estate were free men, but the personal relationship of serf to master had not really changed on the landed estates. Babushka's attitude toward the servants in the Kiev apartment was a carry-over from those days. The bold declaration by the servant girl pointed up for Babushka the great changes in the world around her, which she was reluctant to accept. "That's what the city does to a peasant girl," she would say mournfully to my mother.

The change was blatant in her own circle—Natasha was paying her maids nine rubles a month, and addressing them not by the familiar *te*, thou, used for speaking to menials, but by the polite *ve*, you, as if they were ladies. Babushka did not mind the raise in pay, but to address a maid as *ve*—the world was indeed falling apart!

Yet there was one domestic in our household whom Babushka called *ve* and treated with respect and consideration all through the years. Nyanya was a combination of nursemaid and governess, who was brought from Kiev to our family in Belaya Tserkov when my oldest sister Tissa was born in 1884. She took care of the first four children, and in 1890, when the family moved to Odessa, my mother lent her to Natasha. She remained in Natasha's household until she reached a very old age, when Natasha provided for her in a comfortable home for the aged. Two or three times a year Babushka insisted that the older children pay a visit to Nyanya at the home for the aged and bring her a basket of oranges. Any attempt by them to avoid the visit provoked a lecture on gratitude, consideration and mercy, and a hint that our father would be displeased to hear of this argument. From the one visit on which I accompanied my sister, I remember the beaming happiness on the tiny wrinkled face of a small, very old woman.

Why was Babushka so kind and courteous to Nyanya, who was, after all, a domestic? It must have been because Nyanya came from the burgher class—she was a *dvoryanka* and a graduate of the Institute for Honorable Maidens. Class solidarity was unconsciously operating.

My mother, preoccupied as she was with her dental practice and her infant son, was glad to let Babushka manage the children as well as the household. It was Babushka who saw that we were up on time, properly washed and dressed, breakfasted and ready for school on time. She made our breakfast herself—the coffee with the right amount of chicory added, served with boiled milk, the butter sweet and fresh, the eggs right from the coop. She could seldom send all the children of school age off together on the same day, particularly in winter. One or another would have some complaint. Children were sicker in those days, and parents more fearful—not without reason, since except for smallpox, there was neither immunization nor antibiotics against the dread diseases.

Babushka's idea of prevention was to keep the children from catching cold. They must be warmly dressed—too warmly. She bundled us up like Eskimos. My mother had the more modern approach of dressing children in lighter clothes in all sorts of weather. She even believed in cold morning showers as a preventive against the common cold. Since we had neither tub nor shower, she had a basin brought into the small corridor near the kitchen, and she compelled Misha to get into it while she poured a pail of cold water over him. My turn for the ordeal came after Misha's. Our shrieks could be heard all over the house. Babushka was beside herself. But my mother followed through religiously. In this she was influenced by Dr. Eugene Sklovsky, a family friend close enough to be known to all of us by his pet name, Jeenie. Medically Dr. Sklovsky was, in Russia, far ahead of his time; he insisted that cold air was a friend, not an enemy, to a person's health, and he initiated a municipal campaign for a "drop of milk," free milk distribution daily to the poor children of Kiev.

But though my mother believed in his ideas, it was Babushka, not mother, who dressed us for school. At the vociferous protests of the girls, Babushka relented a little, but she was adamant in the case of my older brother. Poor Misha—he became the battleground between Babushka and Dr. Sklovsky. The *casus belli* was a warm hood called a *bashlik,* with a double layer of thickly woven cloth that enclosed the entire head and neck and much of the face as well. It was usually worn only on the coldest days of the winter, by those who had to stay outside for long periods. But for Babushka, once winter had come, no matter what the weather, Misha had to wear his hood. Despite all his objections and pleadings, she would insist—and win the battle.

One day Misha came home from school with the *bashlik* off his head and lying folded over his shoulders. Babushka was beside herself. How had he dared do such a thing? Dr. Sklovsky, Misha told her, had passed him on his sleigh, had told the driver to pull up, called Misha over and removed his *bashlik* from his head. "Tell your mother," he had said, "never to put this on you again. This is how you catch cold." Babushka was mildly embarrassed—she respected the charming doctor—but Misha was still forced to wear his hood.

Strict and stern as she was when we were well, she was gentle and indulgent with a child who fell ill. Even her voice changed, becoming soft, low and warm. There was nothing she would not do for a child then—it became a temptation indeed to simulate a complaint.

If the child's temperature rose during the day, Dr. Weinzweig would be called in. He lived in the same apartment house, an oldish man, short, stocky, bald, with blue eyes and a pleasant smile. His absentmindedness was a source of amusement to our family. After a thorough examination of the child, he would sit down at the table and start to write the prescription in a deeply thoughtful way as if he were about to write a book. Then he would suddenly stop, raise his eyebrows, look at the worried faces of my mother and Babushka, and solemnly ask if the child he had just examined was a boy or a girl.

Dr. Weinzweig believed in diet. Every prescription he gave was accompanied by a special diet, invariably rich in fat. I recall one that raised great problems: it prescribed breast of chicken, chopped up with a couple of eggs, fried in butter. The difficulty was that Babushka kept a kosher house, and this diet would not only have the child eat *treyfa* (meat and butter together), it would also un-kosher the dishes and cooking utensils. But there were no limits to which Babushka would not go when a child was sick. A corner of the kitchen was set aside with a small kerosene stove for the cooking, and special utensils and dishes that could be disposed of when the diet cure was over.

This diet may have been tasty; it could not have been too easy on a sick child's digestion!

But Dr. Weinzweig could do worse than that. Examining my sister Tissa, he found her undernourished and anemic, and he prescribed a diet of ham to build her up. Though not an observing Jew himself, he could certainly see that Babushka wore a wig and should have taken it for granted that we ate only kosher food. Certainly he was aware of the aversion to pork products even among non-kosher Jews. Yet he prescribed ham. Babushka and my mother were shocked and looked at each other in amazement. Babushka was the first to recover. "Buy it, Bibi," she said to my mother. "I'll take care of it myself."

The ham for Tissa was bought in small quantities, well concealed in layers of paper, and kept in the cold space between the regular and the storm windows in Babushka's bedroom. At certain times Babushka motioned to Tissa to follow her into her room. They locked the door and remained in silence for fifteen minutes. Then Tissa would emerge without saying a word to us. The rest of the children were supposed to be ignorant of these goings-on, but it did not take us long to learn that Tissa was eating ham in Babushka's bedroom, out of the wrapper—no dishes involved.

Because of the mystery, we were all eager to have a taste of the forbidden, intriguing food. Babushka explained that Tissa was given ham as a medicine. But the satisfied look on Tissa's face after taking this "medicine" did not indicate that it was a very painful cure. Pretty soon we were all clamoring for ham to eat. Babushka ignored us, but we persevered, and a mutiny was organized by the rebel, my sister Lyala.

Lyala had led us to revolt before. Once she organized a rebellion against the monotony of our diet. On being called to dinner, we all followed Lyala, not to the dining room but in a march to my mother's office, and there sang in unison our protest, which ran in Russian like this: "*Soup perlovi, myaso s'kartoshkoi, na tretie kompot*" ("Barley soup, meat with potatoes, and for dessert compote"). My mother was outraged and my father seemed unhappy, but for some reason Babushka laughed. During the ham rebellion, Lyala's slogan was: If Tissa may eat it, we all may eat it; what's good for her is good for all of us.

No explanations, lectures or appeals could placate us. We did get ham, finally, not as often as Tissa, but occasionally, and in the same manner—right out of the paper. That is how I became convinced that Jews could eat ham only out of a paper. Once, at Natasha's, I saw the children being served ham on plates, like other food. I was so astounded that I cried out, "Ham on a plate!"

I suppose it was inevitable that Babushka, for all her immediate domestic practicality, should live more or less in a dream of past standards. My mother, who was supposed to be the financial mastermind of the family, never knew exactly how much money she had in her pocketbook. My father, who had a real penchant for orderliness, kept out of household affairs. As a result, the fiscal maneuvers of my mother and Babushka were extremely complicated and worthy of a much greater enterprise.

Take their transactions with Selig, the butcher. Not a day went by in our house without the consumption of meat; it was our staff of life. Every morning my mother sent the cook to Selig's bearing a slip of paper with the order of the day written on it—the precise cut and weight. Selig filled the order, kept the slip of paper, and the cook returned with the meat—very simple.

With most households there was a monthly reckoning, with the bill paid on submission. But with our family Selig knew better. He did not waste time and paper on a formal billing; his system with us was different. Once in a great while—I suppose, when the bill had reached impossible proportions—he would tell the cook to tell my mother that he would soon be coming to see her. For my mother this was a subtle and not at all welcome hint that she should get the money ready for him. My mother would apparently ignore the cook's words, but immediately she had dismissed her she would turn, red in the face with anxiety, to Babushka. "He's coming," she would say.

"A plague on him," Babushka would answer.

Selig's name was spoken only in a whisper, especially when my father was home. If Babushka was to be believed, Selig was no ordinary tradesman, not a butcher at all, but a crook, a robber, a bloodsucker, a devil. Almost invariably the cook's return from Selig's was the signal for an explosion from Babushka. "What a ganef," she would cry as she inspected the meat. "What a crook, what a scoundrel! Look, just take a look! Is there anything here to cook? Is there anything here to eat? Only fat and bones!" Yet somehow, after Selig's meat was cooked and put on the table, there always seemed to be plenty of good meat to go around.

Selig's visits were dramatic—and traumatic—events. His manner and looks belied Babushka's characterization of him. He was a stocky man in his middle forties, with a thick brownish-red beard covering his face and neck like a bib, and he had, it seemed to me, kind brown eyes and a ready smile. I could not keep my eyes off him. Was this man with the kind face and so soft a voice really a bloodsucker? Another thing that puzzled me was why my mother and even Babushka were so nice to him. Not a word was said about "fat and bones." The visits were most cordial. Selig, seated at our round dining-room table between the two ladies, seemed like a friend on a social call. There was leisurely general conversation, small talk and gossip about local matters and mutual acquaintances. Everything was genteel and friendly. But the crucial moment was bound to come— and my mother and Babushka knew it.

Even while paying close attention to the conversation, with smiles and nods, Selig slowly reached deep into his pocket and produced a heap of slips of paper. These were my mother's orders, now smeared with fat and blood and hardly legible as they lay there on our table. He did not advance them even one inch toward my mother for checking and adding. Apparently the wrinkled slips of paper were to serve, at least for a while, as a strategic weapon only. My mother's eyes strayed to the slips of paper. She looked surprised that there were so many of them. Then, as the two ladies continued to talk about this and that, Selig gently moved the heap in my mother's direction. When they were right there in front of her, she fingered a few of them daintily, exchanged a pleasant word or two with Babushka, turned to her pocketbook, and at the same time brought up a new subject for gossip with Selig. Soon from the depths of her purse a number of rumpled rubles of various denominations appeared. These she methodically straightened out so that one could be placed neatly on top of the other. But even before she had handed over the rubles to Selig he began to shake his head. He could tell without counting that the amount was far below what he expected. My mother, ignoring his negative gesture, shoved the rubles toward him. Raising his hand as if to ward off a blow, he pushed the money back to her side of the table. His face, soft and gentle a moment earlier, hardened and turned red. A note of anger came into his voice:

"But no, please, Olga Mikhailovna, please, no! It's impossible! How can I stay in business if I don't get paid? Look, Olga Mikhailovna, look at the amount you owe."

But my mother did not want to see the bill. Presumably she had some vague notion of the amount—probably at least a few hundred rubles—but did not want to face this with Selig sitting opposite her. She looked furtively toward the corridor leading to my father's study. I knew she was nervous for fear he would find out about Selig's visit and the true significance of the slips of paper. This was my cue to run out and see what my father was doing and to reassure her in a whisper that he was busy writing. This relieved her, and she could explain to Selig how things stood with us, with Babushka adding her interjections and my mother promising to do better next time—possibly to clear up the whole account. Once again the money was extended to Selig. He by now was perceptibly weakening. With a deep sigh he accepted it, rearranged the bills again by denomination, counted them, and in a low voice told my mother how much she had given him, to which she asserted with a slight nod. From a pocket Selig produced a worn leather purse, already bulging with paper money, and to the relief of the two ladies, jammed my mother's rubles into it.

This confrontation was apparently an ordeal for Selig too. He perspired profusely and briskly wiped his brow with a red-and-black flowered handkerchief. My mother and Babushka remained seated, waiting for him to rise and take his leave. But Selig was in no hurry now. In a thoughtful mood, he began to apologize for his earlier insistence on a larger amount. It was tough to stay in business these days, particularly when you tried to run a Jewish butcher shop in a goyish neighborhood, with the policemen forever popping in and out to ask for just a few bones—but try and give them bones! It was meat they wanted, and good meat, and for nothing, of course, as though he, Selig, were getting it for nothing. Everybody taking advantage . . .

When the door finally closed on him, Babushka would throw up her hands and say to my mother, "Everybody taking advantage, oh, yes, the poor fellow! I wish I had half the money he takes in, that ganef!

In those days it was Hannah, the custom peddler, who supplied the material for our dresses and school uniforms. She sold on credit, like Selig. Her visits, however, were anticipated not with dread but with pleasure. Hannah was a good soul; she had never worn a school uniform herself, but she had a sympathetic understanding of how a young girl felt when she had to go to school with a patch on her sleeve.

Her visits were usually in the winter and she came well fortified against the cold. She rolled through our door, a heap of shawls—of various faded colors, and all with frazzled fringes, they were wrapped in tiers around her drab cotton coat. Her head, too, was entombed in several scarves that overlapped each other. She had faded dreamy eyes, a deeply lined face, with a dark hairy mole on her lower lip. A slight tic that shook her lower jaw before she started talking made the mole even more conspicuous. She carried a huge basket on her arm, the kind used for marketing, brimming over with fabrics of all kinds.

Once in the apartment, Hannah put down her basket and slowly began shedding her scarves and shawls. This was a lengthy process, as she stopped frequently to reply to a remark from my mother or Babushka. They treated her like an old friend come on a rare visit. For us the conversation seemed as interminable as—to borrow a simile from Babushka—the Jewish exile. We stood motionless at Hannah's side, our eyes fixed on her basket, waiting for the great moment when she removed the covers and displayed the material. We thought the moment had arrived when Hannah's hand reached down and removed one cover—but then she would stop again to respond to a remark of my mother's. This unintentional tease went on for some time. Finally, to our immense relief, the last cover was off and the treasures exposed to view.

Then there was another delay. My mother suggested that Babushka make her selection first. Babushka said no, no, no, she did not need any new dresses. After some expected persuasion, however, she condescended to make her selection, and before long she left the room with yards of material to deposit in her fabulous trunk.

It was our turn at last. But a new hurdle arose now—my mother's budget. While she had no compunction about increasing her debt to Selig, she was very careful not to run up a big bill with Hannah. If she could not make a sizable payment on the old account, she bought only the absolute necessities, in spite of Hannah's urging. Ignoring all money talk, Hannah lifted the coveted bulky brown wool material used for school uniforms from her basket and deposited it gently, like a newborn baby, in the center of the table, so that all the girls could see and touch it. This set us hopping and clapping; it was like showing a sizzling steak to the starved.

In good times my mother smiled and said to Hannah, "Let's see how many yards we need," but in bad times, which were frequent, she said firmly, "Only sleeves this year." This was tragedy, except for the girl whose uniform was really all worn out, so that she would have to get a new one, come what might. Those who were merely to get sleeve replacements complained that as the new material did not completely match the old, new sleeves would only make the uniform look shabbier. I remember my sister Lyala protesting and weeping, being comforted only by the news that Tissa was also to be limited to new sleeves.

There were fewer tears and more arguments in the second act, when Hannah displayed her dress goods—alpaca or cotton prints. Naturally each girl wanted a new dress, but we could see my mother figuring in her mind how much this would cost and how much she already owed. Then, "No, Hannah, not now. The next time we'll take care of dresses." Hannah did not press the matter. Her soft eyes wandered from one girl to another, observing their long faces. Her tic became more pronounced, the dark mole on the lower lip moved up and down. Then a smile came to brighten her face—and our hopes. We had learned to read Hannah's smile. This time it told us that after she left, some of the dress material would remain on the table.

Of all my father's relatives—brothers, sisters, half brothers, half sisters, and innumerable nephews and nieces—not one lived in Kiev, and few ever visited us. But I remember two uncles, younger brothers of my father, who came to see us occasionally. Both lived in Berditchev, were comfortably off, wore modern dress and spoke a good Russian.

Uncle Hershel was popular with us all, but he made himself especially memorable to Misha, to whom he once promised a horse as soon as his mare had foaled. With each of his visits we had more news—first it was a newborn colt, too small to stand on its own feet; next visit it was growing, yes; next, it could outrun its mother. It grew and grew, and so did Misha—for him it was a good dream while it lasted.

A tall, spare man with a ruddy complexion, Uncle Hershel looked like a healthy outdoor man, but he had an annoying, suspicious cough. Babushka and my mother always asked him about the state of his health. He spent his days in a pine forest, supervising a lumbering operation. I often heard him say, "Where would I be if it were not for the wonderful pine air?"

Uncle Vevik was a very different sort of person. He, too, was tall, with a kind face and a ready smile. He was a businessman in Berditchev, a manufacturer of ladies' leather and suede gloves. This was of no interest to Misha or me, but a delight to my older sisters who could use the gloves he brought with him. He related countless stories, not about horses but about the industrial fair in Kiev where he exhibited his gloves. His ambition was to win a gold medal for their quality and workmanship. He never did receive the medal but was given a citation of merit, an elaborate document that looked like a diploma, which he kept unrolling and rolling up and unrolling again to show to my father and the rest of us.

Uncle Vevik learned his trade when in his teens. My father, who was then only twenty-three, wrote him a lengthy paternal letter when he first set out on his own:

"I am glad to hear that you have devoted yourself to learning your trade. Bear in mind that toil never degrades a person. Our sages said, It is better to skin a carcass in the marketplace than be beholden for gratuity to others. Happy is the man who has a trade." The letter went on to give Uncle Vevik advice on how to choose friends in a strange city where it is "no easier to distinguish between one person and another than between trees in a thick forest." He drew the parable of an orchard where each tree bears its specific fruit according to its original seed, and added that the same orchard might contain weeds, nettles and thorns. "You," he wrote to Vevik, "are not like those young men who grow like thorns and nettles. You must remember that you are a son of Menahem Nahum, grandson of Zev-Wolf Rabinowitz and that you bear the name of our grandfather, blessed be his memory. Preserve the honor of our grandfather and be on guard for the honor of our father by keeping on the right track and the finest path."

Then my father exhorted Vevik to be an honest man, so that his conscience would always be clear and his heart pure as gold, and asked him to contact him if ever he was uncertain and needed advice. The letter ends with a reference to Grandfather Nahum:

"Write me if you have letters from our father and tell me what he is writing you. Write him often, and don't be sparing in cheerful letters to him. You must bear in mind that our father, may he live long, derives his sustenance from our frequent and cheerful letters."

On my mother's side we had the Yampolsky family and, of course, Natasha, who, as I previously described, had been brought up with her on the Loyeff estate. Avram Yampolsky was the cousin who had brought my mother and father together again after the forced separation and had helped them to get married. By profession he was a secretary at the German consulate, but his heart was in art. He wanted to be a painter and he painted all his life, though he never received the slightest recognition from his friends, not to speak of the art critics. He took this lifelong frustration stoically.

When my husband, traveling in Russia in 1934, visited Avram Yampolsky in Moscow, he found him still devoted to art. He insisted on painting my husband's portrait and presented it to him when he left. By Soviet law however, no work of art could be taken out of the country. Avram Yampolsky had to go before the Art Commission, exhibit the portrait and convince its judges that it was not art! This he succeeded in doing.

In Kiev, Natasha and her family were, as always, very close to us. She and my mother remained like sisters. Manya, the other granddaughter of Grandfather Elimelech, had had a brief and tragic life. As I mentioned earlier, her mother had left her with the Loyeffs after she divorced Israel Loyeff. Manya was very beautiful and had been engaged to Dr. Eugene Sklovsky, the crusader for fresh air and free milk. But she contracted tuberculosis, usually a fatal disease in those days, and succumbed, as her father had, to an early death. She died in Yalta at the age of nineteen. Dr. Sklovsky remained a close friend of my parents and of Natasha.

For all the love poured out to Natasha by her grandparents, she suffered the pain of having been deserted by her mother well into middle age. Natasha was the prototype for the little girl, Bouzie, in my father's famous story of childhood love, "Song of Songs." At one point Shimek, who loves Bouzie, is flaunting his prowess as they play, running and jumping ahead of her, she trying to follow but tiring and calling for a rest. As Shimek recounts it:

"I am happy Bouzie cannot do what I can do, but at the same time I pity her. My heart aches for her. She seems to be worried. It's Bouzie's nature to be jolly and merry, then suddenly she gets away into a corner by herself quietly weeping. At such moments, no matter how much Mother is comforting her or Father kissing her, nothing helps. Bouzie must have her cry. For whom? For her father who died so young? Or for her mother who remarried and went off without a farewell? Ah, that mother of hers! When you mention her mother Bouzie's face turns all colors. She does not think much of her mother. She does not say one unkind word about her, but she does not think much of her. I know this for sure. I cannot bear seeing Bouzie unhappy. I sit down by her side and try to distract her. . . ."

In Babushka's eyes Natasha's mother was worse than a demon; her name was taboo in our house. But Natasha, instead of condemning and forgetting, nourished a growing desire to find her mother. It was as if she needed to prove to herself that she *had* a mother. When she married and had children, she projected this complex on them. Now she *must* find her mother and have her children see for themselves that they had a grandmother like all other children.

Natasha's marriage had presented a problem to my parents. She had grown into a handsome and accomplished young woman. With the dowry left her by Grandfather Elimelech as part of his estate, she could have made the finest marriage. But when things went badly for my father on the exchange and he was in danger of losing a fortune, she begged him to take her money to save his investments. She did not need it yet, she said, and as for later, we'll see what happens. My father hesitated, but he finally took the money, which disappeared with the rest. Without a dowry, in the bourgeois society of the time, a girl, Jewish or non-Jewish, could not easily find a suitable husband. The Russians even had a special term for such a girl—the *bezpredanitza* (the girl without a dowry), connoting a tragic fate. Natasha found herself in such a situation, and one can imagine how my father, the cause of it, felt.

When a marriage proposal came from a brilliant, prosperous lawyer, a widower with no children, my parents tried to dissuade Natasha from the match. Moyssei Savelevich Mazor, as I have said earlier, was one of the few Jews in the whole of Russia fully admitted to the bar as a counselor at law. But he was twenty-five years older than Natasha. My parents tried to dissuade him as well as Natasha, but they did not prevail, and finally arranged the wedding. It turned out to be a very successful marriage. Moyssei Savelevich never quite forgave my parents for their opposition, but he did not let this interfere with the close, intimate relations between the two families.

Natasha was thirty-two years old and had three sons, aged twelve to eight, when she finally located her mother and began to make plans for her children to see their grandmother. Babushka reacted violently, raged and cried and did not sleep. To her it was like rewarding an assassin. Perhaps she felt it as an act of treason, for she had substituted as a mother to Natasha. My mother was torn between conflicting loyalties and emotions. She did not want Natasha frustrated in this great desire of her life, but she too had an aversion for that "beastly" woman who had never inquired, over all the years, as to whether her child was alive or dead. My mother was worried about the possible disappointment and ill effects of such a meeting on Natasha's state of mind. So she tried to dampen Natasha's ardor for the visit and at the same time pacify Babushka.

In 1903, during the spring holiday, Natasha announced she was going, with her children, to visit her mother in Kishinev. In a terrible scene Babushka swore she would never set foot in Natasha's house again if this happened. Natasha went, regardless, but her visit coincided with the terrible pogrom that raged in Kishinev for two days and nights, when fifty Jews were killed, some six hundred wounded— about a hundred of them severely—and seven hundred Jewish homes destroyed. The pogrom was instigated by the czarist government to "drown the revolution in Jewish blood," with the local police looking on and five thousand troops staying in their barracks. This was one of the pogroms that shocked the civilized world and evoked public protest meetings in London, Paris and New York.

The news of the pogrom reached Kiev almost immediately. The resentment about Natasha's visit to her mother gave way to fear for her safety, for her very life and that of her children. No one was more alarmed and frantic than Babushka. There was no way to communicate with her in Kishinev, no one to turn to on her behalf, and there was no word from her. But three days later, to our immense joy, Natasha and her children returned home. Babushka, her threat forgotten, threw her cape over her shoulders, put on her tiny hat with the pompon at the front—the style for old ladies at the time—and rushed over to Natasha's house.

The talk was of the pogrom and the four days Natasha and her children had hidden in a cellar. The purpose of the trip, the visit to her mother, was not even mentioned. Later she told us that she did achieve her goal—had managed to see her mother and let her children meet their grandmother—but she never spoke of it again. Nor did the children talk about their grandmother. The one memory they retained from their trip was the pogrom.

In 1936, when my mother made her only return visit to Russia, she of course went to see Natasha, by then a widow living in one room of her former luxurious apartment. She brought back a sheaf of letters which my father had written to Natasha. I quote two of these as yet unpublished letters, characteristic of my father in a light vein. They happen to deal with grapes.

Natasha had not been well during 1898, and in the fall had gone to a health resort in southern Crimea called Wonderful Shelter, situated in the wine country of Feodossiya. My father wrote her three letters about sending us some grapes. The first one is dated September 8, 1898:

"Dear Natasha: Your first letter reached us today and we feel deeply for your frozen limbs on the southern shore of the Crimean peninsula. As soon as the first snow falls, send us a wire and we will send your fur coat. Meanwhile my advice is to light the oven and get a pair of high rubber boots. Here in the north it is not that cold, although we do not bathe in the sea. Grapes are fully ripe at the Besserabka market, but devilishly high-priced and almost all rotten. So please send us a basket or a small barrel of grapes as quickly as possible. Do not send bottles of wine, for at Lissidov's you can get a bottle of sourness for thirty kopecks. We see your boys quite often. On the first day of Rosh Hashanah, Moyssei Savelivich was here with Minya [a son] and on the second day he came with Minya and Loussia [another son], who is remarkably smart for his age. I was at your house today and saw your threesome turning it upside down. There were many clients in the office. Moyssei Savelivich is thriving, but he gave me a stomachful, that is, an earful of his pains. Hurry with the grapes, for I am forbidden to feast on anything else. Your Uncle Solomon."

In a second letter he evidently reminded her of the grapes, and in the third, dated September 18, he expatiated further on the matter:

"To darling Natasha: I just returned from Paris, that is, from Berditchev, and found a letter from you. There should really be no trouble at all for you to send us the grapes. First, you take a droshky to the market and buy a basket. Then you go with it to the orchard or fruit market and buy the grapes. You drag it to your Wonderful Shelter. Then you go out to buy a rope to tie it with, and you catch cold. You begin to pack, but it is no go, so you send for the janitor. You quarrel with him, give him fifty kopecks, and dispatch him to hell because he is drunk. All this time, your friend Bertha is sitting there eating the grapes. But don't worry—this won't hurt her! You go to the station to ship the grapes, but there is no porter there, and you postpone the whole thing until the next day. The next day is Sunday, so you ship them on Tuesday, because on Monday you forgot about it. After all this bother, we get a notice in Kiev—very soon, only about two and a half weeks later—that the grapes have arrived. The basket is full of crushed, dried, rotten grapes. Babushka is angry. She takes one into her mouth, spits it out, and declares war not only on the smelly grapes but on all the health resorts, particularly those in Crimea. So, as you see, the affair is not at all complicated, and yet you deprive yourself and us of this great pleasure. You are simply mean, my dear.

"As for your remark about sour grapes setting the teeth on edge, I am inclined to agree with your doctor. It is quite simple: the more sourness, the more the teeth are on edge; the more the teeth on edge, the less appetite; the less appetite the more sourness; the more sourness . . . and so on. It's all so clear, like a sunny day. Don't tell me you don't understand it. Ask the doctor for his opinion of the red, sweet, crumpy watermelons. Are they not better than the Feodossiya grapes?

"By the way, here we don't get the terrific northeast winds and storms you get there in the blessed south, you lucky girl!   Your loving Uncle Solomon."

Another amusing incident of those days in Kiev comes out of a memoir by Osher Beilin, one of my father's copyists. In those times, before typewriters and secretaries, an author had an onerous problem with his manuscript. Any serious writer, then as now, revised his work several times, and it would have been a great drain on his energy and his time to copy the manuscript himself after each revision. Tolstoy, with the almost illegible handwriting that only his wife, Sofia, could decipher, would have been hard pressed if that remarkable woman had not spent long hours of the night copying what her husband had written that day, only to find it marked up again the next evening.

Fortunately my father wrote an excellent hand. His first teacher was a calligrapher, and he taught all his pupils to write the way he did. Still, the copying problem was there. As my father always wrote on small bits of paper, which he pasted together, then kept editing, changing a word here, a phrase there, canceling some lines, adding others, the final manuscript tended to look like a maze. Moreover, as his fame grew and Yiddish publications multiplied, there were demands for contributions from various local periodicals, and he would send the same story to several, perhaps changing a word or a passage in one or another. This required several copies of the same manuscript. My mother was too busy with the children and her practice to do any copying; besides, her handwriting did not have the elegant clarity of my father's. So copyists were engaged, to serve also occasionally as secretaries and answer letters, though my father really preferred to do that himself.

I remember a few of these copyists—diffident, silent young men, awestruck by a master author they had admired since childhood, and also discomfited by the atmosphere of our household, which was strange to them. Most had literary ambitions of their own. One of these was Osher Beilin, who described, after my father's death, what it was like to work for him.

Osher Beilin was the son of an old-fashioned religious Hebrew writer. He had heard from a friend of my father's that Sholom Aleichem was looking for a secretary who knew not only Yiddish but also Hebrew and Russian. At his first meeting with my father it emerged that his father was originally from Woronko, and thus a townsman of my father's. The elder Beilin had once translated one of my father's stories and published it in a Hebrew journal without my father's permission. Sholom Aleichem had written him a very sharp letter. Now he asked Osher if his father was still resentful about that letter.

Osher replied, "If he were, would I be applying for the position?"

My father liked that, and asked the young man to write a few lines as an example of his handwriting. They were satisfactory. What happened later is described in Osher's memoir, with the dialogue running like this:

"Are you doing any writing of your own?" my father asked.

"Yes, I do."

"That's just what I was afraid of. It had to be true. What else? What do you write—poems, stories, plays, or all of these at once?"

"No, none," Osher replied. "None of those. I am writing love letters."

My father laughed. "You are truly an engaging young man. The secretaries who preceded you wore me out with their manuscripts, tired me to death. Now, do you promise not to lose my manuscripts?

The others did. Do you promise, and forgive the question, not to
stick your nose into my personal affairs? The others did. You know
Hebrew? Russian? You do? Good, very good, let us talk terms and
with good luck get down to work."

At first young Beilin worked in my father's study, my father standing at his pulpit to do his original writing, and the young man
sitting at a table nearby, copying. Later, when Sholom Aleichem had
gained enough confidence in Beilin, he trusted Beilin to take the
manuscripts home and do his copying there.

Beilin in his memoir gives an incident from those days when he was
still working alongside my father in the study. This room, he wrote,
was not conducive to mental effort. The massive apartment house
stood in the heart of a main street full of buildings of iron and
stone. The ring of galloping horses and wagon wheels encased in iron
on the pebbled pavement, the bells and crash of the trolley, and all
the other city noises were oppressive and wearying.

One day Beilin got up from the table where he was working and
said to my father, "I am going, Solomon Naumowitz, I am tired."

"Tired already? Rest a while if you are tired."

"No, I want to go."

"Go? Did you ever! A man works two or three hours and is tired.
Shame on you."

"This is all I can do today."

"Murderer! Perhaps you should try a new penpoint—look at the
new penpoints I bought. I've been looking a long time for penpoints
like these. They almost write by themselves. Try one."

But Beilin insists on going.

"Perhaps you are hungry? Of course. Why didn't I think of that
before? You're certainly hungry. So why didn't you speak up? Do you
want fried eggs or an omelet? I advise an omelet. With shmaltz or
butter? No? Why not? Maybe you're thirsty and want some tea?
Which kind, Wissotsky's or Popov's? You can have your choice. No?
Why not? Ah, I understand, it's hard for you to sit on that chair. Take
mine. Here, take it. If it's too low, you can take this big fat book. . . ."

It was half in jest and half in earnest. Then again: "Why am I not
tired, not one bit? Why? Why so silent, young man? Explain to me
why I do not get tired."

"Because your work is more interesting than mine. You are creating."

"A good answer. Very good. Now listen, I am talking to you

very very seriously. My advice is for you to lie down and spit at the ceiling. Try it and you will be convinced that this has been a definite and effective remedy since time immemorial. You will rise a new, refreshed man. Again no? Then perhaps you'd like to get a little exercise by driving some nails in the wall?"

"Good," Beilin said. "I think that the picture of Mendele is not in the right place. Is there a hammer in the house?"

"All right, young man. You may go in peace."

Osher Beilin wrote that often when he happened to pass our apartment house after midnight, he saw my father's study still lighted. "Amid stone and iron, he was still working, creating."

VIII
Summers in Boyarka

AT A SUMMER RESORT called Boyarka (the "Boiberik" of my father's stories) we spent the three months from mid-May to mid-August. This was the happiest time of our year, away from the city sweltering in the heat and having the freedom of cool gardens and woods to play in. There was an old, thick pine forest, with huge pointed trees beneath which pine needles piled up to form a soft carpet under foot, and a fresh, spring-fed pond where we swam. Above all, we had our father with us every day, all to ourselves, except for the rare occasions when business called him to town.

An hour's train ride from Kiev, Boyarka had three definite advantages: it was located in a beautiful natural spot, Jews were permitted to live there, and the rents were comparatively reasonable. While the price varied with location and size, a dacha (bungalow) could be had for as little as one hundred and fifty rubles for the season.

At the first signs of spring, we began to press our parents to go to Boyarka and rent a dacha for the summer. On their return they would report to us what they had found. This would depend, of course, on the financial situation that year. In good times the dacha was in the best location, in good condition, with lovely grounds. In bad years it was second-rate. Since we could not possibly forgo our vacation in Boyarka, my parents rented whatever there was for the money they could afford.

I remember clearly one of the summers that came in a very bad year. After their exploratory trip in the spring, my father was enthusiastic about the dacha they had rented. The garden was beautiful, he said, running right into the woods. There were many trees: a cherry tree—he was not absolutely sure it was a cherry since it was too early to tell, but it was a beautiful tree—and the most marvelous birches, one a weeping birch. Along the fence were shrubs which, he was almost sure, were grapevines. He omitted to describe the dacha, but our mother told us that it was run down and much too small for our family. The kitchen, which had a floor of earth instead of wood, was inconvenient to the dining room; the well was far away, and the outhouse situated at the end of the garden, with a path to it that became a mud track when it rained.

On moving in, we found the place even more dilapidated than we had feared. Worse, the day of the move was cold and dreary, and a downpour of rain brought water streaming through a crack in the roof into the center of the living room. Babushka was positive we would all catch pneumonia. As for my mother, she collapsed into a hard wooden chair in one corner of the room and covered her face with her hands.

But my father was equal to the occasion. "*Nitchevo* (nothing at all), children," he cheered us. "Why, it's fun! Look at it gushing, gushing down." Quickly he produced a bucket for the rain water to fall into and called, "Now form a ring around the bucket, holding hands, and round and round we go dancing." And so we all did, including our father: it was noisy and gay, with riotous outbursts of laughter. After a while, my mother took her hands away from her face and actually smiled.

Usually the dacha was in better condition than this one, but none of them provided much housing comfort. They were all simple frame structures with four or five rooms and a separate shed, often with an earth floor, that served as a kitchen. There were no facilities for lighting or plumbing; the outhouse was in a corner of the garden; water was drawn from the community well. Another community service, missing in the city, was an icehouse—a dugout with a vertical thatched roof, holding in its deep center thick blocks of ice taken from the river in winter and covered with thick layers of moss to prevent it from melting. Each dacha was allocated a corner in the icehouse for keeping food supplies.

In the garden that surrounded each bungalow were a few trees—pine, birch or cherry—shrubs and wildflowers. The gardens of four bungalows merged into one large area surrounded by a picket fence.

One gate in this fence led through the woods to civilization—the railway station and the village; another gate led to the forest in the back. A large pond had been made into a bathing pool with two separate enclosed pavilions for men and women, since bathing suits were still unheard of in Russia.

As the dacha had no furnishings whatsoever, everything had to be brought from the city by horse and wagon: tables, chairs, beds, bedding, linens, kitchen utensils, dishes, silver. In May, a familiar sight in Kiev was a wagon overloaded with furniture and large strong baskets, a mountain of bedding on top, pulled leisurely by a corpulent dray horse along the streets that led to the Boyarka road. Some wagons had a maidservant perched on top of the bedding, precariously swaying with the jerking of the wheels, to guard against theft on the part of the movers. (We never dreamed of sending a maid with our belongings. Even Babushka considered it degradingly suspicious. What could they steal? A pillow?) It took a full, long day for the horse and wagon to reach Boyarka; in August, of course, the move was made all over again in reverse.

A number of the dachas, including the one we rented that summer, belonged to a Ukrainian whom we called Khropatch (his name was actually Khropotchevsky). This man fascinated my father. From his appearance—he was tall, straight, square, with a handsome face, blue eyes and blond beard—and his habit of galloping around on a spirited horse, he might have been taken for a nobleman. He was, in fact, an ignorant, barely literate Ukrainian peasant who could not even speak Russian. My father, who spoke Ukrainian, was the only one in the family who could talk to him.

We all looked forward eagerly to Khropatch's arrival. He came a few times a season, presumably to see if everything was in order. By experience we knew that if there was anything out of order, it would stay out of order. But it was fun to watch Khropatch and laugh along with our father during their conversation. He would tell us later what had been so amusing.

These visits were of special interest to my father, for here was a peasant like any other peasant, who had somehow managed to buy land, erect bungalows and rent them to summer residents. He wanted to understand Khropatch, to find out what made him tick. He enjoyed the flavor of his earthy dialect and would lead him on to talk. At the community well the rope that pulled up the heavy pail of water from the depths was worn.

"Do you think this will hold much longer?" my father would ask. "It might break any moment."

Khropatch would scratch his head and think long and hard, then say slowly and deliberately in his peasant idiom: "*Yak bude derzhat bude derzhat, yak upade to upade,*" which means, "If it will hold, it will hold, if it breaks, it will break."

Or he would be shown the way the chimney smoked in the kitchen shed, and how much it needed cleaning. For this he had a marvelous play on words that delighted my father: "*Yak ne bude kuritsa bude pyetukh.*" With a little mispronunciation the word *kuritsa,* smoke, could also mean chicken, and *pyetukh,* meaning extinguished, could also stand for rooster. His statement meant either "If it does not smoke, it has gone out" or "If it's not a chicken, it's a rooster." My father would laugh at the turn of speech and admiringly watch Khropatch jump nimbly to the back of his large horse and disappear in a cloud of dust.

Many mornings, early, we heard our father's soft voice: "Children, get up! The sun is shining, the sky is blue, not a sign of a cloud, quickly now, let's go to the woods and pick cherries. Quick!" He loved to explore the forest with us, looking for berries or cherries or unusual plants. He pointed out wonders, his blond hair blown in his face by the light wind, his eyes full of astonishment, as if he were coming upon these things for the first time in his life. "Look, look how pure, how green the leaves of this birch are! Look, children, how low the birds are flying, you can almost touch them!" Or he suggested a race, and when we were exhausted, he would get us to lie flat on our backs and look up at the sky. "Watch the clouds floating over us, and their different shapes. Right there, in the corner, don't they look human? Don't they remind you of people you know?" And we saw that, yes, there were people in the sky, and we told him about them. Then he described how he saw the clouds, how they resembled his friends and acquaintances, imitating the speech and mannerisms of these people. We enjoyed this as much as if we were at the theater.

Birds were a constant preoccupation in Boyarka. They were plentiful, especially so near our veranda, attracted by the food that my father scattered—his first ritual act on rising. He welcomed their nests in our trees or in the eaves of the dacha, watching the process of nest building, egg laying, hatching and eventual flight.

"Papulia," we asked, when we were watching, with him, a mother bird feeding her young, "where is the father of the little birds?"

"Why, he's out flying around trying to collect worms for the mother to feed them with."

The birds became as real to us as human beings, and we shared his anxiety for them. I remember a stormy night with thunder and lightning—the Russians call it a "sparrow night" because it plays havoc with the sparrows—when my father was as concerned about the nests and the chicks as if he himself were responsible. When the next morning came and all was quiet and warm, with the sun shining and the grass and leaves freshly polished, we did not have to be called. We had gone to bed worrying about the baby birds, and no sooner had we opened our eyes than we jumped up to find our father and check on the nests. Near the veranda a small bird lay dead on the ground. A grimace of pain crossed his face, and without a word he went into the house and returned with a small box. Gently he placed the baby bird inside saying, "We're going to bury him."

Funeral fashion, we proceeded to the end of the garden, where our father went down on his knees, dug a hole with his hands and buried the box. He covered it with earth and a few wildflowers that grew nearby, put a stick at the head of the small mound, and said, "This is the grave of a bird; remember not to step on it."

Sadly we returned to the dacha. And we never did step on the grave.

We had two strange neighbors in Boyarka—one Christian and one Jewish—who are still vivid in my memory. A short distance from our bungalow was another with a huge chimney, a sign that the people lived there throughout the year. It belonged to a Ukrainian peasant family: father, mother, a married daughter whose husband was away in the army, and a host of smaller children. The father worked a patch of land behind their house in corn and vegetables, the women took in washing from the summer people. They stood in their bare feet in a narrow swift stream at the edge of their land, beating the soapy clothes with a semicircular piece of hardwood against a large stone in the stream. As they whacked away, they sang in unison, keeping time with their work. I remember the words of one of their songs: "Oh, why did my mother give birth to me? And why did God create me? For the one I love God did not give me!"

I liked to be near them, and they seemed to want me around. The married daughter, who had the same name as mine, Maroussia, was fond of me. She would look into my scrawny face, brush my hair over it, and say, "No, you won't last long in this world." I was puzzled by her remark but not concerned.

I saw things going on in that family that I had never seen before. There was the nursing, for instance. The mother sat on a low stool, holding the newest baby, which was at least nine months old and quite big, feeding it at one breast while the older child, perhaps three years old, stood close to her holding the other breast and sucking at the nipple. This was how a peasant woman solved the jealousy and insecurity of siblings.

The married daughter, Maroussia, was a handsome woman, big and strong, with apple cheeks, blue eyes and long flaxen braids tied up with red ribbons. She often wore her gaily embroidered *sarafan*—usually only worn on special occasions.

Her mother scolded her for this: "I know who you're dressing up for, you good-for-nothing! It's for Piotr. You think I don't know you're running around with him? Take it off, you fool! Your Vanka [the soldier husband] will be back on furlough any day now, and will he give it to you! He'll kill you or Piotr, or maybe both of you." But Maroussia only laughed, slapped her thighs and ran out singing.

One day Vanka did arrive. Whatever the reason—news of his wife's behavior or just plain drunkenness—his first greeting for Maroussia was a cruel beating right in the road outside the house. He knocked her down and thrashed her as she hugged his feet, crouching like a beaten dog. I was standing close by, trembling like a leaf. Then a man passed by, stopped, and shouted at the soldier, "Stop it, you drunkard, you don't beat a woman like that!"

To my great astonishment, Maroussia rose to her feet and snapped quickly at the passerby, "It's none of your business, you busybody! He's not beating just a woman, he's beating his own wife!"

I made the serious mistake of asking my mother why our neighbor Maroussia was running around with a man named Piotr when she already had a husband. My mother was very disturbed and forbade me to visit the family again. I obeyed—but the ban did not preclude my joining them at the stream when they were washing their clothes.

The Jewish family, our other neighbor, also had a bungalow with a large chimney and lived there throughout the year. They seemed strange too, both to my parents and myself. The father was known by his surname only, Medvedovsky, for no one dared call him by his first name. He was large and powerful, like a tower of darkness with two lights. His thick hair was black, his full beard even blacker, and his eyes burned like two fiery coals.

Medvedovsky was the terror of the community. He was feared by the peasants and avoided by the local police officer. Even during the pogroms he went unmolested, not even insulted—the one Jew who escaped trouble. It was not that he was a bully, but just that he feared nothing and kowtowed to no one.

Nobody really knew why he was so feared. One story ran that he had once killed a man and was not even brought to trial; another that he was a favorite of the governor of the province. One thing was certain: there was no man he could not beat up.

During the summer, Medvedovsky taxied the vacationists and their guests to and from the railway station. This was a highly lucrative business in which many of the other peasants joined, standing in line with their carts to meet every train. These carts were square wooden boxes mounted on very large wheels, and were filled to the top with straw or hay. Even with the aid of the suspended bootstep, it was an athletic feat for a woman in a long city dress to climb into the cart, and once there it took no less agility to keep from sliding off the hay. If the horse started to gallop, or if there was a sharp turn in the road, the passengers shrieked with dismay, sure that the inevitable tumble was coming, but the driver barely bothered to turn his head to see if his passengers were still there. The dirt road was sandy in dry weather, covering horse, cart, driver and passengers with a thin layer of white dust. After a drenching rain the sand turned into muddy clay; the wheels sank deep into the mud (perhaps that was why they used such large ones), and the poor horse shook its mane and strained to keep the cart moving.

As a cab driver Medvedovsky belonged in a category by himself. He dressed in city clothes and wore a black derby like the coachmen in town. He drove a droshky, the only one in Boyarka, and charged double. But the comfort and safety of his droshky were worth the extra money. At the station he waited quietly among the carts of the peasants, confident that he would be noticed. He knew the summer people by sight and could tell in advance who would want him to drive them. The peasants kept their distance and held their tongues, not daring to compete with him.

Medvedovsky was as much feared in his own house as he was in public. When he came home, his booming voice could be heard all the way to our dacha. Barely inside the door, he would shout furiously, "Chaim, come here for your two slaps on the face and get out!" Chaim was the oldest son, a quiet, polite and gentle boy of twelve. He was my brother Misha's friend. When he played with other children, he never took advantage of his father's reputation. He used to bring along a little sister, to Misha's annoyance, but Chaim would say she was only a baby and could hardly walk and had no one to take care of her.

When Chaim saw his father coming home, he rushed to get busy with some chore—cutting the grass or fetching water. This often saved him from the slaps his father loved to give him. Medvedovsky's bellow mobilized the other children into frantic activity, and they scampered like mice before a cat to all corners of the house.

For his wife, he had only one word: "*Eats!*" She, unkempt, slovenly, usually pregnant, said nothing, not even turning to look at him. At her slow pace she brought to the table a loaf of black bread and a big bowl of the Ukrainian borsht of cabbage and meat, after which she retired to the kitchen, leaving her husband always to eat alone. For all her placid obedience, she often appeared with a black eye; she said nothing about it and no one asked.

There was apparently only one person toward whom Medvedovsky showed any deference, and that was my father. As his wife, my mother shared to a slight extent in this honor, but they were the only summer residents who rated a greeting and a polite bow of the head from the burly coachman. Medvedovsky would turn other passengers away if he saw my father in the distance descending from the train. My father appreciated this special favor, and on the way home he would discuss current events with him and, after paying the fare, would shake hands as though they were old friends.

The first days at Boyarka were full of confusion and excitement, but soon life began to fall into a daily pattern not unlike that in the city. The writing stand was not moved to Boyarka, and, of course, there was no study. My father did not write in the night, but he did rise very early, and after a walk around the grounds, he would find a place in the garden or on the veranda to write. He could write anywhere, at any time and under all circumstances, even while walking. He had a black notebook which he himself had devised, narrower than the palm of his hand and a bit longer, a tiny clipboard, really, backed with a strip of wood covered with purple plush and a band through which he passed the four fingers of his left hand. Standing or walking, his pen in the right hand moving fast across the page, it looked as if he were writing in the palm of his own hand. In the country, all of his time, except when the family occupied his attention, was spent in writing.

Although the lack of domestic help entailed more work for our mother with us children, she did not neglect her dental work. Her instruments—except for the drill apparatus and the velvet chair—came with her to Boyarka, and she gave free service at a clinic a few miles away, which she herself had founded and set up for the peasants. A cart took her there and back, and often Misha and I went with her, both for the ride and to see the clinic, which fascinated us.

The dental service took place in an ordinary room in an ordinary peasant hut. The patient sat in a simple wooden chair, and the only clinical note was the white napkin spread out on the table for my mother's instruments, which she kept wrapped in a white towel in a small straw case.

This was one place where my mother did not have to wait for patients. They waited for her—old and young, men, women, seated on a long bench in the anteroom, standing in corners or crouching on the floor. The greatest demand was for extraction—most of the affected teeth were too far gone to be saved, even if my mother had had her drill. Only the minor cavities could be filled without the drill. The Ukrainian peasant was a patient, long-suffering human being—arriving at the clinic hours before it opened, waiting his turn, then undergoing the ordeal of the treatment without a pain reliever, yet always leaving grateful and happy. Each patient bowed his head low as he slowly backed out of the room, the older ones bending down to kiss my mother's hand, which embarrassed her and made her blush, no matter how often it happened.

This free service occupied a lot of my mother's time in Boyarka. My father was very proud of it, and awaited her return each time with great curiosity, never tiring of hearing just what she had done for each peasant, and how he or she had reacted, etc. Only after he had obtained from her every possible story in connection with her day at the clinic would he tell her what he had written during her absence.

There was very little social life in Boyarka, but I do remember one function that my father arranged, not at our dacha but in one that had a very large living room. This was a party to hear a nine-year-old musical prodigy and to raise funds for him.

It all began with an unexpected caller, a short stocky man, so nearsighted that his thick glasses reduced his eyes to tiny blurred specks and made his short chubby nose look even shorter and rounder. He and my father were closeted together for some time, and when my father showed him to the gate he was wildly excited and lit up. His caller, he told us, had a little boy who was a musical genius. The grandfather had been a fiddler, and the father was also very musical. The latter was convinced that his son was another Paganini, who had amazed the world with his violin performances when he was only nine. His son could do the same if only he could gain the ear of the musical world. But the family was very poor and did not know where to turn.

This affair could not have been closer to my father's heart. Next to writing, music was the great passion of his life. He relaxed best by sitting down at the piano to improvise, though he had no formal musical training. A popular children's story of his called "The Fiddle," is about a boy who hungered for a violin, loved to hear it played and wanted to play himself. Since there was no hope of buying one, he tried to make one out of the wood from an old piece of furniture and, of course, ended up disappointed and heartbroken. In his autobiography, my father tells how tempted he was to steal money from one of the guests at the inn so that he could fulfill his own ambition to play the violin. Music runs through the stories of his childhood and youth; one of his greatest joys was to make friends with music-makers. His first two novels deal with the experiences of two young geniuses, Stempenyu, a violinist, and Yosele Solovey, a singer who stole the hearts of women and gained great fame among men with the spell of their music. In the last years of his life, when he was writing the American experiences of his beloved child hero, Motel, the son of Paysie the cantor, he planned that Motel should develop into a talented musician.

It was inevitable, then, that my father should respond enthusiastically to this appeal by the father of a prodigy. He immediately turned impresario. He found the right place in Boyarka for the boy's first concert, inviting and personally prevailing upon many people to come, and raising money for a handsome gift to the young artist.

The boy violinist made his first appearance before his first audience in bare feet, the pockets of his trousers bulging with nuts which he had been offered at one house before coming to the concert. He performed masterfully, and the audience was admiring and enthusiastic. After the concert my father gathered together a few friends to discuss the boy's future with his father. Their advice, which the father took, was to travel with the boy to Western Europe, where he would find the right teachers as well as benevolent patrons to lend material aid. These friends also provided money for this initial move.

A few years later, in 1904, at his first concert in Berlin, the same boy, now not quite thirteen, was acclaimed an artist of great promise and launched on an illustrious career. The boy was Mischa Elman. Some years after that, when my father was in London for a public reading of his work, Mischa Elman's father came to his hotel to thank him for the crucial aid he had given in Boyarka.

Babushka occasionally used a racy Yiddish idiom: "Stand in water and beg for a drink." This described perfectly our food situation in Boyarka. We were in the heart of a farming district, yet it was not easy to get provisions. The village market was too far away, unless we wanted to hire a cart or droshky, which was expensive and bothersome. So we had to wait for the food peddlers to come by.

To buy chickens, we waited for Baba, a peasant woman in bare feet, with a yoke that was padded with a quilted material over her shoulders and a basket of live chickens suspended from either end. The chickens were inside a tight netting through which they stretched their heads and necks. Their protest against this cramped position announced Baba's arrival from a distance. She would stop at our veranda, lower the baskets to the floor and remove the yoke. Then she would display her wares, extricating one chicken at a time to hold it in front of Babushka and blowing the back feathers to show how fat the chicken was.

Babushka would buy several and let them loose in the back of the kitchen. But they preferred our veranda, and it was our job to chase them back where they belonged. We became adept at this and we knew every chicken by sight, even naming them. It was in the kitchen that their nemesis came in the person of the *shochet,* the ritual slaughterer, a bashful young man with rosy cheeks and the first sprouts of a beard. We were allowed to catch a few chickens for him; he walked off with them, and that was the last we saw of them.

Curiously enough, when we had chicken for dinner, we never made the connection.

Procuring vegetables was a much more intricate process. Nobody brought them to the dachas. You had to go out on the road, spot a peasant carrying vegetables to market in his cart, intercept him and try to buy some. The peasant would stop willingly, glad to sell, but unable to master the financial complications. He knew two facts: there was a load of vegetables on his cart, and he was to sell it for three rubles. You got the vegetables, he got the three rubles. But my mother presented him with disturbing ideas. She selected what she needed from the vegetables in his cart, held them in her hand, and tried to negotiate. This is how it went:

Mother: How much?
Peasant: Three rubles.
Mother: Three rubles for what?
Peasant: For the vegetables.
Mother: For this much?
Peasant.   For all the vegetables.
Mother: But I'm only taking a few of them. . . .

At this the peasant shrugged his shoulders and did not reply. My mother took a ruble and a half out of her purse and put it in his hand. He held the money in his palm, looked at it and shook his head, saying, "Three rubles."

My mother tried again. "You take this money for the vegetables I take, then sell the rest in the market, and you will end up with more than three rubles."

But he slowly gave the money back to her, took the vegetables out of her hand and, putting them back in his cart, said, "Three rubles, *up!*" The last was for his horse to start moving.

Next time my mother knew better than to argue with a Ukrainian peasant. She gathered two or three neighbors, paid him the three rubles, and each woman took whatever she wanted, leaving the rest in the cart. The peasant looked back at what the women had left, counted his money again, shrugged his shoulders and returned home.

What a relief and joy it was, after such experiences, to buy from a Jew—articulate and friendly, though just as close to the soil as a Jew in Russia could be at that time. Babushka would even invite him to sit down on our veranda, but he always declined and remained standing, keeping his distance, despite the fact that he had been coming to us every summer, year after year.

He supplied us with all our dairy products, which, like meat in Kiev, were the staff of our life in Boyarka. His wares were delicious. Our Ukrainian borsht had a different taste with his cream; his pot cheese was a delight; we ate his sour milk by spoonfuls; we spread his rich butter on fresh black bread and it was a meal in itself. Even his ordinary milk was better than any other. No wonder we especially looked forward to his visits.

Yet it was more than that. There was something about the man himself that made his coming a rewarding break in the routine of our country life. He was short and slight, and I remember particularly his black beard that grew contrariwise—beginning normally at the sides of his face, it slipped under his chin and left the chin itself bare. His lips were thin and moist. He would halt his horse at the gate of our dacha, then trudge in like a walking dairy carrying all the wares he knew we wanted: a wooden pail of milk covered by a towel in his right arm, his whip under it; over his other arm a number of wooden containers of sour milk, sweet and sour cream, and varieties of cheese wrapped in cheesecloth, all covered with a thick piece of linen. He deposited all these on the table with the utmost delicacy, as if they were most precious and fragile.

Our business with him was over in a few minutes, but he was in no hurry to leave nor we to see him go. Babushka and my mother liked him to stay and tell them about summer residents, particularly those they knew from Kiev. But he was really waiting for my father, who loved to talk with him, often chuckling at a remark he made, something in Hebrew, which we did not understand but which was evidently very funny to my father. Occasionally during the conversation, my father would take out his little notebook and jot down a few words.

The name of this delightful man was Tevyeh, and my father gave him the Yiddish nickname *Der Milkhiger,* which means The Milky One, not "dairyman," as it is often rendered in English. (For dairyman there is a trade word, *pakhter,* also "milkman." *Milkhiger,* milky, has a humorous connotation, but friendly and affectionately bantering.) Tevyeh was the prototype of Sholom Aleichem's famous character by the same name.

We were still going to Boyarka in the summer, and Tevyeh was still delivering our dairy products, when my father's Tevyeh stories began to appear in newspapers and magazines. They were popular enough to reach the summer residents in Boyarka, and Tevyeh learned that he was "written up in the gazettes." At first he resented it and complained to Babushka that the stories had brought him great embarrassment, for wherever he went among the summer people they called him The Milky One and laughed at him. But in time he began to enjoy his fame and admitted it was good for business, too. Some people became his customers merely to be able to tell their friends in town that in Boyarka they were served by Tevyeh, The Milky One.

It is interesting to compare the original Tevyeh with his literary counterpart. As far as the stories about Tevyeh's daughters are concerned, there is absolutely no resemblance to fact. As he himself said to Babushka during his first period of resentment, "He writes stories about me and my daughters! I have never had any daughters!"

These famous daughters were pure figments of my father's imagination, reflected through the prism of the soul of a Jew like Tevyeh. Whether the stories about the man himself before he became a dairyman, and about the dramatic way in which he became one, were based on real life, I regret to say I do not know. There is no one left who could throw any light on the matter. But as one who knew Tevyeh, I can say that these events could have happened to him, and if they did, Tevyeh would have reacted in just the way my father described.

The literary Tevyeh, however related he was to our friend at Boyarka, was very real to us. We were so fond of him that we often forgot he was fictional and regarded him as a member of the family, sorrowing with him in his troubles and rejoicing in his moments of happiness. We were always affected by his genuine warm humanity that knew no bounds, whether directed toward his creator in heaven or his horse on earth.

Though Tevyeh's faith in God is an active force in his life, he is continually needling Him for the injustice with which He administers the world. When Tevyeh tells of his terrible straits as a drayman, before he became a dairyman, he says, "With God's aid, I starved to death. . . . A Jew must hope, keep hoping, and if in the meantime his life is full of grief and disaster, well, that is what we are Jews for, chosen from all the peoples of the world, all of them envying us. . . ."

When he stands, tired and hungry, watching the sumptuous dinner being served at the rich man's cottage in Boyarka, he thinks of his wife and children going to bed hungry at that very moment and says to himself, "What is dropped to the floor here would be enough for my children for an entire week. . . . Oh, God, dearly beloved, are you not the Lord of long forbearance, the great God, the good God, with mercy and equity, how can you give one man everything and nothing to another?"

He refuses to listen to the imploring of his daughter, because she had married a Gentile and converted to the Jew-hating religion. But afterward he says to himself, "What harm would it have been to listen to her? Maybe she wants to return home? Perhaps she is suffering unbearably in her life with her husband and was trying to ask me to save her." Then strange thoughts come into his mind. "What is it, really, this being a Jew or a non-Jew? Why did God create Jews and non-Jews? And if he did create Jew and non-Jew, why did he make it so they should keep apart, have no regard for each other as if one was from God and the other was not?"

At the end of his rope, when he is about to go to the land of Israel, Tevyeh sells his horse to a water carrier who makes uncomplimentary remarks about the animal during the bargaining. Tevyeh says later, misquoting as usual: "I could swear my poor horse understood every word, as the Prophet said, the ox knoweth his purchaser, which is to say that every animal feels it is being sold. I could see it. For as I closed the deal, and shook hands with the water carrier, wishing him luck and blessing, the mare suddenly turned her face to me, looking at me with its dumb eyes, as if to say, in the words of the Holy Book, Is this my portion for all my toil, is this how you thank me for all my service to you? I looked at the mare as the water carrier took her in hand for hard labor, and thought to myself: Father in heaven, how wisely You manage Your world! You have created Tevyeh and you have created his horse, and both have the same fate on earth, except a human has speech and can at least complain, to get it off his chest, whereas the horse—what can it do, dumb creature that it is? As the Holy Book says, for the vantage of man over animal. . . ."

My father always read his stories aloud to us before sending them out for publication. The completion of a major work, like a novel or a play, was a family festive occasion, the children participating in the gladness of their father-author. (On one such occasion, when he finished his long novel *The Bloody Jest,* the story of which we, of course, knew as he was developing it, he offered a prize to any of us who would guess whom the heroine, Betty, finally married. We were living in Switzerland then, and the prize, fifty francs, was won by Emma.) I can still remember my mother's heartfelt cry, "Goldie died!" as my father, reading from one of his *Tevyeh* stories, came to this sad event. Indeed, all of us felt it as a personal loss.

Perhaps there was a deeper reason why we felt Tevyeh to be a member of our family. Consciously or unconsciously on my father's part, Tevyeh turned out to be the exponent of my father's philosophy of life, of his attitudes toward God and toward other human beings. In our family, philosophy in the abstract, in disembodied principles, as it were, seldom came up for discussion. With us it was the life situations, the characters real or fictional, that seemed to matter. But if we had translated our attitudes into terms of social philosophy and ethics we would have arrived at much the same general view that Tevyeh enunciates in his own articulate folk-Biblical speech.

Recently as I leafed through a book of my father's stories in a Chinese translation, I wondered what could interest the Chinese in a character like Tevyeh. Only a few of the six hundred thousand who bought the book in China would have read any part of the Bible or ever seen a Jew. How could they put themselves in the place of so typical a Jew, so drenched in Biblical lore, as Tevyeh? It occurred to me then that perhaps they go beyond the parochial frame, and see in Tevyeh the dignity of the lowly, of people much like themselves. He may be low on the worldly scale, but he can think for himself, have a view of himself and of his situation in the general scheme of things. They feel in him, too, man's compassion for all living beings. For him no one is too benighted or poor or evil to be excluded from man's humanness. They hear in his voice the universal outcry against injustice which stirs man in the rice paddy as much as in Tevyeh's Anatevka.

Above all, readers can laugh with Tevyeh at the pomposity of the powerful and the meanness of the mighty. They realize with him that the evil around them derives not from the nature of man but from the circumstances men have made—and what men have made, men can remake. There may be such a thing as salvation by laughter. Human frailty and vanity dissolve in an outburst of laughter, and only the good and warm heart remains.

Tevyeh was much on my father's mind all through the years. He wrote the first Tevyeh story in 1894, the last in 1914. At the beginning of 1914 he dramatized his Tevyeh stories and had solved the problems of the dramatization.

In a letter to my mother from Nervi, dated February 25, 1914, he wrote: "I dislike writing about the weather, but when you get up in the morning and look about and find it's not Nervi but Nervichke, you can't help talking about the weather. . . . Yet, there is joy in my heart. I am happy. Do you know why? Because I am finishing the play. What do I mean by finishing? Just that. After you read it I rewrote it completely. That is, I wrote an entirely different play along the lines I told you about. You will see. Today I am writing the fourth, the last act. It came out as you said it would—four acts and seven scenes. The first three acts are rather long; the fourth short, but moving. Especially when Tevyeh takes leave from his four bare walls, kisses them, and takes pity on the orphaned cat, says it can't be left there for one must have mercy on all living creatures. Non-Jews (if the play will ever be produced on the non-Jewish stage) might feel embarrassed by this—the Jew who is driven out by them takes pity on a cat. . . ."

IX
We Leave Russia

THE YEARS 1903–1905 marked the most eventful and significant period in my father's literary life: they were to be his last two years in Russia. 1903 was the year in which he finally realized his lifelong aspiration to be only a literary man, giving up his business activities and living entirely by his pen. This step had great meaning for him; he was always proud that he belonged to the writing trade, and just as the tailors in his stories call themselves "folk of scissors and iron," so he referred to his pens as the tools of his trade.

Business brokerage had become increasingly irksome to my father over the years, especially since his popularity as a writer grew while business was continually shrinking. He was able finally to break away and take the decisive step of being a writer exclusively, primarily through the growth of the Yiddish literary reading public, which promised at least some financial support. This step meant a reduction in our standard of living—a move to a more modest apartment, the sale of some of our furniture—but my father was a much happier man. Suddenly he had thrown off his chains, emerged from prison, and come into his own. Sadly, he had only thirteen years of life left in which to devote himself completely to writing.

More than ever now, our lives were swayed and marked by changes around us, as Russia entered the twentieth century, emerging from its medieval hibernation and pushing forward with a mighty spurt. The Russian mind, sunk in superstitious resignation on one level, and enervated by too much soul-searching on the other, at long last confronted reality. Economic development, industrialization, and the cultural push became driving forces, compelling even the feudal church and state to be dragged along. With these developments came social changes and the release of rebellious feelings which had been frustrated for nearly a century. Agrarian organizations, trade unions, liberal groups, Socialist parties sprang up everywhere, seething, fervid, destined to produce a revolution that was abortive in 1905 but would be victorious in 1917.

The new spirit of the age was reflected in its literature. The giant Leo Tolstoy was still in his glory, though by now resting on his laurels; but the idol of the young intelligentsia was the new man of letters, Maxim Gorki, who came from a rung of the social ladder as low as Tolstoy's was high. Gorki was more interested in describing the living conditions of the lower classes than in dissecting the souls of the idle. While some writers, like Andreev and Chekhov, depicted the moral disintegration of the gentry and decadence of the middle classes, others, under Gorki's influence, oriented themselves to the proletariat and aligned themselves with the revolution.

The great changes throughout the country penetrated into the large Jewish centers, and even filtered through to the small towns. People became more aware of the outside world; they began to want secular knowledge; a mood of resentment and revolt against social evils took shape, and an absorbing interest in literature emerged. Political Zionism evolved simultaneously with Jewish socialism, which was based on anti-Zionism; between the two extremes, intermediate political positions were formed. Desire for secular knowledge competed actively with absorption in Talmudic study. Modern literature in both Hebrew and Yiddish emerged, the latter appealing particularly to the new liberal intelligentsia. Reading books began to take the place of studying religious treatises, and public recitations of poems and short stories became the accepted form of cultural entertainment, even as the sermons of the itinerant preacher, the *maggid,* had served the older generation.

Before 1902 there had been a single Yiddish publication in the whole of Russia, despite a Jewish population of six million, 90 per cent of whom spoke Yiddish. In that year two more publications were added. The next year, the first Yiddish daily newspaper in Russia made its appearance in St. Petersburg. Before long there were journals and newspapers in Warsaw and other cities. More literary outlets appeared for Yiddish writing abroad, in London and most of all in the United States, where Yiddish newspapers with mass circulation had existed since the latter part of the nineteenth century.

In this rising tide, my father was in his element. He became even more productive, and some of his best stories were written at this time and published simultaneously in many Yiddish magazines and papers. He also contributed to Hebrew publications. Translated into Russian, Polish and German, his writing was now beginning to reach non-Jewish readers. The first collection of his writing, entitled *The Complete Works of Sholom Aleichem,* in four volumes, appeared in Warsaw. Another enterprising publisher in that city began to issue single stories by Sholom Aleichem in brochure form at the very low price of five kopecks each. Called *Books for All,* this series was exactly that. Even the poorest man, who perhaps had never bought a book in his life, could now buy a Sholom Aleichem story for the Sabbath. On a Friday morning in almost any sizable Jewish community, one could see a woman carrying a basket of food for the Sabbath, fish, *challa,* vegetables, etc., with a story of my father's on top of the heap. The story was meant for family reading, the man of the house reading it aloud to his wife and children after the meal as part of *Oneg Shabbat,* Delight in the Sabbath.

The great literary critic Baal Makhshoves put it this way: "Sholom Aleichem is an old dear friend in our Jewish world. Among our people there is not a family occasion, a *mazel tov* of some sort, a holy day celebration, or just a gathering for the evening, at which the host will not offer his guest a bit of Sholom Aleichem as he offers them a good glass of wine or a fine piece of cake. Long ago our people discovered the sweet taste of Sholom Aleichem's works. Thanks to this Jew of the Ukraine, our sad, depressed people, with bitterness in its heart and tart words on its lips, learned to laugh."

In 1905, my father saw his first work on stage—*Scattered and Dispersed.* It was originally only a story written in dramatic form, like several similar dramatic pieces which he had previously written, not especially designed to be plays. It was translated into Russian and produced in Warsaw. (Yiddish theater was still banned in Russia at that time.) He was invited to the opening by the theater and was overwhelmed by the enthusiasm that the production aroused. He described it in a letter to Tissa dated April 14, 1905.

". . . What shall I tell you about yesterday's triumph? I myself have participated on occasion in crazy ovations for beloved artists. But I have not seen anything like this, even in my literary fantasies.

After the first act I was literally strewn with flowers. Then after every act I had to come out to receive repeated curtain calls. During the fourth act the audience simply went wild, applauding every phrase that had any bearing on the subject of the play. As the last curtain came down, hats began to fly in the air, and an enormous elemental force moved toward me, as if to swallow me up. For a moment I thought the roof would come down. I became frightened of demonstrations. I do not know how to account for it, whether it was actually the popularity of the folk writer, or because the Jewish audience hungers for a Jewish stage, or simply the unrestraint of the crowd. At the exit a thousand-headed mass awaited its victim. But on the wise counsel of the chief of police I was kept in a closed loge for half an hour, and then they let me out through a back door into another street. Good God, what would have happened if it were possible to play it in Yiddish? My fate and your future (I am referring to my progeny) are closely bound with the Jewish theater. Put it down on your calendar. And for now let me kiss you, dearest. Ah, how I wish to be with you on your birthday! Whether I will manage it I do not know. For as to money—there is not a centime. The fruit is picked by others, not by me."

My father was not being modest when he looked for reasons outside his play itself for the tremendous reception at the Warsaw theater. He was never blind to flaws in his writing, no matter how popular a piece became with the public. In his preface to the second edition of *Scattered and Dispersed,* he told how he wrote it as a sketch, not dreaming it would be produced on a stage, and how it was translated and produced in Warsaw. And he added, "True, the audience gave the play and its author a rousing acclamation, and the balcony clapped bravo, as usual. But the louder the audience applauded, the sorrier was the author. He felt that the play lacked much more than it had to offer; he felt that what was produced on stage was a *feuilleton* rather than a play. My torment then was a veritable purgatory. Nobody knows, it is said, whose shoe is pinching. I was perhaps the only one in the theater who booed the author of the play."

So he began to revise it, and the revision was so drastic that it turned into a new play, but with the same theme and characters. He wanted his first work on the Jewish stage to have some professional resemblance to a real play, so that if the balcony was unable to control itself and would sometimes clap and cry Bravo, it would be applauding for some good reason. He ended with a quote from Chekhov that young dramatists should be applauded less and booed more.

The story of Sholom Aleichem's connection with the theater will be told later on in this book. But as an indication of the exuberance of the time, it should be mentioned that in 1905 my father joined up with two enterprising and prominent Jewish actors, Jacob Spivakovsky and Sam Adler, to establish a Jewish art theater in Odessa. They were about to obtain the necessary license for the theater when would-be competitors maligned them to the police, who then withheld the permit.

My father also wanted to publish his own newspaper, and he went to St. Petersburg for the required permit. He spent a lot of time and energy on this project, but it never materialized. The czarist government was in no mood to allow the expansion of the Jewish press. While in St. Petersburg, my father met the new Russian writers Gorki, Andreev, Kuprin and others. He had already been in contact with the luminaries of the older generation, Tolstoy, Korolenko and Chekhov, albeit under unhappy circumstances.

These circumstances are a well-known part of history. In 1903, the czarist policy changed with regard to the general restiveness of the people. Rather than meet the demands of the masses at least part of the way, as he was urged to do by his more liberal advisers, the czar turned to the reactionaries around him, who advocated suppression of all opposition with an iron hand. Their solution to the revolutionary movement was to create a blood bath—primarily of Jewish blood; this was a diversion to shift the wrath of the masses from the czarist regime to the Jews. The new policy was inaugurated with a sadistic and brutal pogrom in the capital city of a province inhabited by many Jews—Kishinev. This was the same pogrom Natasha had experienced the time she went to find her mother.

The Jewish intellectuals in Russia undertook the publication of a book to be called *Aid,* the proceeds of which were to go to the victims of the pogrom. My father was given the task of inviting leading Russian writers to participate in the publication, which would not only add prestige and popularity to the book, but would also identify these writers with the protest movement against the instigators of the pogrom. In his letter to Tolstoy, my father wrote:

"As you have always been sensitive to trends and events in the life of people and nations, you could not have passed by without due concern the most despicable acts, incited by evil men like Krushevan and his ilk, which were perpetrated in the days of the 'resplendent' Christian holy day in the capital city of Kishinev. When you read about it in the newspapers you could not but be anguished at the thought that in our epoch there should still be possible such bestial horrors as murderous attacks upon Jews for two days under the very eyes of the police and the local intelligentsia, hideous rape of girls with their parents forced to look on, the brutal killing of small children, and similar horrors of the age of barbarism."

Tolstoy responded at once with a warm letter and a promise to write something special for the relief publication. This led to an exchange of letters between my father and Tolstoy. It took a few letters to get the aging author (then past seventy-five) actually to write a piece. Then my father undertook to translate the three brief allegorical stories which Tolstoy finally sent in, and this in turn led to an exchange of letters about words and expressions which were difficult to render in Yiddish and required change in connotation. My father also corresponded with Tolstoy's literary agents abroad about the publication of these stories in the original Russian and in English translation, for all royalties from them were to go to the relief of the pogrom victims.

Apparently my father was seeking to influence Tolstoy, indirectly, of course, to take a public position on the persecution of Jews in Russia. In his second letter to Tolstoy he wrote:

"The sympathy that is pouring out to our unfortunate brethren from Christians all over the world is surprising, and touches our hearts. We heard from New York and Philadelphia; both Jews and Christians sent thousands of dollars to Kishinev. The speech of Mayor Lewis in Philadelphia stands above all dollars. Without a doubt our calamity touched a sympathetic chord in the hearts of all the best people in our time. This brings consolation to my unhappy people who are great in a suffering which has been unequaled in the world— for the persecution of the entire nation, proud of its past and hopeful for its future renaissance, goes much deeper than all discrimination, even than bloodshed, as in Kishinev. Though I, for example, was not in Kishinev during the days of the Holy Easter and thereby saved my life and the lives of my children, yet does not my heart bleed even here, when I read what the newspapers write about us, or when I hear what people around me, pretending to be of the intelligentsia, say about us? Or how does my boy feel when not only the students but the teachers too harass him only because his family name is Rabinowitz? And how should he feel when he learns that he has passed his entrance examination with the mark of 'excellent' in all his subjects and yet has been rejected because of the 'percentile situation' for Jewish children?"

The correspondence about the subtleties of translation was extensive. Here is one small and simple example: Tolstoy had used the Russian word *zdokhnet,* which means "he expired," but in the colloquial it is more like "he croaked." My father wrote him that Yiddish had a similar word from the Hebrew, *paygert,* but that it did not give fully the ironic-contemptuous connotation Tolstoy had in mind, so he had translated it as "his kosher soul was emitted." Tolstoy must have acquired a fairly good taste of the Yiddish idiom from these letters.

Events in Russia were leading in a chain reaction toward a severe crisis during the period between 1903 and 1905. The year 1904 opened with the Russo-Japanese war, a most unpopular war waged by a most unpopular regime. Committed to a struggle for the most elementary human rights against a doddering, corrupt government, the Russian people could not get excited about a piece of land in Manchuria and some Chinese spoils. Rather than uniting the people behind the rulers, as wars often do, this one had the opposite effect. It only increased the hostility to the czarist regime, particularly as the news of colossal defeats exposed the inefficiency, rot and corruption even in the military establishment. Many came to realize that a victory at the front would spell defeat at home by bolstering up the reactionary group around the czar. A decisive defeat would discredit it and force the czar to turn to the more liberal advisers who wanted him to meet the demands of the masses at least halfway. The embittered and frustrated Russian people were close to praying for the defeat of their own armies. This was most prevalent among the oppressed minorities, who had reasons to fear for their physical security if there was a fresh reactionary surge.

My father expressed this sentiment in an allegorical story called "Uncle Pinny and Auntie Raizi." The dull Russian censor who once banned a story of my father's as blasphemous because a character in it misconstrued a Biblical quotation, did not catch on to the double meaning of this 1904 story. He took it literally as the tale of a married couple, even though the names of the small, lithe, able husband and the big, clumsy shrewish wife were so close to *Japan* and *Russia*. The story was published in brochure form and sold in the hundreds of thousands, making literally millions laugh. The publisher made a small fortune; my father received only one insignificant payment for it.

The war dragged on until September 1905, ending in an ignominious peace at Portsmouth, New Hampshire which would have been even more humiliating without the intervention of Theodore Roosevelt on Russia's behalf. All through this period, as the news from the front ran like a serial of disaster, the people pressed for changes in the czarist regime. Early in February 1905, a demonstration of common folk, led by a priest named Gapon bearing a cross, while other marchers carried icons and pictures of saints—it looked more like a church parade than a political group—marched to the Winter Palace to present a petition to the Father Czar for relief from their grievances. They were met by a fusillade from the palace guards which killed seventy of them and wounded two hundred and forty. This massacre, which went down in Russian history as Bloody Sunday, shocked the entire country and aroused the people to take action. The palace was showered with petitions; there were innumerable strikes and open outbreaks.

Belatedly the czar made a niggardly gesture toward appeasement. In March he issued an edict promising to convoke a duma, a consultative assembly; to cancel part of the peasants' debt, money they owed for the land which their forefathers obtained from the feudal lords half a century earlier; to permit the Poles to use their own language in their schools; and to give some vague relief to Jews.

The March edict pleased nobody—it merely proved that nothing substantial could be obtained from the czar with the means employed so far, and that he was beginning to show fear of the people. Instead of subsiding, as the czar had hoped, the spirit of revolt burst into seething fires. Not a city was without a strike or some revolutionary manifestation; ambitious police officers were assassinated; the workers of St. Petersburg organized the first soviet; during the summer months, mutinies occurred in both the army and navy. In October a general strike paralyzed the entire country. Finally the czar yielded, and on October 20 he issued a manifesto granting the full demands of the people—a constitutional government. The new constitution would give the people all the basic liberties and legislative powers.

Russia would no longer be an absolute monarchy but a constitutional monarchy like Germany and England. Pessimists thought this was too good to be true; optimists saw a new era opening up for the Russian people. My father was among the optimists.

Like the majority of Russian writers he was sympathetic to the revolution, although he had not participated in the revolutionary movement, nor did he identify himself with any particular party among the Jewish revolutionaries. But he frequently appeared as a literary guest at public meetings indirectly arranged by all these parties, reading his own works, and his readings attracted large crowds. He was also in great demand for literary functions in general, which had sprouted and increased during the cultural evolution that ran parallel with the political revolution.

Even at that time there were actors and amateurs who specialized in public readings of Sholom Aleichem's stories. But it was universally acknowledged that my father was his own best reader. His voice was soft, not very deep, but his diction was excellent and his voice carried, even in the large halls that held a thousand, all the way to the highest balcony. He did not act, except for reading the funniest parts with a serious face; he did not raise his voice or overemphasize. He read simply, naturally, as the character himself might have spoken. But he had a brilliant sense of timing. A momentary pause at the dramatic turn, a slight motion of the hand or even of a finger at the psychological moment, could bring the house down.

His arrival in a town for a reading was an occasion of great excitement. A multitude of enthusiasts would come out to welcome him at the railway station. A large crowd would mill around his hotel, waiting to follow him to the lecture hall, and would press around him on his way back. This created two problems: one was that the police saw in any gathering of people a sinister political rally; the other was the physical difficulty of getting him to and from the hall in safety. Mostly the youth of the town—the college students and older high-school boys—saved the day, by forming a human chain around him to keep off the crowd, and cutting a path through the surging mass of fans.

The artist Marc Chagall tells how my father came to his home town, the city of Vitebsk, when he was a boy, and how much he wanted to hear Sholom Aleichem read his stories but did not have the forty kopecks for admission. So he climbed on top of the fence that encircled the hall, hoping for at least a glimpse of Sholom Aleichem, but all he could see was a thick, milling confusion of people.

After such a triumphant tour my father returned home tired, worn out by the slow and uncertain trains in those days of intermittent strikes, and also sad and depressed. He took the admiration of his audiences modestly—it was their plight that affected him. For all his own deprivation in youth and the experiences of want that he described in his stories, he was shocked by what he saw in the small Jewish towns—poverty, hunger, distress, and, worst of all, the hopelessness that only a real change in the regime could destroy.

That is why he was so elated about the October Manifesto that granted a constitution. As soon as he learned about it, he went from friend to friend bearing the glad tidings. He even sent a congratulatory telegram to Tissa, who was then teaching Russian in a private school in Mohilev-Podolsk. A new day was dawning for Russia, and especially for Russian Jews.

A dawn had indeed appeared, but the new day did not materialize. The crack of light was followed almost immediately by an even blacker darkness. A torrent of reaction and terror, arrests and suppression, was unloosed all over the land. This was intended to create an atmosphere in which the Manifesto could be revoked in practice, if not officially by declaration, and the back of the revolution be broken. The major feature of the repression was again a pogrom, but it far exceeded the previous one. The secret police organized bands of hoodlums, called the Black Hundreds, whose slogan was "Kill Jews and Save Russia." Local authorities were ordered not to interfere with these bands and also to see to it that the Jews were taught their lesson. Local hoodlums and anti-Semites did not wait for the Black Hundred, but set about their own barbaric performances. There were pogroms in six hundred and sixty Jewish communities, large and small.

In his story "Get Thee Out" Sholom Aleichem's hero Tevyeh tells of his own experience in a pogrom. There had been pogroms in many cities and towns, but none at his village. Nor did he expect one; he had been living with his gentile neighbors on the best personal terms and they trusted and respected him. They called him *Batyushka* Tevel, Papa Tevel, and if any of them needed advice they went to him: in case of sickness, they went to Tevel for a remedy; if they wanted a loan (without interest), it was to Tevel they went. In fact, when the wave of pogroms started, they told him he had nothing to fear—they would not permit such a thing.

Yet one day, when he returned home, he found in his yard a crowd of peasants and the entire village council from the *starosta*, the head official, to a mere shepherd—all looking threateningly ready for a festivity. Tevyeh met them in his usual cordial manner. "Welcome, welcome, good neighbors, what brings you here? Any good news?"

The *starosta* spoke up immediately. "We've come to beat you up."

"*Mazel tov*, how come, children," said Tevyeh, "you thought of it so belatedly? In other places they have already forgotten it."

In great seriousness the *starosta* replied, "You see, Tevel, the Council has been deliberating all this time whether to beat you or not. Everywhere the Jews are being beaten; why should we pass you up? So, the council decided to beat you. Only we don't know ourselves what to do with you, Tevel, whether we should only break your windowpanes and rip up your featherbeds and pillows to let their feathers into the air, or burn your house and barns and the rest of your homestead."

And Tevyeh replied with these words: "Listen to me, my dear neighbors. Since your council so decided, there is no use arguing about it. I suppose you know best if Tevyeh deserves to have you destroy his homestead and livelihood. But do you know that there is a power even greater than your council? Do you know there is a God in Heaven? I am not saying *my* God, *your* God, I am talking of the God of all of us, who is right there above us and sees all the evil down below. Maybe He Himself has marked me to be punished, absolutely innocently, by you, my best friends. Again, it may be just the opposite, and He does not want anyone to do any harm to Tevyeh at all. Who among you can undertake to tell which is His wish? Anybody who thinks he can let him speak up."

Finally the *starosta* said, "Well, Tevel, it's like this. We really have nothing against you. True, you're a *zhid*, but not a bad man. But the one has nothing to do with the other. We have to beat you. The council so decided and so it must be. But we will only break your windowpanes. This we *must* do, for then anyone passing through here will see the signs that we have beaten you, otherwise we might be punished. . . ."

How did we children feel through all this? Growing up during the last decades of the czarist regime was, of course, an ordeal for Jewish children. We had met anti-Semitism at every step—in the classroom, on the school grounds, among our playmates. Born to it, living with it since birth, we had got used to it, as people do to foul air. As for the pogrom, that meant to us killing—but always somewhere else, anywhere, everywhere except where we were.

It had never occurred to us that Jews would be harmed in our city of Kiev. Yet the dread day was approaching. There were open calls for a pogrom, and the first signs of its preparation were indicated by the appearance of strange, suspicious-looking characters in the streets. We could not go to school for fear of being hurt. Our maid packed up and left; it was not safe for her to stay with us at such a time. There was fear in the house, and dejection, a lowering of voices, frequent talk of moving from Kiev, of possibly leaving the country.

This idea had been in the air for some time. Now that my father lived entirely as a Jewish writer, residence in Kiev, far from a cultural Jewish center, was a handicap. He urgently wanted to be involved in the thick of the creative Jewish life, in close touch with the Jewish masses. That was why he was so anxious for a connection with a newspaper or a theater. Had his project for a Jewish art theater been realized, we might have moved to Odessa. Or if the Yiddish newspaper had materialized in Vilno, we might have moved there. Other possibilities were Warsaw which was then, like all Poland, a part of Russia, or New York. Natasha, our closest relative, urged us not to leave the country but to move instead to Warsaw. But my father was not enamored of Warsaw. He liked some of the writers there, but there was something in the literary atmosphere in that city that dampened his enthusiasm. Perhaps he had lived too long in a different world.

The impending physical danger brought a pressing reality to our plans for leaving Kiev, but the immediate problem was to escape the pogrom. Natasha and her family lived in a gentile neighborhood, and the other families in her apartment house were all gentiles. This meant her house would not be molested. But our apartment house was known to be inhabited by Jews, and certainly would not escape the hoodlums. It was suggested that we move to a hotel until the danger was over, which we did, choosing the Imperial, a nearby hotel whose proprietress, a Mrs. Epstein, received us with open arms, gave us three of her best rooms, and provided us with meals.

The very next morning we were awakened by a terrifying noise, a confused racket of clatters and crashes, of loud shouts and shrill cries.

We ran from our beds to the windows on the street and looked down on a scene of brutality and murder—a gang of hoodlums beating a poor young Jew with heavy sticks; blood was running over the face of the young man, who was vainly shrieking for aid. A policeman stood nearby, casually looking on and not moving a finger. Our mother quickly pulled the shade down, sent us back to bed and ordered us never again to go near the windows. But what we had seen was enough to give us nightmares for weeks to come.

The Kiev pogrom lasted three days, three terrible days and nights during which we were unable to eat or sleep, walking in silence and fear that our fortress, the Imperial, might be broken into at any moment.

Worried as we were about our own safety, we were in greater anxiety about Tissa in Mohilev-Podolsk, a town in the eye of the storm. There was no way of communicating with her. Nobody could leave the hotel to post a letter or send a telegram, and even if it had been possible, the strikes that had broken out simultaneously with the pogrom had paralyzed communications. Most likely Tissa was herself in hiding—if only she had a place to hide. Our fears for her grew. Then, like a hurricane ending, the rage of hate and evil finally subsided, and it was safe to return to our apartment. I remember my father shaking Mrs. Epstein's hand, telling her he would never in his life forget her kindness in this critical moment. My mother embraced her, and even Babushka, who was rarely demonstrative, did the same. On our way home, our father obtained a newspaper that listed the cities where pogroms had taken place; Mohilev-Podolsk was included. I can still see his ashen face, and hear my mother's refusal to believe the worst. They kept it from Babushka.

Communication was gradually restored. Trains still ran irregularly, with uncertain schedules and many delays, but the telegraph and the post functioned again. And we finally heard from Tissa. Like us, she had lived through the pogrom in hiding. Fortunately her fiancé (mentioned earlier as the Hebrew-Yiddish writer Isaac Dov Berkowitz, and always called "Berkowitz" in our family, rather than by his first name) arrived from Vilno on the eve of the pogrom, and they were together during those critical hours. Now they were coming home to be married, but Berkowitz's family—parents, sisters, brothers—were already in America and he had it in mind to join them there with his bride.

Life returned to normality, although it was never to be the same again. When we went back to school, to the same classes, the same schoolmates, we Jewish girls kept to ourselves, not mixing with the others as we used to do, even avoiding our best friends if they were gentiles. There was curiosity in the eyes of the "others," as if they wanted to ask us questions, but we looked away from their glances. We did not blame them. Their fathers had taken no part in the pogrom. Yet they had done nothing to stop it.

The pogrom was a harrowing experience for my father in more than one way. It caused an abrupt change in his life—it forced his decision to leave the country. All the hopes he had entertained about establishing himself somewhere else in Russia were snuffed out. There was no basis for material existence under the new regime of brutal oppression. Neither could he function creatively in the atmosphere of hopelessness and nihilism that pervaded the entire country, trapping even the revolutionary youth in its spell. It took twelve years and another disastrous war for the Russian people to regain the faith and courage to march forth in another and final revolution.

Fortunately nihilism was not common among the Jewish population. For them, the failure in Russia was replaced by the hope of success elsewhere, primarily in the United States. In America freedom and equality already existed, and the Jews enjoyed the same opportunities as the rest of the population. Above all, anybody could at once find employment; a day after arrival one could have a job. True, there was exploitation there too, perhaps even worse, but it was a free country and they could help change that.

An unprecedented wave of emigration to the United States poured from Russia, reaching well over one hundred thousand a year. Since the steerage passage, cheap as it was, could be raised by most families only with great difficulty, the oldest or strongest usually went first. The father or the eldest son, once arrived, saved up money to send a steamship ticket (purchased often on installment) and a few dollars to bring over another member of the family, the two of them then saving money to send for the rest.

My father expressed this general hope for a future in America in a lullaby, and mothers sang their children to sleep with it in many thousands of Jewish homes in Russia. It told of the father in America, where they eat *challa* on weekdays, who would send twenty dollars and his picture too, and in time would send steamship tickets which would reunite the family in that wonderful land:

We Leave Russia

Sleep, My Child

Sleep my comfort, my beautiful one,
Sleep, dear son.
My crown, my mourner, sleep.
Lu-lin-ke, lu lu.

By your cradle sits your mother,
Sings her song and cries,
Perhaps one day you'll understand
The reasons for these sighs.

To America went your father,
Your father, little one.
But you're a child, a tiny child,
So sleep, *lu lu.*

This America, they say,
Brings great fortune, joy to all.
And to Jews it's Paradise,
Incomparable.

They have no Exile there,
No shackles, strife,
No fear—so sleep, now sleep
My little son, *lu lu.*

The Jews are rich there,
Blessed, they say.
All are equal there,
Have prospered too, they say.

Sabbath loaves they eat there,
And on weekdays, too.
Chicken soup you'll have,
So sleep, now, sleep, *lu lu.*

But for the moment we must hope,
Just hope—what more to do?
I'd sail out and find your father
If I knew where to.

My Father, Sholom Aleichem

God willing, he'll send us
Letters, my little son,
And be sure to meet us.
So sleep, now, sleep, *lu lu.*

Twenty rubles he'll send us,
And his picture too.
Then to the States he'll lead us.
Oh, may he live long, and true.

How he'll clutch us and kiss us,
Dancing with glee.
And tears I'll shed, silently,
Happy and free.

But until that day comes
You must sleep, dear son,
Sleep—it's the easy way through.
Lu-lin-ke, lu-lin-ke, sleep, *lu lu.*

—English adaptation by
Jeremy Robson

For my father, the material advantages of America were of
secondary importance. He saw in his own emigration to the Golden
Land a symbolic act. He was going along with his own people; the
folk writer, as he liked to call himself, would journey with his own
folk; he would be with them, with his pen and his heart, as he had
been with them all these years in Kasrilevka and Yehupetz.

But the going was easier said than done. We were now ten—
Babushka, our father and mother, six children and Berkowitz. Even
a second-class passage would run into a considerable sum, which we
did not possess. Berkowitz wanted to return, after the marriage, to
his post at the Hebrew daily newspaper in Vilno, to save up enough
money for the fare for Tissa and himself. But my father would not
hear of it. Married, Tissa would still be his child, and her husband,
particularly Berkowitz, for whom he had already developed a literary
affinity, would be his son. The entire family must emigrate to America
together.

In this difficult situation my father turned to a newly acquired
friend, an American tourist he had met the summer before in Warsaw

at the home of the famous Hebrew publicist and Zionist leader Nahum Sokolov. This man was Dr. Maurice Fishberg, an immigrant himself, who had risen quickly in two fields, medicine and physical anthropology. A clinical professor of medicine at New York University, he was a pioneer in the treatment of tuberculosis; his book on this subject was the standard work in the English language for many years. He was also the chairman of the department of anthropology and psychology of the New York Academy of Science and had written studies of the physical anthropology of the Jews. He was a consultant to the Congressional Committee on Immigration, and had been sent abroad by President Theodore Roosevelt in this connection. Dr. Fishberg was an important figure in the New York Jewish community.

When they met in Warsaw, Dr. Fishberg described to my father Jewish cultural life in America, going into special detail on the Yiddish press and theater. Noting my father's interest in the theater, Dr. Fishberg offered to contact the two stars and directors—Jacob P. Adler and Boris Thomashevsky, of the two leading Yiddish theaters in New York—on his behalf. Soon after that, my father sent Dr. Fishberg two plays to offer the theater directors, one a revised text of *Scattered and Dispersed* which had been such a success on the Warsaw stage, and the other a dramatization of his novel *Stempenyu*. Later he sent him a third piece.

After the pogrom, my father wrote to Dr. Fishberg, telling him frankly of our plight, and asking him to contact a theater or newspaper that might advance him the necessary amount to bring the family to the United States. One of the American Yiddish newspapers, *The Tageblat*, owed my father money for material published, and he hoped that Dr. Fishberg could at least collect this sum for him. This would take time, of course, and our father wanted us to leave Russia at once, so it was decided that we wait for Dr. Fishberg's reply across the border in Austria, in the city of Brody. My father turned over his library to the Zionist reading room in Podol. The furniture would be sold by Natasha after we left. We began packing our remaining belongings to take with us, waiting only for the arrival of Tissa and her fiancé, Berkowitz.

It was a strange homecoming for Tissa and Berkowitz. As our departure was only a few days away, the apartment was in a state of great disorder. No sooner had Berkowitz been introduced to Babushka and the children—who had not yet met him—and answered our questions about the events in Mohilev-Podolsk than he began packing our clothes. It was odd to see the newcomer, in our house only a few hours and for the first time, packing our suitcases. My first impression of him was of a handsome young man—he was just twenty years old then—who spoke only when absolutely necessary and when he had something important to say, and who was nimble-handed. His packing was excellent. My father at once accepted him as an older son with whom to discuss all family matters.

The matter in question now was the wedding. In their first letter from Mohilev-Podolsk, right after the pogrom, Tissa and Berkowitz had written that they intended to be married there before coming home. But my father insisted that the ceremony be performed at our home in Kiev. In spite of the pogrom, he wanted a formal wedding with announcements and invitations, and friends and relatives at the ceremony. As it turned out, there was no time for any of this. Only the family was present at the marriage ceremony, which was performed by the Official Rabbi, Solomon Arcadevitch Luria, a friend of my father's and a writer of sorts himself, while the droshkys waited downstairs to take us to the railway station.

That was how we left Russia forever, late in December 1905. My father was to return there twice (once with my mother) for reading tours, during which he enjoyed great adulation. The first of them was disrupted by a sudden violent sickness.

Now, we thought, we were on our way to America, but as a family we did not get there until nine years later. In those nine years we were practically homeless, living in hotels or furnished apartments, part of the year in one country, and part in another—Switzerland, Italy, Germany—with our father in sanatoriums part of the time. But Russia remained inside us. Our language at home was Russian, our mother tongue; we were tutored by Russian tutors, although we later attended French universities; the literature closest to our father and to the older children was the literature of Russia; and as strangers in strange lands we still had our own territory—the world of Kasrilevka and Yehupetz. Our father had always maintained close, intimate contact with Kasrilevka and Yehupetz, wherever they were located— in Russia, America, Britain, Australia—and the Yiddish newspapers came to our quarters from all parts of the world, in whatever part of the world we happened to be.

X
Homeless Abroad

BRODY, in Austrian Galicia, was only a short distance from Radzi-will, the town in western Ukraine which was our last stop in Russia. But between the two places lay centuries of progress. Brody seemed to us a different world. The stores were clean, modern, their windows displaying a profusion and variety of beautiful objects, small comforts, household goods, knickknacks, at moderate prices. But over and above the standard of living we noticed the atmosphere of ease and relaxation, the sense of freedom: no one seemed to be afraid, whether of the government, the police, or their neighbors.

The local Jews were no less surprising. They spoke Yiddish, but with an accent of their own, a sort of cockney Yiddish, and in a singsong. *Ay* came out as *eye,* for instance; *eye* sounded like *ah,* and *o* like *ou.* It pleased my father to talk with them in their own accent and rhythm. They suffered no official discrimination—there were no specific anti-Jewish laws on the statute books. All the educational institutions were open to them, and if qualified they could enter the civil service, at least the lower grades. Austria-Hungary was a multinational state which embraced a few previously independent nations, and its government had to walk gingerly on the rim between autonomy and suppression in order to hold the Empire together. The Jews loved their Kaiser Francis Joseph, calling him affectionately Efrayim Yossel and swearing by his life—*Der Kaiser zoll lebn.*

Equally surprising, and depressing, was the extreme poverty of the poor Jews. The social and economic contrast between rich and poor, modern and old-fashioned, was greater in the Jewish community in Galicia than in Jewish Russia. There were Jews in modern dress, beardless or with side whiskers like those of the Kaiser, sitting in the cafés reading the highbrow German newspapers of Vienna and Budapest; in contrast, there were Jews with long, thick *payes* (earlocks) wearing Hasidic garb—large circular stiff hats, long jackets that reached to their knees (even on the youngsters), with white socks and black slippers—but all this incredibly worn and ragged. My father, who had seen much Jewish poverty in the Russian *shtetl,* was shocked by the threadbare tattered clothes of most of the Jews on the streets of Brody.

We were there only a few days, but one incident remains in my memory. The Jewish intelligentsia of the town, among whom the students were especially active, arranged a public reading for my father. This took place in the largest hall in town, which filled up quickly, with hundreds of people outside. The audience was enthusiastic and exuberant, their admiration as great as that of their Hasidic elders for their favorite Rabbis. At the end of the reading, the students rushed onto the stage in a surging mass, lifted my father up in the air, and carried him on their shoulders through the hall over the heads of the applauding crowds outside and into a carriage. The horse was unharnessed and the students themselves pulled the carriage all the way to our hotel.

We were left behind. We could not even get near the young men who were carrying our father; we could hardly catch a glimpse of him through the mass of humanity that quickly filled the slightest gap in the crowd. My brother Numa kept crying, "What are they doing to my papa? Will they give me back my papa?"

Such a reception was, of course, gratifying, particularly since it came from the young generation. But we could not exist on admiration alone. We were living on money our father had borrowed before leaving Kiev, which soon began to run low, and there was still no word from America. In his indomitable optimism my father had expected to find, on his arrival in Brody, at least some of the funds he had asked Dr. Fishberg to procure for him. Now he waited daily for letters. He had assumed he would hear directly from the theater directors; he had taken for granted that there would be waiting for him both word from Dr. Fishberg and, at least, the money due him from *The Tageblat* in New York, which would have covered our fare. He cabled to Fishberg and to *The Tageblat*—still no reply. Finally, in exasperation, he wrote a heartrending letter to Dr. Fishberg, complaining that his letters and cables from Brody had gone unanswered, that a friend of his in America had quoted to him the announcement of *The Tageblat* that it had sent Sholom Aleichem twelve hundred rubles to come to America (it owed him two thousand rubles for material already printed), but that actually it had sent only three hundred rubles, which had soon been swallowed up by the expense of leaving Kiev. Now he was stranded with his family without a source of livelihood or any means of getting to America. "I am going out of my mind. To whom shall I turn? Are all my plans, all my castles in the air, to go up in smoke? What is to become of my family?"

His desperation can well be understood if one considers the situation from his point of view. He had hesitated to leave Russia while his people were being persecuted; he felt he would be leaving them, as it were, in the lurch. He finally left only in the general exodus of his people from Russia to America, managing to get out in the nick of time by catching the last train across the border before the new wave of pogroms and strikes. This escape saved his own family's life. He felt unjustly prevented from continuing his journey to America, where there was his own money due him for his writing. Moreover, he felt that an advance on the plays he had sent to the Yiddish theaters could have been obtained, and, as a last resort, he had so many devoted admirers and readers in the United States that it should have been possible, he thought, for a person like Dr. Fishberg to find one sponsor, or get up a committee to raise a loan for him, which he could pay off soon after he arrived. Instead, he was now stranded, forsaken, helpless, vainly waiting every day for a letter from America and watching the last of the little money he had brought from Russia melt away.

The realities of the situation were quite different. The directors of the Yiddish theaters in New York were happy to receive the manuscripts that Sholom Aleichem sent them through Dr. Fishberg, but not willing to part with money, at least not until they were ready to go into production. Dr. Fishberg, although a very busy man, was ready and willing to organize a reception committee that would lay out the money for the passage, to be repaid after his arrival. But *The Tageblat,* an Orthodox, conservative paper, did not want radicals outside its own sphere to take over the famous writer—one of its frequent contributors—so it announced that no committee was necessary inasmuch as it was sending Sholom Aleichem one thousand dollars for his passage. (As we have mentioned, the paper actually sent only three hundred rubles—one hundred and fifty dollars.) Thinking all was arranged, Dr. Fishberg became involved in other matters.

We packed up and went to Lemberg, where the devotion of my father's admirers came to our rescue. In this modern city, with its considerable Jewish intelligentsia, there was even a local Yiddish newspaper. Its editor, a well-known Russian Zionist and Hebrew journalist, knew not only Sholom Aleichem's writings but also his efforts on behalf of Zionism before the movement took form. Even before the notice of our arrival appeared in the newspapers, our presence in the city became known and a stream of admirers came to our suite in the hotel. They were professionals, intellectuals, students, all very polite, devoted, eager to be of help. They arranged a reading in a large hall and one of the young admirers found a furnished apartment for us.

It was cheaper than the hotel and not so cramped, with more—though not enough—privacy. For though we assumed when we sublet the apartment that it was to be all ours, the morning after our arrival we were amazed to see the door of a room we had not yet explored open and a tall lean Jew in nightclothes emerge and head for the bathroom.

Babushka asked him what he was doing in our apartment.

He blandly replied, "What am I doing here? I live here." It turned out that he was a permanent roomer with the family that had sublet us the apartment. We simply had not been told that he would stay on—which he did through all our months in Lemberg—a quiet person, but an embarrassment to the girls when they had to go to the bathroom in their nightgowns, with towels over their shoulders.

With the public reception for my father, a gala affair, a new field of activity and income was opened.

He was uneasy about his first public appearance in Lemberg. He knew, of course, that he had readers and admirers in the city, but he thought they might be merely a small group, a fringe of the city's intellectuals and sophisticates. Now he was to face a large mass of people, plain ordinary Galician Jews, and he was uncertain how they would react to his stories. They were not, like the Jews he was expecting to find in America, former Russians; they were born and had lived all their lives under the liberal Austrian rule. The plight and vicissitudes of the Jews in his stories might seem strange and of no interest to them. On the eve of his appearance, therefore, he was nervous, silent, restless, biting his fingernails.

But his nervousness was unjustified. Despite the large hall, many had to be turned away, and the audience, most of whom were wearing traditional Hasidic garb, applauded thunderously when my father appeared on the stage and responded with enthusiasm to his every word. Geographical, political and cultural differences did not seem to affect the popularity of his stories or modify the audience's response to their author. The news of this reception soon spread to other cities and towns, and requests poured in for Sholom Aleichem to visit them, too. The group of admirers who had arranged the Lemberg reading formed a committee to manage his tour through Galicia.

The mass reception in Lemberg was followed by a banquet for the elite, unlike anything my father had ever experienced in Russia. It was organized by Zionist student groups, who were dressed in formal student garb, with sabers at their sides, wearing their fraternity insignia— white-and-blue caps and white-and-blue sashes across their chests. When the speeches were about to begin, the student organizers knocked their sabers thunderously on the table and shouted *Silencium!* in student style. The speeches themselves, in Yiddish, Polish and German, reflected the various ideologies current among the Jewish intellectuals—bourgeois Zionists, Socialist Zionists, and those groups which stressed involvement with their own nation, particularly in the approaching elections in the Empire. Each speaker took from Sholom Aleichem stories a corroboration of his own ideology, claiming that my father's deep insight into the psychology of his characters and the circumstances of their lives had led him indirectly, without theorizing or discussion, to recognize the same problems and suggest the same solutions as that particular speaker's own party or political group.

My brother-in-law, Berkowitz, who was present at that banquet, described it in his memoirs of his years with Sholom Aleichem and gave the substance of my father's replies to the various speakers. My father began with the familiar Biblical story of Jacob running from his hostile and stronger brother Esau to his Uncle Laban, and having to spend the night on the road. My father then added the equally familiar Midrashic legend that the stones of that place wrangled among themselves for the honor of serving as a pillow for the holy man. It must have been very unpleasant for Jacob, he commented, to try to rest there with the stony multitude in altercation around his head. So what did God do, according to the Biblical legend? He took the quarreling stones and formed them all into one stone.

"This is the parable," my father said, "and as is customary with sermons and preachers, it does not exactly apply to the situation here. I do not regard myself as a holy man, far from it, but in one respect I may liken myself to our Father Jacob. I, too, am running from my brother Esau—the Russ constitution and the Russ pogroms—and I am running to our rich Uncle Laban, the Aramaean, in America. And so it comes to pass that I have made my first rest stop en route with you in Galicia . . . and I must tell you that I found among you a very good and very pleasant rest stop, and even the pillow is not too hard. Now you have in addition tendered me a splendid reception to make my stay with you even more pleasant. But what? You are contending among yourselves, engaging in disputation, over me. One says, Let Sholom Aleichem rest his head on me—Sholom Aleichem has to lead us to the land of Israel; and another says, No, Sholom Aleichem has to lead us to the political orientation here; and a third says, You're both simpletons, Sholom Aleichem will lead us, God willing, to proletarization. Therefore, brethren, if you will only listen to me, let's make of all the stones one stone, and we had better sing, all of us together, a Jewish song, from the best of our folk songs, to reduce the dullness and enhance the jollification."

The parable was greeted with laughter and applause, and the banquet ended in community singing of folk songs and joyful Hasidic melodies.

My father's reading tour through various Galician cities and towns was balm to his worried and weary heart. Little did the people of those places realize what their ardor meant to their beloved author. Their enthusiasm and gratitude tempered his feelings of isolation and homelessness. He was comforted by the realization that where there were Jews he could not be friendless, that any Jewish community could be home to him, and that he was never alone in the world but belonged to his people and was part of their life wherever they were. Moreover, the income from that tour and a tour of other parts of Austria-Hungary such as Bucovina eased the financial situation for a while and opened vistas of tours in other countries which might make it possible for us to reach our destination, the United States, under our own steam.

The rest of the winter and spring we remained in Lemberg. Early in the spring my father traveled to Rumania on a reading tour and later went on special engagements in Paris, London and Switzerland. None of these proved as gratifying as his tours in Galicia-Bucovina. In Rumania the Jews lived under better economic conditions than those in Galicia, but their interests tended to be more epicurean than cultural. The students in Paris and London compensated for the depressing audiences they brought to the readings—recent Russian Jewish immigrants who had found meager opportunities available for impoverished newcomers, and were tired and downhearted.

But in London my father had the pleasant surprise of finding not only that the Yiddish newspapers welcomed him but that the English press also took notice of his visit. Despite the fact that no book of his had as yet appeared in English translation, *The London Jewish Chronicle* and writers in the general press had some knowledge of his writing.

On our father's return, at the beginning of the summer of 1906, we moved to Geneva—Switzerland was then, as ever, an international haven for emigrés. Mendele, our father's favorite author, was also in Geneva at that time, which made it additionally attractive. June was peaceful but clouded by my father's impending departure for the United States in the fall. We could see he was reluctant to go. His exasperating experience with the Yiddish newspaper and the New York Yiddish theaters had undermined his decision to settle in America; he was now uncertain about the whole idea and hesitant to move the whole family there immediately. He himself had to go—it was the only hope. The Russian Yiddish newspapers did not pay for the material he sent them, and he could not go on reading tours forever: he wrote very little while on the road, and for him this meant either physical exhaustion or very low spirits.

Worse still, he had to make a reading tour in Great Britain to replenish the dwindling sum made from earlier tours, and his first visit to London, for all its favorable publicity, had not whetted his appetite for another. He decided that he could not undertake this long jaunt to England and America alone; he needed at least a part of the moral support he always derived from his Republic, as he called his family. So he took my mother and my younger brother, Numa, to England and America. My older brother, Misha, was to stay with Natasha and her family in Kiev and finish his studies at the Gymnasium there. The rest of us would remain in Geneva.

Like most intellectuals of Eastern Europe, and particularly of Russia, my father held Great Britain in great esteem. France had her charm, Germany her comfort, but Britain was the cradle of modern civilization. The great lights of his youth were Shakespeare, Dickens, Darwin, Spencer and Buckle. Then, too, England was considered a paragon of democracy, with individual freedom unsurpassed anywhere, and its name was synonymous with industrial progress and an advancing economy. Of greater import to the Jewish intellectual was the absence of anti-Semitism in England. France had been the first country in Europe to emancipate her Jews, during her great revolution; she had had her Crémieux—but she had also had her Dreyfus case. Britain had no such blemish, and her Disraeli was a source of pride to Jews not only because of his domination of the European scene but also because he was a substantial man of letters. Learning was still regarded as the supreme human virtue.

However, in actuality, particularly at the turn of the century, Britain was not very attractive to a man like Sholom Aleichem. The snobbery of the rich, especially the *nouveaux riches,* and the abject poverty of the poor were disillusioning. Even more disappointing and depressing was the situation of the Jews in Britain. Leadership was concentrated in the hands of a small group of wealthy Sephardic families whose ancestors had come to England after the Puritan revolution—proud, haughty, overbearing and Orthodox, cherishing the memories of the grandeur of their forebears in pre-Columbian Spain, sensitive to the unhealed wounds of the Inquisition. Only with great condescension did they on occasion admit to their circle, as a marginal, second-class member, a German Jew who had arrived much later but had managed to amass a great fortune.

Then there was the small segment of East European middle-class Jews, merchants or shopkeepers, who tried in their small way to ape their economic superiors. The great mass of Jews, however, consisted largely of recent immigrants from Russia, who were there by second choice. They had wanted to go with the other Jews to the land of promise, America, but lacked the means or the courage to venture to that distant, turbulent land. London was for them a station, a stopgap on the road to the future. It did not cost much to get there from Russia, nor was the sea voyage so long and harrowing. In London they meant to find work, save up the passage money, and prepare for life in America; it was a sort of economic rehearsal for the real struggle to come.

Some of these immigrants did manage to collect both the money and the courage to go on to the United States. Most of them, however, remained and settled both in and for England. And while the expansive spirit and social mobility in the New World widened the scope of the immigrant and encouraged his ambitions, the experience in England tended to have the opposite effect. There the Russian Jew was a little immigrant among little Englanders, assuming the negative virtues of his new environment, pinching pennies rather than fight for a higher income, engaging in ventures that were more safe than imaginative, subduing his native ebullience, keeping to himself as though his small, dark, cold flat were "his castle," in imitation of the British.

Even the crimes associated with the Jewish section of Whitechapel, as compared with the rest of that slum area, were of minor scope. There was one street called Mile End, a stretch of about four blocks, lined with two rows of pushcarts, with a motley crowd milling between the rows. There was a saying that by the time a visitor passed the first block his watch was stolen, but when he reached the last block he could buy it back off a pushcart.

Ten years later, in New York, my father told my fiancé this amusing incident of his first visit to London. A Yiddish publication there had been reprinting my father's stories as they appeared abroad; it had been doing this for years, not sending him any payment for them or even asking his permission. Now that he was in London, my father decided to call on the editor and try to collect some of the royalties due him. His arrival by cab on a side street in Whitechapel caused a commotion in the neighborhood. People did not come there in cabs. Neither did they look so distinguished as this stranger with his long hair, high hat and cape. The women decided this must be some "big professor" coming to see a very sick patient. One woman conspired with another to intercept the "professor" on his way out and try to take him to a very sick neighbor—just to have a look at the poor man. After all, wasn't the professor on the block anyway?

The editorial office of the publication was in the anteroom of a printing shop in a damp cellar of an old house. As my father went down the rickety stairs and opened the door, he saw a tall, heavy-set, uncouth-looking man standing in the middle of the room. This personage did not come forward but waited for the stranger to walk up to him and tell him his business. Yes, he was the editor of the publication; true, he had been publishing the stories of Sholom Aleichem. Hearing that the visitor was Sholom Aleichem, he nodded respectfully, but expressed no welcome nor did he invite his guest to sit down; the two remained standing in silence. Then my father said that inasmuch as he happened to be in London, he had come to collect the royalties due him for his stories.

"Royalties?" the editor asked, surprised but not disconcerted. He turned a bit aside, as if to hide his next move from my father's direct view, pulled a wallet from his hip pocket, extricated a one-pound note and handed it to my father.

The general atmosphere of Yiddish culture in London was as different from that of Galicia as the English climate was from the Central European. The weather was damp and penetrating, the skies always cloudy. My father's tour of Britain in that fall of 1906 was successful enough with respect to attendance and income, but it left him cold and lonely. Only the presence of my mother and little Numa sustained him morally during the ordeal.

"Colossal, grandiose, depressing, devastating, cold, damp, gray, smoky, hard-working, free, illimitable, cultural, wild, foggy, strange, frightening—this is London." My father thus summed up in one sentence in a letter to Tissa and Berkowitz his first impressions. And while on tour through other cities of England, he wrote us all an amusing letter, dated Leeds, July 6, 1906:

"Dear Children: Before I begin to describe to you our sojourn in provincial England, I feel I must swear to you that all you will read here is the absolute truth, that is, not a *feuilleton* but an actual occurrence. We left Manchester hurriedly, without breakfast, and arrived here about two o'clock, starved—like Lyala in the sixth class, or like Misha when he did not have his dinner the night before. The Zionists—give Kaufman a glass of water—[Kaufman, Lyala's fiancé, belonged to a Jewish anti-Zionist group] who met us took us first to one hotel and then to another, which took another hour. The first question they posed to the hungry travelers was the following: How do the Russian Jews regard the split in the Zionist movement after the death of Herzl, and does the Territorialist movement have a future in Russia? My answer was that not only have we eaten nothing, we have not even had a glass of tea. They took this subtle hint, and one of them said in his British accent, 'As to food, you may rest assured, our Mr. F. has placed his dining room at our disposal for your entire stay in Leeds.' Mr. F. himself arrived in due time and asked us how our trip was and invited us to his house. We started walking to his place. We walked, we walked. We arrived. Sat down. Talked of this and that, mostly of Zionism. The man had a boy of fourteen, also a Zionist. He recited a poem, 'Zion,' of Luboshitzky, by heart, excellently. 'Hey, Sam,' the father called to the boy, 'come here, do another recite of "Zion" for the dear guests, but pour it on!' The fourteen-year-old Sam again began reciting the poem 'Zion,' which caused a gnawing sensation in our insides, and poor Numchick began whispering, 'Mother, I'm hungry. Mother, a bun.' This duet continued not for long, only about forty-eight minutes, and finally at long last we were introduced to the lady of the house, who had been occupied with her toilette all this time, sat it out with her for twenty minutes discussing the climate of the city and the most pressing problem of England (servants), and then we simply rose from our seats, not waiting for our host, and finally followed the lady of the house to the dining room. To our great misfortune we had to pass a piano, and Mother, trying to be friendly, remarked to the lady of the house, 'Do your children play the piano?' The lady of the house was all but offended. 'What a question! Of course they do. And how well they play. Hey, daughter, come here and play a bit for the dear guests, and from the book!' At once a creature in long loose hair appeared, bowed, and sat down at the piano, banging away ferociously, endlessly. We were almost frozen in position, for we were on our feet all the time. Only Numchick disturbed the harmony, declaring loudly from time to time, 'Mother, I don't want music, I want to eat.' (What a rascal!) But all things come to an end. I remarked to Mr. F. that perhaps the second part of the musical program should be left for after dinner since the child was hungry, and we ourselves had not had even a glass of tea. We went down a stairway into the dining room. The table was set with small plates, with one platter of *truskavki* [tiny cheesecakes] and another containing a few pieces of bread smeared with soft, yellow butter (just what I like, what I adore!). And nothing more! 'What would you rather have, soda water or lemonade?' I said neither the one nor the other, but if possible bread, just bread, without butter. The lady of the house replied, 'Why, don't you like bread and butter?' I was going to say, 'This is goo, not butter,' but Numchick anticipated me by saying to Mother, 'This is what they call dinner? Some dinner!' . . .

"Epilogue: Eight o'clock in the evening the quiet inhabitants of Leeds could see two emaciated travelers, with a little boy between them, roving the streets aimlessly, helplessly, stopping peaceful Englishmen to ask them in their broken English where they might find a restaurant.

(THE END: not to be continued)

"The Zionists called. I am still hungry. It is midnight. We have not found a restaurant. I am thinking of a Browning (revolver). It is desolate to be in a strange land without dinner. I kiss you all.

Your Pa"

Nevertheless, my father's time in London was not without bright moments. Just to be in Dickens's country was an experience for him— he often sought Dickensian types in the throngs in the streets. And as before, the press took generous notice of his visit, with tributes to this remarkable, very popular Jewish writer. He also met a number of British celebrities, among them Israel Zangwill, then at the height of his social prestige and fame as an English man of letters and hu- morist writing of Jewish life. Zangwill invited my father for a week- end on his country estate.

Berkowitz wrote of this visit in his memoirs, *Unsere Rishonim:* "Zangwill knew of Sholom Aleichem from the little of his work that had appeared in English translation, and possibly also from what had been read to him in the original by others. His attitude toward Sholom Aleichem was most cordial, as to a colleague working in the field of humor, close to the mainspring of Jewish life, and he invited him for several days to his rich summer place outside London. Sholom Aleichem accepted the invitation, visited the Zangwills at their coun- try home, but remained there no longer than was absolutely necessary for the proprieties. Sholom Aleichem must have felt the humiliating contrast between these two Jewish humorists, the one deriving from the poverty of Whitechapel having climbed to the position of world fame and English gentleman, in the ease and security of his estate in the beautiful countryside, and the other, a rich man of Kiev who had given up a life of wealth to serve 'Whitechapelly' people in poverty and homelessness." Berkowitz may have exaggerated my father's mood a little, but it was certainly in his character to extricate himself from such an atmosphere as soon as it was politely possible.

My father did find a congenial atmosphere in the home of a Dr. Frank in London. This was a non-Jewish family whose daughter had become enamored of Jewish literature and had learned enough Yid- dish to translate stories by my father and other Yiddish writers into English. Her translations were most inadequate, practically a verbatim rendition, but they helped at least to call the attention of literary people to the burgeoning Yiddish literature.

Years later, in *Motel, Paysie the Cantor's Son,* my father described the vicissitudes of a couple of related families leaving Kasrilevka and making their way through several countries, with the aid of immigrant-aid societies, to America. He had them stop en route in London. They did not like the Jewish community of London, either. The title of the chapter about their sojourn in the city came from an outburst by one of the women characters: "London, why don't you burn?"

XI
America, 1906

My FATHER, with my mother and Numa, left for the United States
with a heavy heart. The idea that we should all settle there immediately had been abandoned, and the trip was merely exploratory in
nature. But the circumstances were unpromising, and there was no
anticipation of a rewarding reception. He was depressed at leaving
part of his family behind, and having to sail on the 13th of October
added to his depression. Rationalist though he was, my father had a
superstitious reaction to such portent-bearing occurrences, and much
as he might make light of them they still affected him. To add to the
misery, the voyage at that time of year was particularly rough, and
none of the three had ever crossed the ocean before.

As he reflected on it, even his best friend in America, Dr. Fishberg,
seemed to be existing in a world of different values and sensibilities.
Early in 1906 he had written to urge my father not to delay his visit
to America, for interest in the Russian pogroms was waning and this
might affect the success of a possible lecture tour. My father had
replied to him in a letter dated February 23, 1906:

"You do not begin to understand me, and I do not understand
you. I do not recite anything dealing with the pogroms and I would
do no such thing, utilizing the moment, in America for money. I read
only from my own works, stories and sketches of Kasrilevka, Maze-
pevka, Berditchev, and the like; and the audience is bursting with
laughter, and occasionally drops a tear, and this is the important

thing. These readings reflect all phases of Jewish life in the bloody land, also the pogroms, the constitution, etc. Art, my dear friend, never loses its worth, pogrom or no pogrom, Europe or America. . . ."

For the benefit of all of us who were left behind, he kept a diary on board the *St. Louis* which he called "From London to New York." It began with a notation on Monday, October 16, 1906, the third day out:

"My dears: I am writing these pages to you lying in a cabin, second class. This is the first day it has been possible to hold a pencil in hand. Saturday all was quiet. We walked, we ate, we drank, we made acquaintances. Sunday morning we heard the bell for breakfast. We rose, dressed, went on deck, intending to get to the table. But this was out of the question. The ocean was on a rampage. It heaved the ship like a splinter of wood. People were nauseated; women were suffering; children were suffering. Perched in a soft chair on one of the more secluded decks, Mother was in anguish. In a hard chair on the main deck, I held my own. I took Numchick on my lap, telling him a long story with no end. He napped, awakened, complained of headache, nausea. No desire for food whatever. The ocean was raging. A terrible gnawing. With great pains we got down below. Barely managed to undress, went to bed. Fell asleep in a daze. Up again Monday A.M. Bad. Ocean tempestuous. We could not get up. We rang. A steward and nurse came in. Brought coffee. Who could drink it? We live on water, oranges and wine (Madeira). Numchick woke up with a question, 'Where are we?' He does not want to go to America. He wants to go back to Geneva. The heart is bleeding . . . tears flow in silence.

"Today, our fourth day, Tuesday, we woke up at seven. No desire to get out of bed, but Numchick begged. We dressed him lying down. Now he is on the floor, sighing, playing dominoes by himself, painting without stop. We have shaded our windows well, not to see the stormy waves of the raging ocean. Turned on the lights. Forty-eight hours like one long night. . . . We are cut off from the world until Thursday. On Thursday we will wireless to New York, and they will meet us at the port.

"They brought in the dinner. Could eat only soup and ice cream. The impression—as if we were a hospital for prisoners. And Gargantua is plowing ever nearer and nearer to the Promised Land, wrestling with the mountainous waves of the angry ocean. The thought that this is already the fourth day pours courage into our hearts. Ah, only four days more!

"Hurrah! Toward evening I got up, and went up with Numchick for dinner. Mother did not risk getting up. We brought her fried herring with potatoes. The joy was boundless. Think of it, herring, and fried, too! I am not joking. After the English cuisine a fried herring is a delicious dish. I think our seasickness is subsiding.

"Wednesday, 17th, our fifth day: The bell awoke us at seven in the morning and at eight we were called for breakfast. I and Numchick got up, dressed, even though the ship was still rolling and we could hardly stand on our feet—I must interrupt.

"We have wrapped Mother up, taken her on deck, seated her in a chair. The ocean like a mirror. The view is wonderful. The weather gorgeous. Numchick and I are observing the card games all about. Americans play cards. Germans are guzzling beer. Englishmen gourmandize. A Slav is plucking away at his balalaika. Joy in the heart. Appetite enormous.

"On deck. The ocean—quicksilver. The ship—you want to know what the ship is? It's a small, moving colony, with streets, alleys, houses, families, children, noise, bazaar; there is a bar, a barbershop, a post office, a bank, a kitchen, a colossal dining room. The population of our colony is said to be 3,500, in short, a small Boguslav!

"We are talking about you, my dears. Did you receive our letter with money from London? Tomorrow I will wireless to New York that we are arriving Saturday afternoon. For this reason, you will not receive our cable before Sunday. And our letters, alas, only eight or ten days after the cable. We will be writing you as often as the ships depart for Europe, thrice a week, I think. But you write every day.

"Wednesday evening, 8 P.M. Few Jews on board and for this reason it's dispiriting. Jews are peculiar in that way. If there are many, they are not easy to bear; if they are not there, you long for them. You should see Numchick, how he has set up his own abode on the floor between the beds in the cabin. The child sitting and singing O–ce–an, O–ce–an. By the way, all passengers are children.

"Thursday, 18th, morning. I am writing on deck in a chair, with gloves on, Numchick in my lap. The joy of the passengers at the knowledge that land is near is beyond bounds. Tomorrow, they say, we'll see land. Just sent a wireless to New York.

"The ocean has calmed. We are still in our special boat, our cabin, where it is quiet, warm, bright, and rolls less. To make it more cheerful we steal oranges and apples at the table in the dining room and eat them here. About twelve o'clock I went down to the third class, to the 'people.' My God, what a horror! People are regarded there like cattle. Rather than go third class better travel first class. At once the Jewish colony gathered about me. The attendants noticed it immediately and ordered me back to second class. After this visit, our own tent, second class, seemed like the Garden of Eden. Moral: Son of Man, look below to those beneath. . . .

"Important announcement: Today's dinner consisted of the following courses (Lyala, Maroussia, you love to read menus, don't you?): 1. bread. 2. salty vegetable soup. 3. whitefish, hot, with sauce. 4. pâté. 5. lamb with celery. 6. chicken liver with peppers. 7. sweet potatoes. 8. salad. 9. toast. 10. ice cream. 11. marmalade. 12. oranges. 13. coffee.

"Of all this we could eat only soup, fish, ice cream, potatoes, coffee, one orange eaten, two more stolen. We also stole a bun to keep for the evening. When we get hungry we will have a bun and an orange. Generally the commandment Thou shalt not steal is not observed on the ocean. Everybody steals, from the captain to the humblest steward. A sorry example for the passengers and the new growing generation. (N.B.: Numchick asks me, 'Papa, how many oranges did you steal today?') It came to such a pass that when we began stealing oranges, Numchick called out, in a voice that could be heard all over the dining room, 'Papa, we have to steal an orange for Babushka!' Happily the English do not understand Russian.

"Evening, 18th. An incident. A man from Warsaw going to America via London, where he attended one of my readings, had great desire to go on same ship with me. Since all accommodations in the upper classes were sold out he bought a third-class ticket. On the fifth day he wanted to come up to see me, but they would not let him up. On the sixth day I remembered my poor admirer (who is, by the way, richer than I am) and went down to third class to find him. Found him and took him upstairs. His bliss had no end. He was eating Sholom Aleichem, like a hungry wolf, till dinner. Then we parted. In the evening a steward searched high and low in second class for a Jewish writer, Sholom Aleichem. You can imagine how frightened Mother became. What happened? Some of 'ours' informed the authorities they should search a certain Sholom Aleichem for contraband, a passenger from third class. Fortunately for the contraband victim, he had been back in his own cabin in third class for some time. It looks as if the incident were closed.

"Friday, 19th, 7 A.M. What dreams! I dreamed of Count Tolstoy. He blessed me, like a father. Mother still sleeping. Numchick on top of me. In the next cabin the English are jabbering. Mother is waking. Thank God, it's Friday.

"8 A.M. We are on deck, all three of us. God, what a view! Pure sky. The ocean, blue, glitters like a mirror. Imagine the lake of Geneva magnified a million times, and you will have an image of the ocean at this moment. In half an hour the first call for breakfast. The appetite is whispering into our ears a ditty about fried herring and potatoes. . . . What would have become of people if they had to dream for ten years in this glorious blue of ocean about fried herring and potatoes!

"The same day, on deck. What wonderful weather, unbelievable. As in a dream. Summer, warmth, the sun is bright. The sky crystal. The water bluestone. As in a tale for children. We are writing postcards daily.

"2 P.M. Just received a wireless from New York, from a new Yiddish paper, *The Jewish American,* with this to say: '*The Jewish American,* a new journal which has recently begun publication, bids you welcome and sends warmest greetings. Please wireless collect immediately purpose your visit, situation in Russia.' My answer was: 'Thanks for wireless greeting. Regret seasickness prevents reply at length. Object visit is study situation our brethren in America and tell about real situation Russian Jews through narrative also to get acquainted with Yiddish theater and possibly work for it. Best regards to all colleagues.'

"Well, my diary, if such it may be called, is nearing its end. I intend to close it early, get stamps and mail it early. I beg you to send it on, after reading it, to Kiev to Natasha's address. Poor Misha, he has also been without a letter these ten days. I am going down to shave and pack.

"Same day, 8 P.M. The night is warm, starlit. There is music in third class, choral singing. Still, nothing can dispel the despondency and the gnawing in the heart. Like a fog settling upon the soul. The ship is still rolling. Hard to write.

"Saturday, 20th, 8 A.M. Finally! We lived to see it. They say that at two we will be in New York. Last night was the longest, the hardest. We are going to breakfast. No land in sight yet. The appetite growing.

"12 noon, 20th. Hurrah, land, land! This is how the sailors of Columbus shouted in 1492. This is how Numchick shouted in 1906. The joy of the passengers is indescribable. Bell is ringing for dinner. What happiness to anticipate the closeness of ground, hard, unshaking ground! We are going to have dinner. Today nobody would think of stealing even a single orange.

"The last minutes. Leafing through these pages I was astonished. Not my style, not my handwriting. So disconnected, illogical, difficult to get through. I think that under such circumstances one's mind does not function normally. In another hour we will send a cable home. We worked all morning on our wireless [to *The Jewish American*] and it came out foolish in the end.

"8 o'clock, 20th: At last we are in New York. The port is full of people. The ship is approaching slowly. A high voice calls, *Heydod!* [Hebrew for Hurrah]. Hats fly in the air, many hats. What is happening? The shouts 'Sholom Aleichem!' make it clear. The people at the port are delegates from Zionist and other groups. We are surrounded by representatives of the Yiddish and English press. I am lifted into the air, over the heads of the people; Numchick cries. News photographers direct their cameras at the three of us. From the crowd of people embracing and kissing me emerges a young gentleman with a small yellow beard. It's my brother Bernard. That gentleman shouts, 'A cable, Tissa gave birth to a daughter!' The occasion could not be more exultant. I am closing, and, as Lyala says, I put down a period."

While my father was on board ship, sea-tossed and miserable, plans for his reception in New York were brewing furiously. An unprecedented national committee, drawn from all segments of the Jewish community, had been formed, spurred on by two personal friends— Dr. Fishberg and an old friend of my father's Odessa days, Avrom Eliahu Lubarsky. The latter was the picturesque representative in America of the famed Russian tea firm, Wissotsky and Company. Leading the list of notables was Dr. Judah L. Magnes, even at that time a celebrated and controversial figure.

Reform Judaism, then opposed to Zionism and deprecating the idea of Yiddish culture for Jews in America, was represented on the committee by the prominent and popular Rabbi Samuel Schulman.

Others from the religious world were the British scholar and anthropologist Joseph Jacobs, professor at the Jewish Theological Seminary of New York, center of Conservative Judaism, and Reverend Z. H. Masliansky, the very popular Orthodox preacher and Zionist propagandist. The academic world had provided, among others, Richard Gottheil, head of the department of Semitics at Columbia University. The editors of the four daily Jewish newspapers in the city were on the committee, also the directors of the three leading Yiddish theaters, Jacob P. Adler, Boris Thomashevsky, and J. Schachner (of the Kalish Theater), as well as a host of literary people, including Abraham Goldfadden, the father of the Yiddish theater, and Eliakum Zunser, the venerable and beloved bard of an earlier age. Louis Lipsky represented the American Zionist Organization; there were the leaders of other Zionist groups. Union leaders came—among them the labor leader and orator Joseph Barondess, who rode a white horse in the May Day parades—and leading lights from other Jewish movements and societies.

It was this committee that had arranged the welcome my father described for us in his diary. A special revenue cutter carrying dignitaries and newsmen plowed through the rough waters down the bay to the Narrows where the *St. Louis* was anchored for quarantine. Most of the people on the cutter boarded the *St. Louis* to cheer my father and join him on the last lap to port, while at the dock a crowd of four hundred men and women waited for him to land. After a brief ceremony he was carried aloft over the cheering crowd to an exit. My Uncle Bernard then took my mother, father and Numa to his house on Jackson Street in the East Bronx.

Before long, a gala public reception was held at Adler's Grand Theater on the East Side. The program, beginning at 8:30, ran until midnight—musical numbers from the Choral Union of the Yiddish theaters, speeches, greetings, presentation of bouquets of flowers from the Actors', Composers' and Choral Unions and others, and finally a reading by my father. This public reception was followed immediately by a banquet in his honor. Three hundred or so guests were present, mostly from the theatrical and literary professions, and it lasted until five o'clock in the morning. When we learned about this reception from our father's letter we felt both excited and sorry for him, imagining the grueling strain he must have been under during that long evening and night. Our mother, we knew, would have taken it in her stride, being blessed with more stamina. Through all the ovations for my father, as she stood beside him and shared in the glory, her concern must undoubtedly have been that he should not get too exhausted or catch cold.

This was followed by a reception at the Educational Alliance, the Jewish community center the German Jews maintained on the East Side, given by the German-Jewish elite. Among the notables who attended were Jacob H. Schiff, President of Kuhn, Loeb and Company, his son-in-law, Felix Warburg, Nathan Straus, and the pride of the American Jewish Community, Judge Samuel Greenbaum, vice-president of the Bar Association of New York, trustee of the New York Public Library, founder of the Young Men's Hebrew Association, and leader in a host of top Jewish associations. A most distinguished guest at the reception was Mark Twain. It was Justice Greenbaum who introduced my father to the great American humorist as the "Jewish Mark Twain," to which Mark Twain graciously replied, "Please tell him that I am the American Sholom Aleichem."

The press reflected the exuberance of my father's New York welcome. The Jewish papers had carried the story of his embarkation at Southampton on their front pages, and even *The New York Times* reported it on an inside page. After his wireless from the ship stating the day and time of his arrival, he was again on the front pages and one paper editorialized: "Next Saturday the Jewish world in America will be enriched by a great literary personality that may well compare with the greatest luminaries among the nations." On the day of his arrival, the Jewish newspapers carried his picture, one with a caption, "Sholom Aleichem comes to extend 'Sholom Aleichem.'" The same paper wrote, "For the first time in the history of Jewish life in America a Jewish genius, a Jewish great man will be greeted on his arrival here, and honored at the beginning of his career among us; for the first time in the history of Jewish literature, a great literary man will be received here with the honor due him."

All the papers carried reports of the ovation at the pier, and one, *The Tageblat,* in an editorial, even foretold for my father a political future in this country, politics then being very much on that particular editor's mind. William Randolph Hearst, with two large newspapers in New York City, and his Yiddish newspaper by not so strange coincidence just established that October, was making his desperate bid for the governorship of New York, with his eye always on the White House. He was running, with his Tammany enemy's tacit approval, as an independent against Charles Evans Hughes. The *Tageblat* editorial read: "In five years, he [Sholom Aleichem] may become a citizen, like the rest of us; and if he retains the people's love which he now enjoys on his arrival, he could become a candidate for political office like those at present monopolizing the enthusiasm of the people."

Similar glowing and lengthy reports appeared after the public reception and banquet. "A Triumph for Our Literature," ran one of the headlines, and "Writers, Artists, Scientists, Businessmen, Leaders in Judaism Join into One Enthusiastic *Shalom* to the Great Literary Guest. . . ." The story was given without a detail omitted, including the presentation to my father by Avrom Lubarsky, for the Reception Committee, of a golden pen.

About a week later a statement by my father appeared in the newspapers; it filled nearly two columns and was intended as an expression of gratitude for the warm reception, particularly to the committee that had arranged it, and to the press. The statement contained so much observation on the Jewish-American scene that a few newspapers headed it "What Sholom Aleichem Thinks About Us." Considering the comparatively low status of American Jewry at that time, Sholom Aleichem's statement seems now to have had a prophetic ring. He had the feeling that "very soon American Jewry would begin a new and glorious epoch in our long history." Then he added, "I underscore these words, for in all sincerity I must tell you that back home the press and the people entertain quite a different notion. America to us there is synonymous with business, American Jews are peddlers, American liberty, license, and the Jewish press, my colleagues please forgive me, is what you here call 'humbug.'" He himself, he wrote, had had such an image of America, and was now confessing and asking forgiveness "in the words of the ancient prayer, 'for the sin that I have committed' by being prejudiced. . . . Those who have changed the verse of 'From Zion will come forth the Law and the word of the Lord from Jerusalem' to read 'From Kiev will come forth the Law and the word of the Lord from Amsterdam,' will now have to change it once again to read: 'From America will come forth the Law and the word of the Lord from New York.' . . . I, who often indulge in jest, mean this very seriously."

My father was, of course, quite sincere—he was incapable of deception—and no less enthusiastic in his letters to us. He was not blind to the obvious grievous shortcomings of the Jewish press, theater and other sectors of Jewish life in America, of which he had been aware and to some extent had been a victim, but now he saw

American Jewish life whole and in its potential as a historical process. What impressed him most was its vitality, dynamic energy and spiritedness; he had not lived in such a Jewish community before. Kiev contained so few Jews, comparatively, and many of them assimilated, without any of the institutions by which Jews were bound together in New York. What he had seen in Warsaw during his brief visits was a puny, impoverished, petty and harassed Jewry in comparison with what he found in New York. And then it must be remembered that he became immediately involved with the theatrical profession, for which he had a close affinity, and which took him to its heart with all the glow and exuberance natural to the theatrical personality. So, for the moment at least, it was like the dawn of a glorious new period, with limitless channels for his creative talent, in which he would for the first time come into his own.

There was only one fly in the ointment, one sour note in this paean of mutual approval—an editorial comment in the Anglo-Jewish weekly *The American Hebrew*, mouthpiece of the German-Jewish establishment and Reform Judaism, which was largely assimilationist. Their remarks were not directed against my father, whose literary position they respected, but at the Jewish community of the East Side. For while non-Jewish New York intellectuals of the time were apt to admire the cultural fervor and social unrest of the new immigrants, the established *American Hebrew* looked with disdain, if not with alarm, at the teeming activity of the East Side. It disliked the Jews there for their East European origin, which in their view was far beneath a German origin, though unfortunately the gentiles confused the two. It deplored the persistence of these East Europeans in retaining their native languages, although many of the German Jews still spoke German. It felt, on the whole, disgraced by the poverty, clamor and vociferousness of these regretted brethren on the East Side.

The editorial said Amen to the praise of Sholom Aleichem but questioned whether the East Side would have a place for such an author after the hullabaloo of the reception subsided. What will Sholom Aleichem do then, go to work in a sweatshop or join the peddlers in the street? How would he make his living? These remarks went unnoticed by the Jewish masses, who had never heard of the existence of *The American Hebrew*. But one Yiddish newspaper editor came upon the editorial and heaped abuse upon the organ of the *Yahudim*, as the German Jews were derisively called on the East Side.

However, as events turned out, the question so crudely posed by *The American Hebrew* was not entirely unrealistic. I doubt if even in the golden haze of the reception my father gave a thought to settling in America. He did, however, hope to establish connections with the theater and press that would open outlets for his creative writing and give him some measure of economic security. And he struggled very hard to achieve this.

The net proceeds from the reception at the Grand Theater was one thousand dollars. This was meant to go to my father, and actually he had earned it, since those who filled the theater had come to see and hear him. Yet the treasurer of the Reception Committee was reluctant to part with the money. He ignored all requests, until finally my father called on him himself, when, most ungraciously he handed it over as if he were giving a donation out of his own pocket. Half of the money was sent to us in Geneva to live on. With the rest, my father and mother rented a furnished apartment not far from Uncle Bernard in the Bronx, and settled down to temporary living in New York.

Illustrations

Earliest photo of Sholom Alei-chem, at the age of 18. The Yiddish inscription, in his own handwriting, bears his characteristic signature (Sholom Aleichem) of later years and is dated Kiev, 1877; the same date written according to the Hebrew calendar also appears.

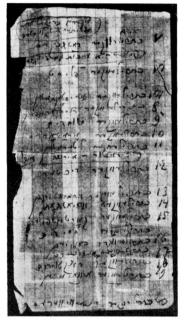

Part of a Sholom Aleichem manuscript containing chapter headings for "Old New Kasrilevka," which he was writing in 1910. Some of these chapters, like "Flirtation in Kasrilevka" and "Kasrilevka Poets," were never written.

Sholom Aleichem in 1915 in his apartment in the Bronx, writing in his little notebook—the way he did most of his creative work. The hanging bunting is one of the decorations at Carnegie Hall for his reception there.

Sholom Aleichem and his father (seated), Kiev, 1885.

Grandfather Elimelech, Babushka Rakhil, circa *1870. Olga with her half-brother's daughter, Natasha,* circa *1890.*

Sholom Aleichem and Olga at their wedding, May 12, 1883.

Sholom Aleichem, Olga, with their first three children, Tissa, Lyala, and Emma, 1889.

Tissa with her Russian Nyanya, 1886.

The Sholom Aleichem children before the birth of the sixth child (Numa). Left to right, Maroussia, Emma, Tissa, Misha, Lyala; the older four are in their school uniforms.

The house Sholom Aleichem lived in at Belaya Tserkov, 1884–1887. The house, still standing, bears a plaque in Ukrainian indicating that he lived there.

Olga at the age of five and in her teens.
Below, as a young mother.

Sholom Aleichem in 1905.

Sholom Aleichem and his son-in-law, Isaac Dov Berkowitz, discussing a new story he had just written. Wiesbaden, 1913.

Left to right, Sholom Aleichem, Numa, Olga, and Moyssei Savelevich Mazor.

Sholom Aleichem with his entire family, which he called his "republic." Front, left to right: Numa, Emma, Sholom Aleichem with his granddaughter Tamara on his lap, Misha; back, Berkowitz, Tissa, Olga, Lyala, Michael, Maroussia. Badenweiler, 1910.

Sholom Aleichem with fellow writers, Geneva, 1907. Left to right, Mendele (grandfather of modern Yiddish literature), Sholom Aleichem, Ben Ami (Jewish writer in Russian), Bialik (famous Hebrew poet).

Sholom Aleichem and Baal Makhshoves (a well-known Yiddish literary critic).

Sholom Aleichem with the popular Yiddish novelist Sholem Asch. Belmar, New Jersey, 1915.

Sholom Aleichem, I. L. Peretz (the classic Yiddish novelist), and Jacob Dineson (a popular writer of the day). Warsaw, 1914.

Sholom Aleichem and Emma, New York, 1916.

Maroussia and Ben, New York, 1917.

Misha in his school uniform, Kiev, 1908.

Sholom Aleichem and Olga, Riga, 1914.

Sholom Aleichem with his two grand-daughters, Tamara (right) and Beloch-ka (Bel Kaufman). Montreux, 1912.

The last photograph of Sholom Alei-chem, Bronx, New York, 1916.

His calling card (including his real name as well as his pen name) in his own hand.

The remains of Sholom Aleichem carried from his last residence, 968 Kelly Street, Bronx. His funeral was the largest seen in New York.

XII
Sholom Aleichem and the Theater

My father's heart was in the theater, but when Hearst's paper, *The Jewish American,* offered him a contract for five thousand dollars a year, the promise of financial security made it a temptation. At that time the amount was handsome, especially for a Jewish writer. Some of his friends urged him to accept, pointing out that no other newspaper could or would guarantee even half that sum, and that the connection might mean my father's stories would be published in translation by other Hearst publications. Other friends, however, dissuaded him. *The Jewish American,* they said, was only an election-campaign gimmick and would fold soon after the election. And Hearst was so hated by the radical Jewish masses that any identification with one of his publications would be offensive to them and might alienate their affection for my father. So the offer was rejected.

No other Jewish newspaper made a substantial offer of a permanent connection—which, indeed, my father would not have wanted, as it might have proved a hindrance to his theater career. To become a regular contributor to one single newspaper might mean a lack of publicity and an unfriendly attitude toward his theatrical projects on the part of other newspapers. He knew that he had to keep himself above the battles going on within the East Side if he were to count on the theater to make his American visit a success.

Why was Sholom Aleichem set on the theater?

All through his literary life my father had hoped and striven to see his work produced on the stage. His own history in dramatic writing began long before there was any Yiddish theater of an artistic nature in Russia or anywhere else. As far back as 1887 he wrote a one-act play, *A Doctor,* which satirized a *nouveau riche* family tussling over the profession of a husband who was to be ordered from the matchmaker for their daughter. The father, a practical man, wanted a merchant for a son-in-law; the mother, in search of status, insisted upon a doctor. Meanwhile, the sophisticated, cynical daughter, who was not being consulted, had her own marital plans.

A few more minor dramatic efforts followed in the next five years, and then my father wrote his first full four-act play, *Yaknohaz,* which was mentioned earlier. This play belongs to the period in which "Menachem Mendel" began to appear; it is a devastating criticism of the stock exchange, of its personnel, methods and routine. On a flimsy pretext—a blasphemy charge—*Yaknohaz* had been forbidden publication by the czarist censor. This is the play that my father adapted for Adler's New York theater; he changed its title to the hero's name, *Samuel Pasternak,* and to this title Adler insisted on adding the words, *or The Scoundrel.*

In the two decades between the original *Yaknohaz* and its rebirth as *Samuel Pasternak,* my father's output in dramatic writing was profuse—skits, playlets, one-act plays, and full-length dramas and comedies. His last play, written the year before his death in 1915, was a delightfully entertaining comedy called *The Great Win,* sometimes produced as *200,000,* hilarious but like all his humorous writing touched with sadness. It was the story of a poor tailor who thought he had won a fortune of two hundred thousand rubles in a lottery, and who lived for a while under this misapprehension that he had become suddenly rich.

My father's preoccupation with the stage never left him through the years when there was no theater for his work, and no possible chance of production. That his ambition to see a play of his own on stage remained alive in spite of hopeless conditions may be traced to several factors. One is that he actually saw, heard and felt his characters live, in action, with all the minutiae of their characteristic personal mannerisms and speech. All novelists experience this to some extent—but in my father's case the dramatic element was the strongest, and he only needed to allow his characters to step from the pages of his books to the living stage for story to be transformed into play.

Another was my father's longing to be in close personal contact with his own people, and for this the theater was the ideal medium: not only on stage but also in the orchestra and the balcony, he was surrounded by Jewish folk. But most of all, his innate love of theater itself, his own sense of mime and enjoyment of it, made it inevitable that he should write drama. In his youth he had read classical drama avidly, and by the time he came to write his own works, he had seen much of the best repertory of his time. Acting was his second, if suppressed, nature, which at times burst out; on one festive occasion, a banquet for the famous Hebrew poet Hayim N. Bialik in Geneva in 1907, he impersonated one of his own characters. This was Reb Alter (from the playlet *Mazel Tov*), an itinerant bookseller, an old bachelor who imbibes more than he can carry while in jovial company in a wealthy household and who ends up proposing to the widowed cook.

While there was no Yiddish theater in Russia, the Russian theater had been stimulating and full of creative force ever since the czarist ban on private theaters was lifted at the turn of the 1880s. With the removal of this ban had come a spurt of new theaters, new plays, new acting and staging ideas. The theater became the medium of expression for the emerging bourgeoisie who allied with the intelligentsia against the lethal influence of the sterile, parasitic aristocracy and the stupidities of the czarist bureaucracy. The realism, the outcry against injustice, the deriding of bluster and pomposity were like food and drink to my father. Kiev, citadel of the new bourgeoisie-intelligentsia, had two repertory theaters and an opera company. And they played not only Gogol, Ostrovsky and the other Russian classics, and Shakespeare, Molière and Ibsen, but also the modern plays of the time by Gorki, Chekhov, Hauptmann. I doubt if my mother and father missed a single new production in any of the three houses then in Kiev; theater was a regular part of our lives. School children could get tickets for ten kopecks—balcony seats, of course. Barely thirteen when I left Russia, I had seen the best of European and Russian repertory.

My father came to America not many months after the wild success of his play *Scattered and Dispersed* performed in Warsaw in translation. As he wrote in his letter to Tissa, quoted earlier, the whole performance, including that of the audience, had convinced him that while his knowledge of theater techniques was still limited and while his play, as a play, had serious defects, yet his "fate" and his "family's future" lay in the theater. If a Polish audience responded so enthusiastically to a play that was in his own view so poor, and in translation besides, a Jewish audience seeing and hearing his work in Yiddish should be even more receptive.

New York was obviously the answer to his needs and his passion. There were three major Yiddish theaters in New York, with six or more minor ones, and a potential audience that increased with every steamer landing at Ellis Island. Surely there should be a demand for plays. In America, too, he would be working with the directors of the theaters right on the spot, and thus would be able to overcome his technical problems. He would no longer merely be writing dramatic literature; he would be writing for the theater directly.

My father's eternal optimism and trust in people was only too buoyed up by the fantastic reception he had received from the theatrical profession when he landed in New York. Jacob Adler, admittedly the greatest actor on the Yiddish stage at the time, star and director of his own theater, begged Sholom Aleichem for a play. So did Boris Thomashevsky, who was also star and director of his own theater for musical comedy. Each offered an enticing advance of one thousand dollars, and as my father needed money badly, for subsistence in New York and for the rest of us in Geneva, he accepted both offers, undertaking to supply both theaters with a work for the coming season. Each director was in a hurry to put on a Sholom Aleichem play, and each wanted to be first with his own production. Consequently my father had to run frantically from one theater to the other to give his plays the supervision they required.

For Thomashevsky my father dramatized his first novel, *Stempenyu*, the story of a handsome, debonair young musical genius who, with his violin, captivates the hearts of old and young, especially of young women. Don Juan though he was, genuine love followed on his flirtation with the beautiful, innocent, romantic Rokhele, who had been married early to a nonentity. Like *Pasternak—The Scoundrel* which went to Adler, *Stempenyu* had its subplot, and its basic feature was the specifically Jewish milieu and speech that, as in his other writing, only intensified the universality of his characters. The more genuinely a person is drawn as an individual, the more evident his humanity.

In his introduction to *Stempenyu,* first published in 1888, my father called it a Jewish novel, making the point that a Jewish novel must be different, because Jewish life, and especially the circumstances of Jewish loving, are different and distinct from other cultures as are the specifics of customs and manners. In *Stempenyu* the specifics meant the situation in a small Jewish nineteenth-century town, where musical expression, however great the talent or the love of music, was limited to liturgy and weddings. The cantors in the synagogues monopolized the liturgical music; the music at weddings was the function of *klesmers,* the local or roving bands of string, wind and brass performers, who played by ear. Some of them, like Stempenyu, were musicians of great talent who achieved renown in their little world. The great musical world outside, however, lay beyond their reach. A Stempenyu could never become a Paganini. They reacted, like other frustrated artists, by becoming bohemians, a nonconformist set with slight regard for either piety or feminine virtue.

For Rokhele it was the world of the small town, where the boys and girls stopped playing together at the age of six or seven, and boy and girl could never be alone together again until their parents arranged their marriage, practically not before the very ceremony. It was after marriage that attachment and love developed between the sexes, and it was ingrained in all that adultery was a most horrible sin which no married woman would contemplate. Yet the flesh was weak, the spell of the fiddler often overwhelming, and what a modern woman would regard as a harmless flirtation was an emotional crisis for a woman like Rokhele. Stempenyu himself, despite amorous escapades, became emotionally involved with her in her innocent but very real inner struggle.

The people who attended Thomashevsky's shows had only recently come from the world of Stempenyu; they would recognize it and identify with his tribulations and those of Rokhele. The play was bound to interest them and fill them with nostalgia.

Samuel Pasternak, which Adler was to produce, was also about a specific Jewish group, the small-time brokers who engaged in speculation with neither the money to indulge in such sport nor the least notion of how it operated. In the crooked mirror of Pasternak's small-town brokerage, one could begin to see the crookedness of the whole system.

The audiences in Adler's theater had never been inside a stock exchange nor did they have any knowledge of its operation, but the evils of Wall Street had been made very real to them by radical propagandists and they could easily identify with *Pasternak's* idealistic children.

The race between Adler and Thomashevsky to be the first to open with a Sholom Aleichem play ended in a draw; through the intervention of a mutual friend, both agreed to open on the same night. The next day my father wrote this letter to us in Geneva:

"New York 2/9/07. My dears: Well, I passed the examination, and, I believe, gloriously. The trouble was that it was impossible to obtain a complete impression because I had to split up into two. I attended two acts in one theater and two acts in the other. At both theaters I was called out several times for great ovations. The audience seemed to me to be satisfied. In any case, there was so much novelty that they had more than enough. *Stempenyu* made an impression of something poetic and patriarchal. *The Scoundrel,* on the other hand, compelled the audience to keep its mouth open and laugh all through the performance until the last drop of the curtain. This, too, was new here, for the customary buffoonery and hokum has become boring, and the humor is so poor that one must take pity on them. . . . They buy "jokes" for money, or lease them from one another. Today we will see the whole of *Stempenyu* and tomorrow the whole of *Pasternak*. Then we'll write you something definite. As far as the press is concerned, I am confident about the non-Jewish press, since it is more honest than the Yiddish; the Yiddish is partial, and I expect nothing good from it. But that's not worth a farthing—the main thing is the public, the masses. . . . As you see, we live here in a separate theatrical world. Circumstances have pushed us into this world, and I still have many hurdles to pass, a great struggle, but I hope to come out victorious. I embrace you all, and Tamara [Tissa's new baby].

Your Pa."

My father's intuition about the attitude of the Yiddish press proved accurate, but "the masses" turned out to be a weak reed to lean on.

The newspapers were divided along what might be called socio-religious lines. The two that represented the middle-class religious community (although also read by workers) praised both plays highly. *The Tageblat* wrote that with these two plays "Sholom Aleichem opened a new world for the theater public." *The Jewish Morning Journal* said that "the hopes that were placed upon Sholom Aleichem that he would bring a new spirit into the Jewish theater of

America have been fulfilled." The drama critics who wrote for these newspapers had harsh words for the current Yiddish theater, charging that it was not a real Jewish theater but consisted of adaptations and imitations of plays in other theaters, with "all roles stolen and falsified." In my father's work they saw "the work of a real artist," genuine Jewish humor surging from a fresh spring, comedy that is not corrupted by crude imitations of Shakespeare and Sudermann. . . . The audience was laughing continuously, yet was learning something, becoming acquainted with new types of people. . . ."

The press that represented the Socialist and labor communities which were intimately connected with the literature and theater of the time was sharply critical of both productions. Abraham Cahan, who as editor of *The Forward* monopolized its literary and dramatic criticism, found all sorts of faults with *Pasternak*. No banker, he complained, would call stocks by the name *yaknohaz,* a word derived from the first letters of the names for articles used in the synagogue on holidays, such as wine, candles, etc. The play was much too long . . . actually a variety show instead of a play . . . not a true picture of life but an amusement piece put on just for laughter. He could not take it seriously, but he had to admit that Sholom Aleichem well understood the theater, knew how to create a "hit," with each act ending with a bang . . . abounding in scenic creation and fun. There was no review in *The Forward* of *Stempenyu,* possibly because Cahan did not want to hurt the interests of his friend Boris Thomashevsky.

L. E. Miller, the editor of the other radical newspaper, *The Warheit,* wrote in his review of *Pasternak* that he had made use of his privilege to leave in the middle of the play despite the fine acting of Jacob Adler. He was amazed that Sholom Aleichem, coming from Russia where they had produced *The Inspector* and *Power of Darkness,* could have put on such a play here. Another writer on *The Warheit,* Joel Enteen, wrote that this was the worst play ever produced in the New York Yiddish theater and could not find sufficiently abusive epithets for it. Yet another critic, in the labor journal *Der Arbeter,* found the play beneath criticism, adding that all great novelists turned out to be failures as dramatists. As for *Stempenyu,* he wrote that while the novel was original, full of types, characters and scenes that impressed themselves on one's heart and mind, the play was merely a kaleidoscope of figures who had no reason for being there; every now and then one felt the glow of Sholom Aleichem's talent as a novelist, but soon Sholom Aleichem the dramatist extinguished it.

Against these onslaughts by the radical press, *The Jewish Morning Journal* took up cudgels for the two plays, ascribing their hostile reception to political and personality struggles within the literary and theatrical community. The radicals, the paper's editor said, were using the theater as a propaganda medium and saw their ideas threatened by the arrival of a new master presenting true life. It was natural, he continued, that the young guard surrounding Jacob Gordin (an outstanding dramatist and propagandist of his time) and connected with *The Warheit* should come out against Sholom Aleichem, since he was a potential competitor of Gordin's. The latter was afraid that true characters on the stage, possessing both positive and negative qualities, might push his characters with their purely negative qualities out of fashion. And the old guard, the anti-Gordin group of *The Forward* also had their reasons, he said, for opposing Sholom Aleichem. They would not mind the blow struck at Gordin, but these plays were a threat to their own brand of so-called realism.

This editor was not too far off the mark. For it seems that the same commentator on *Der Arbeter* who declared *Pasternak* to be beneath criticism, and then proceeded to criticize it, made a point of taking umbrage at a remark made by my father between the acts which he regarded as a reflection on the Jacob Gordin theater. My father evidently said that new currents were sweeping the Yiddish theater, that travesty and raw comedy were giving way to art. Perhaps he had been encouraged to make this outspoken remark by the attitudes and opinions of Jacob Adler, who was then in a fight to the finish with Jacob Gordin.

Thus, although my father avoided identification with any single newspaper or special group, he did not manage to steer clear of the parochial feuds of the theater within the East Side.

Two decades later, reviewers felt quite differently when the same plays were revived. The late Soviet critic, for instance, Professor N. Auslender, wrote about *Yaknohaz* (*Pasternak*) that this first full four-act comedy by Sholom Aleichem "gives an exhaustive picture of a certain environment," and this was seconded by the scholar Bal-Dimion, who said that the play not only presented real people "but actually characterized living people of a specific milieu. . . ." As for *Stempenyu,* A. Mukdoni, a leading dramatic critic of later years, wrote about that play's revival by Maurice Schwartz: "Here Sholom Aleichem has given us a wonderful picture of the first artists in Eastern Europe and of the environment in which they lived. . . ."

As my father said in his letter to us, the audiences were most enthusiastic, and this was more than corroborated in a conversation between Jacob Adler and Berkowitz the following year. Adler said that *Samuel Pasternak* was a wonderful comedy—never had an audience in his theater laughed so heartily—and not only the audience, even the actors themselves could not repress their laughter. This was particularly so when he himself played the role of Pasternak, the miser—the walls of the theater shook in the storm of laughter.

Nevertheless, both plays were failures. They ran no longer than two weeks, with disastrous effect on the hopes of my father. His plans to make a living in the theater were wrecked. These two failures also discouraged further efforts to put on Sholom Aleichem plays in America. It was not until several years after his death that his plays became one of the mainstays of the Yiddish Art Theater in New York as well as of the one in Moscow, which lasted under the Soviet regime until 1948, and returned to the stage after Stalin's death.

What was the real cause of the disaster in 1907? Primarily the plays were a casualty in the collision between two cultures. My father came from a country where the theater had reached artistic heights. Kiev, as I have said, had the best of Russian and continental drama, classic and modern. In these plays it was the psychological insight, rather than the plot, that mattered; what the characters felt, thought and said and how they expressed their feelings were more important than what happened to them. The American theater, on the other hand, was in a state of temporary decline and in the hands of theatrical syndicates operating in a purely commercial spirit. Most dramatists of the time yielded to what the syndicates regarded as popular demand, which was for melodrama, action, and happy endings. In 1905, when Paul Olenov, a leading actor of Stanislavsky's Moscow Art Theater, came to New York with his troupe to play *Brothers Karamazov* in Russian, the critics found it dramatic enough but complained of the unhappy ending.

While the American theater was in a temporary decline, the Yiddish theater in America had not yet come into its own. Sholom Aleichem came a decade too soon. The father of the Yiddish theater, Abraham Goldfadden, the man who founded (in Rumania) the first professional modern Yiddish theater in the world, was still about when my father came to the United States in 1906. In fact, he was one of the speakers at the reception, symbolically relinquishing his reign over the Yiddish stage to the distinguished guest. Yiddish actors were only one generation removed from minstrels and mummers. When Jacob Gordin produced his first plays in America, he would strike actors with his cane for making up their own lines on stage instead of speaking from the script. None of the actors, not even such leading lights as Adler, Thomashevsky, Mogulesco, Kessler, had received any professional training; they had risen to the top by sheer native talent and by observing actors on the non-Yiddish stage. Even Adler, the most intelligent and responsible of them all, thought nothing of making changes in the text of a play according to his own whims, or to cutting other roles in order to highlight his own.

The only forms that could be called traditional in the Yiddish theater then were the Goldfadden operetta, a milestone on the road between the minstrel show and the modern musical; the Lateiner broad farce and sentimental melodrama, seasoned with song, dance and burlesque (Lateiner had founded the first Yiddish theater in America in 1883); and the Gordin dramas, free adaptations of classic and modern continental plays, such as the *Jewish King Lear* or *God, Man and Devil* (adapted from *Faust*). In manufacturing Jewish situations to fit these classic and modern plots, a difficult feat at best, Gordin was handicapped by his estrangement from Jewish life and by a journalese Yiddish removed from the living tongue of the people. The Gordin play was an artificial product with regard to the dramatic situation and the psychology of its characters, foreign to the Jewish mentality, cast in black and white, good versus bad, without any of the shadings of reality.

The New York theater world then as now was hard, hectic and ruthless, and it was into this world that my father came, an innocent abroad. He had built his hopes on it; he was committed to it by the advances he had received, which kept the family afloat both in New York and Geneva. He bowed to the dictates of that world because he realized that he was not an expert and had much to learn about theatrical techniques. Yet he dreamed of changing the face and substance of the Yiddish theater in America as he had changed Yiddish literature in Europe, and of finding success in the end.

But he had reckoned without his hosts. It was not enough for the theater directors that he yielded to their demands for textual changes. They made many more on their own. Jacob Adler was a great admirer of Sholom Aleichem's, even after the failure of *Pasternak,* and when Berkowitz brought him a new play by my father, Adler glowed with excitement. As Berkowitz described it, the great actor exclaimed,

"A new play by Sholom Aleichem! Father in heaven, quick, quick, let me see it, let me hear it!" and, as he turned the pages of the manuscript, he kept saying, "The dear hand of Sholom Aleichem! What a golden hand! What a golden language! How he writes! How his characters talk!" Yet the production script of *Pasternak,* which Berkowitz happened to see, contained many lines where the "golden language" had been changed, in Adler's handwriting, to a banal one. And he did not accept the new play offered by Berkowitz because there was not enough in it for the star "to do" on the stage.

The tampering was even worse in the case of *Stempenyu.* In his memoirs published in *The Forward* in 1929, Thomashevsky wrote that upon first reading the script he had told Sholom Aleichem there was nothing to play and had asked him to rewrite it, but that the author had merely added a couple of scenes and changed a few lines. Since he had to open on the same night that Adler opened his (!) there was no time to work on the script—presumably Thomashevsky meant he had no time to revise the play himself, placing the blame for the failure on Sholom Aleichem. Yet one of the leading actors in that theater, Mogulesco, is quoted in the memoirs of Joseph Rumishinsky (the Yiddish theatrical composer) as telling him immediately after the first reading of the play to the cast by my father, that if the actors played only half as well as Sholom Aleichem read it, the play would be a great success. But Mogulesco feared it would not be a success "because the production would not have the tone, the Sholom Aleichem atmosphere."

Just what that meant Rumishinsky explained through his own experience: he had been called in by Thomashevsky to score a melody that Sholom Aleichem was to sing for him, so that it could be used in *Stempenyu.* The melody was so beautiful that Rumishinsky was tempted to request Sholom Aleichem to sing more folk songs but was diffident about asking him to do so. "Both melody and words were delightful, with a thousand charms—but on stage it came through like cheap doggerel. All its folk quality, its Sholom Aleichem charm, was gone. New words were added, so-called lyrics, and new bits of melody injected, which drowned the folk quality. . . . The entire piece was drowned in cheap theatrical effects."

Nor was the cheapness confined to the productions themselves. To give an idea of the kind of people my father was dealing with, Boris Thomashevsky, who was certainly not the worst of the lot, had the audacity to write in *The Forward* in 1929, while my mother was right there in New York, that he had twice sent Sholom Aleichem money, once to Kiev and again to Switzerland, for a play which he never received. Then, he said, he brought Sholom Aleichem and his family, at his own expense, to America, where he gave him a thousand-dollar advance to dramatize the novel *Stempenyu*. But meanwhile, he said, Sholom Aleichem had become involved with Jacob Adler. My mother published a sharp reply in the same paper, saying that there was not a word of truth in the story, except that Thomashevsky paid the thousand-dollar advance, but not until the play had gone into production.

To round out the story of my father and the Yiddish theater, let me quote from two men who were recognized as the most authoritative drama critics in the Jewish field both in Europe and America. Writing in 1940, in New York, Dr. A. Mukdoni dwelt on the sad fact that Sholom Aleichem had had no luck with the theater during his lifetime and was theatrically discovered only after his death. He added:

"The true story is this: Sholom Aleichem has been a Jewish theater himself. For forty years Sholom Aleichem has been played continuously in thousands upon thousands of Jewish towns and cities. For forty years his stories have been continuously recited at thousands of cultural events, meetings and gatherings, in public and private family meetings. No writer in the world, not only among Jews, has been played and recited as has Sholom Aleichem."

The Soviet-Yiddish dramatic critic J. Dobrushin, of Moscow, in a study published there in 1928, discussed Sholom Aleichem's fifteen dramatic works and their hundred and thirty-six roles and remarked: "Sholom Aleichem was the first to introduce the principles of the theater in Yiddish literature; and in order to achieve clear, expressive theatrical images, he deviated from his own wide range of novel and short-story themes and created simple theater action; he created theater through literature rather than literature through the theater, as his predecessors had done."

The closing of the two plays after so short a run was a bad shock for my parents. My father had staked too much on them, both morally and financially, to take their failure in his stride. The advance money soon ran out, and no further income could be expected from the theater. Again came the frantic search for a means of livelihood, and again, the most immediate and direct source seemed to be a reading tour—this had worked well in other countries. And, of course, there were the newspapers, as there was no longer any reason against a connection with a particular one. But neither idea proved lucrative.

There were no agencies, no impresarios at that time to arrange Yiddish reading tours, and the local Jewish communities were not so organized as they later became. Moreover the immigrant Jews who settled in cities outside New York were generally the less sophisticated, mostly shopkeepers with overlong business hours. The engagements were not many, and the income low.

As for the newspapers, only a novel, run serially, could assure at least a momentary steady income, whatever it might be. Here again, Sholom Aleichem was faced with the demand that he adjust to the so-called public taste. L. E. Miller of *The Warheit,* who negotiated for a serial, insisted that however literary it might be, it must possess plenty of action and suspense. My father reluctantly agreed to take this into consideration.

Simultaneously, he arranged with the *The Tageblat* to provide stories which they would run weekly, and with the publisher of *The Jewish Morning Journal,* Mr. Saperstein, to publish other stories in his popular weekly, *Der Amerikaner.* On the face of it, this looked like an achievement, and one that would bring him a considerable income. But the novel brought very little; *The Tageblat* paid even less, relatively, per story, and sometimes the stories were not printed. Mr. Saperstein was a personal friend and admirer of my father's, but the editors of *Der Amerikaner* were evidently out to prove their editorial independence and superior literary taste by finding fault with some of my father's stories and complaining to Mr. Saperstein that Sholom Aleichem gave his best to the other publications. They rejected one story that soon became, and has remained ever since, one of the most popular stories he ever wrote. Maxim Gorki wrote to my father that he had laughed and cried when he read it. The story was "Motel, Son of Paysie the Cantor"; Mr. Saperstein overruled his editors, but only because the story was scheduled to appear in the Shevuoth holiday issue and he would not spoil that holiday for Sholom Aleichem.

As in other times of trouble, my father sought spiritual nourishment from his family. His letters to us from America, written in haste and under harassment, had overtones of longing and sadness.

"Mother wrote you yesterday, and I am writing today. I suppose by now you are used to this kind of letter. If fate had taken you to

America (or if the same fate had kept you in outcast Russia) you would know and understand that no other kind can be written from here. Letters are written by one who is alive and feels his living. But we do not live here at all, only find ourselves on the road, on a train, noise and rush, everybody hurrying, and we too, not knowing where to. Did you ever try to write letters in a railway station? Imagine we have spent the entire winter at the depot waiting for the train—to Geneva! If only that longed-for train had arrived!"

In response to our cabled greeting on his forty-sixth birthday, March 3, 1907, he wrote us:

"Your cable brought forth a tempest of memories, thoughts and sentiments. In our minds we were back where we all—though in difficulties, yet together—celebrated this day, on which each one of you felt happy and festive. Yes, it is sad, very sad. I never thought that on 18 February [March 3 in the Gregorian calendar of Russia, and Sholom Aleichem's birthday] I would be far away from you. Yesterday, Purim, we also spent sadly. And you can imagine what Passover will be like! You know how elated I feel on this exultant holiday, Passover! I am sending you Numchik's drawings—his only pastime here. Ah, how he is longing for all of you! Tamara [then ten weeks old] is the only happy one—she does not yet know this sentiment of longing. . . ."

My mother was more outspoken and bitter about the conditions under which my father had to work in New York. "America compels Pa to write Paul de Cocque novels for $30 a week." Actually the novel, *The Flood,* which he wrote for one paper was not nearly so bad as those of that popular French best-selling novelist of the day. But it was written hastily and carelessly enough for my father to re-write it and change the title before publishing it in book form.

As if to save his soul, and retain his balance, my father wrote, even under those trying circumstances, some of his very best stories—parts of the *Tevyeh* series, and some of the series *Motel, Son of Paysie the Cantor.* These raised him above the depressing situation, as his own fictional heroes so often did, and allowed him to recapture his natural mood. We began to receive diverting letters in Geneva, like the one he wrote to his first granddaughter, when she reached her fifth month:

"Darling Tamara: I am sending you, my dear lady, herewith five dollars (25 francs) as a gift for your personal needs, like cosmetics and similar necessities as may be needed by a young lady like yourself who has reached the age of five months. You will use it, I trust, wisely, and will not spend it on trifles. I am cautioning you particularly not to make loans right and left. For instance, your Aunt Lyala will no doubt desire to borrow some change for a short term; or your Aunt Musa will begin flattering you to persuade you in regard to chocolate that can now be bought at the store very cheaply, with coupons, to boot, and such. After a while, draw up an account and send it to me. Give my blessings to your papa and mama, to your aunts and grandmother. Your Uncle Numa sends you his best regards. He is burning with eagerness to make your acquaintance, to push his hand at first opportunity into your face, to attempt to poke out one of your little eyes with his finger—just out of curiosity. I warn you also against a certain poet S. who no doubt has a desire to lift you high in the air with one hand. Your Senior Papa."

In the midst of all his preoccupations, frustrations, and disappointments in people, my father did not hesitate to undertake the formation of a committee in New York to celebrate the seventy-fifth birthday of Mendele for the purpose of raising a fund for the publication of Mendele's works. His friends in Odessa, where Mendele resided, had written to my father about this occasion and of their endeavor to raise such a fund. In his first letter in reply he chided his friends for being such greenhorns as to advise him only two weeks before the date, not six months before, as would be required here to organize such an activity. In a second letter he informed them he had issued a call, under his own name, in the press for a Mendele celebration, and a committee of prominent persons was organized for this purpose, with a plan for a gala concert that would bring two thousand dollars clear profit, making four thousand rubles for the publication project. Of course, nothing came of this.

In June 1907, after eight months of heartbreak and hard work, my parents managed to get away from America and return to us in Geneva—not without borrowing the money for the fare.

XIII
A Parting in Geneva

IF OUR FATHER compared their life in America to living at a railway station, the life of the remainder of his family in Geneva was like staying at a post office. Our preoccupation and thinking, our dreams in the long lonely nights, revolved around the letters arriving from our parents in America. What was happening to them there, their decision as to whether to settle in America or make a permanent home elsewhere, would direct the lives of us all, even though some of us were grown up, I myself pushing the teens. Spiritually and psychologically we had always been completely involved with our father: his life, his comfort, his interests, had never failed to take precedence over our own.

Materially we were also dependent upon him, for in those days in Europe it was still regarded as improper for girls of "good families" to go to work. We were not trained in any useful occupation that could make us self-supporting. Our mother, however, did believe that girls should acquire a profession, as she had done, and her influence was manifest in the case of Tissa, who followed in my mother's footsteps upon her graduation from the Gymnasium in Kiev. Tissa never practiced dentistry, however, preferring to teach school instead. Undoubtedly my mother hoped that we other girls would also study a profession, especially while we lived in Switzerland, where education was easily accessible. But she was too much engrossed with our father's struggle to achieve some basis of a livelihood from his writing to actively direct our education, and we were left largely on our own.

Lyala, having graduated from the Gymnasium in Kiev before we left Russia, entered the University of Geneva, took a stab at law, switched to medicine under the influence of the medical student she was later to marry, and finished by reading literature. For my sister Emma and myself, the two younger girls, a Russian student at the University was engaged to teach the required gymnasium subject for admission to college. We were taught in Russian, for this was the language we knew best, our mother tongue, and most suitable since our place of a permanent home was still undecided. (My older brother, Misha, who remained with the Natasha family in Kiev, was a student at the Gymnasium there.)

With the birth of my niece, Tamara Berkowitz, there were seven of us in Geneva, living as though we were stranded on an island, waiting for our rescuer who would also determine our future. Then Babushka began ailing, but was too proud to complain of her physical discomfort, and would not undergo treatment until her daughter returned. Meanwhile the Berkowitzes had plans of their own, for Berkowitz was anxious to be out in the literary world on his own, as he had been before his marriage to Tissa. But he could not take a decisive step without consulting our father; moreover he was the only man left in our family in Geneva. Lyala, too, may have had dreams, if not plans, for her life with her fiancé, but for the present she remained with the two of us, Emma and myself, as we lived vicariously with our father's vicissitudes in America and waited to learn what path he would take on his arrival.

We were all at the depot when our parents, with little Numchik, returned from America, and with this joyful reunion our months of loneliness in Geneva came to an end. We cried almost as much as when they left, but this time the tears were of happiness. Yet, we were apprehensive, too, for Babushka by now looked pale and thin, as though she had shriveled since their departure. My mother and Babushka embraced each other, not kissing, but hugging and crying, the longest embrace I had ever seen. My father seemed to be struggling to overcome a distraction, or perhaps trying to convince himself that this homecoming was not a dream. He looked each one of us up and down as though checking for a possible change in us, and when we reached home he went through all the rooms, opened the wardrobes, picked up objects, just as if he were there for the first time.

So, at long last, we were all happily together, each finding security in the presence of the others; our father needing the warmth and shelter of his Republic no less than we, its "citizens," needed the protection of the presence of our President. Individually, we were reassured, but collectively not at all secure. We realized that our father's arduous efforts and harrowing experience in America had not solved our economic problem, although he endeavored to give the impression, perhaps to convince himself, that he needed only to complete his projects and plans for his livelihood to be secure.

Considering his experiences in America, it would not have been surprising if Sholom Aleichem had left New York in frustration, with resentment in his heart. But such a state of mind was foreign to his nature, and certainly so for a long period. Disappointment, failure, crisis brought sadness occasionally mixed with a drop of bitterness, but this did not last for long. Then came the rebound, the birth of new hopes, renewed faith, further effort, with fresh, bright dreams of success.

My father came from America with harsh words for some of the leaders of the cultural community; and there were aspects of American life of which he strongly disapproved. Yet, he brought back a deep respect and admiration for the vastness of the American scene, the hope, the vision, and the drive of the lowly of all nations, who came to America to create a new life. This attitude was in accordance with the philosophy that lies at the basis of his writing: nothing is inherently wrong; evil is a mistake made by man under the force of circumstance and can be corrected by a change of circumstance. In contrast to Mark Twain, my father never quarreled with the human race; he only made fun of the pettiness of some of its members, which he blamed not on their human nature but on the artificial circumstances surrounding them. His world never closed in on him; there was always the horizon, and the great beyond; and the time was always the dawn. America was much too large to be judged by a few isolated instances, and, while he rejected some of the parts, he accepted the whole.

Instead of resentfully shaking the dust of America from his feet, as another man in similar circumstances might have done, my father saw the best in the situation and departed on friendly terms with everybody, telling his friends and the public in his farewell that he was not saying goodbye, but au revoir. He was returning to his family to discuss the possibility of settling permanently in America.

Was this only politeness, or did he really mean what he said?

In the long run, he certainly meant it. He mistook the suavity of the actors and producers and the respect of the publishers for genuine friendship, and he translated this imagined friendship into prospects of cooperative action. He could, he thought, work with these people, despite all the disappointments, now that he knew them personally and realized their own problems. He had lost the first battle, but he could still win the war. He reassured himself with the thoughts that Jacob Adler was still anxious for another play; that even Thomashevsky had said, Better luck the next time; and that he could send the plays from whatever part of the world he might settle in. Moreover, now that he knew the theaters better, his plays could be angled to have more chance of success. The newspaper publishers expressed readiness to publish his material regularly, though at low pay, and agreements had been made with them. If these expectations were fulfilled, he would receive a steady basis for a livelihood, catching the phantom he had been chasing ever since he had made writing his only source of income. Since he had gained, as he was trying to make himself believe, this goal by sinking his anchor for a short time in America, why not settle there in due time? America was the land of the future, and his face has always been toward the future. However, he saw that until these hopes were truly realized, he must return to his family in Switzerland and settle somewhere in a measure of comfort so that he could complete his part in these arrangements.

In my father's lullaby, quoted earlier, the mother tells her child of the wondrous things that will happen after its father in America has sent for them. But meanwhile, she tells the child, until God permits him to send us the lucky paper (the steamship ticket) bidding us come, sleep my child, for sleep is the great reliever. This relief my father could not have, he could not sleep and forget, he had to work, to write the plays for the producers and the stories for the newspaper publishers, not without some doubt that they would really stand by their arrangements.

My father's return home was overshadowed by Babushka's illness, which was soon to take her away from us in her sixty-sixth year.

Babushka maintained her matriarchal status to the end, but she mellowed after we left Russia. If she did not become more tolerant, she at least yielded before superior forces to the extent of not deigning to do battle. Besides, both the territory of her dominion and her function as its ruler were sharply diminished by our way of life abroad. Living in a furnished apartment, with all household services provided for, did not leave much of a menage for her to rule. The children had grown up sufficiently to look after their own personal needs, and the sole exception, Numchik, the last of her wards, was temporarily removed from her domain by our parents' taking him to America. Even her own food, which was kosher, was ordered from an Orthodox family living in the city. She must have felt like the proverbial hen who hatched duck eggs and thought them to be chickens until they arrived at a pond and swam away, leaving her alone on the shore.

Within the range of her dignity she endeavored to adjust in a sort of noblesse oblige. She addressed the maid as mademoiselle, even condescending to say on occasions, *s'il vous plâit.* She treated the children as though they were children no longer and tried to counsel rather than order. Perhaps her illness subconsciously contained a measure of relief, perhaps was an excuse for her withdrawal from the center of the stage.

Babushka's illness was, of course, the immediate problem after our parents' return. Geneva was then a noted medical center whose distinguished physicians were famous far beyond the borders of Switzerland—like the celebrated Dr. Roux, to whom people came for surgery from all corners of Europe. Babushka had the benefit of the greatest physicians in the city. Their diagnosis was carcinoma, and the advice—immediate surgery.

Naturally, my parents wanted Dr. Roux to perform the operation, but he was an old man, was booked up for surgery many months in advance, and no respecter of persons. Once a princess came to his office, and he told her casually to take a seat, as he would anyone coming to his office. The princess was shocked. Was it possible that Dr. Roux did not know who she was? She said, "But, Dr. Roux, I am a princess." *"Alors."* Dr. Roux smiled. "Take two seats." My mother sent Lyala to beg Dr. Roux to perform the operation on Babushka; he received her with his kind smile, and listened to her halting French with great patience. But when Lyala told him that our family would feel confident of Babushka's survival if she were in his hands, Dr. Roux did not relent. Instead he sought to belittle his competence: "Really?" he asked. "What about the people I operated on who did not survive? Did you ever hear of them? You heard only of those who did. Besides, is it always in the hands of the surgeon, or does not the Almighty have a bit to do with it, too?"

Babushka was operated on by another surgeon, whom Dr. Roux recommended. On the third day after the operation she died.

We felt our loss deeply and grievously, for we loved Babushka as she loved us and admired her stamina and fortitude. Many incidents of the past now came to mind, which pointed up her selflessness and her devotion to us all. There had been tensions in the family; there was in particular the relationship between her and my father, which has already been indicated. They hardly ever talked to each other and avoided even formal greetings. Yet my father treated her with the utmost respect, yielding to her the seat at the head of the table and primacy in family affairs in other matters. She seemed disinterested in, or unimpressed by, his fame as a writer; yet she would have leaped fiercely to his defense if it were necessary.

Reflecting on this in later years, it seemed to me that Babushka suffered from an overwhelming resentment against my father which she could not forget, and could not or would not conceal. My father suffered all the more deeply in that she never voiced her antagonism: she was the mother of his wife, the grandmother of his children—but not his mother-in-law. What could her objections to him have been? Not to his person, as a man, husband and father, but as the cause of the financial degradation of her daughter and family. No personal qualities, no literary fame could assuage that wound. Babushka was not money-minded, but she was comfort- and status-minded. When my father lost my mother's inheritance in the market crash, Babushka did not hesitate to pay his debts out of her own share and to advance him money to start anew. But when he lost this money, too, so that his family lived in need through the years that followed, the blow, which she took personally, she could not forgive.

That my father was aware of this we saw, although at the time we were too young to understand it, in the Ivanoff affair. *Dyelo* Ivanoff was a lawsuit that grew out of my father's early business transactions: it had dragged on for years and years, and its origin lay too far back in my childhood for me to ever know it.

The Ivanoff affair hovered like a fluttering angel over our heads, holding out the prospect of riches and, for us children, special gifts promised by our father after the case had been heard. But we were concerned with *Dyelo* Ivanoff not only for selfish reasons: we knew that this lawsuit involved a lot of money, and if our father were to win it his financial difficulties would be eased. This uncertain state of hope continued for a long time. Occasionally the case was about to be resolved, then another postponement, or some other legal device, occurred, which removed it from the daily conversation. Finally the case was judged, and my father won it, as he had always believed he would. This day stands out clearly in my mind.

To have a smiling and gay demeanor was not unusual for my father, but that day his face was beaming with happiness. He hugged his briefcase to his body when he came home, and for a time he was closeted alone with my mother in his study. Then he emerged, holding a large brown envelope in his hand, and with my mother accompanying him, did a most unusual thing—he walked with my mother right into Babushka's room. I could not remember ever seeing him enter her room before. As usual, I followed my parents, so that although I was too young to understand the conversation, I saw my father's shy smile as he handed over the brown envelope to Babushka. Babushka's face was flushed, she seemed embarrassed as she accepted it, and after my parents left, she opened her trunk with the large key and deposited the brown envelope inside it. I ran to my mother, pressing her to tell me what was in the brown envelope, but all the information she gave me was a brief lecture that little girls must not want to know everything, for this would turn them overnight into old women. But I learned soon enough that the brown envelope contained all the money which my father received from the *Dyelo* Ivanoff.

Why did he turn it over to Babushka?

To my father this act must have been a token of his financial obligation to Babushka, a partial repayment of the money she had advanced him many years earlier. To Babushka the possession of the money was a means of bolstering her sense of independence—she was now a woman of means in her own right. But what did she do with the money? Not a kopeck of it was spent on herself. She kept it all as a sort of bank for my mother, and whenever my mother needed money she went to Babushka, who unlocked her trunk and took out the brown envelope. Babushka did it gladly, for she wanted to be able to give to her daughter.

My father was away at the Hague for the Zionist Congress when Babushka went to the hospital for her operation. He was there not only as an honored guest, but also as an official delegate of the Zionists in America, no doubt enjoying this special function where he would meet old friends from the early Zionist days. He hurried straight home upon hearing Babushka's condition had worsened, and he was as distressed at her passing as was my mother. Despite their strained relationship he felt and reacted as though he were her son. His dear friend and literary "Grandfather," Mendele, read the prayer at her interment, and my father recited the Kaddish, as a son would, and as she had expressed a wish before her death that he do. All through the seven days of mourning we had a *minyan* at our house, my father reciting the Kaddish for her. He even observed the lesser period of mourning, the mourning month, refusing invitations to make public appearances during this period.

That this was not a passing sorrow is shown in a letter my father wrote to Lyala on the occasion of her wedding in 1909, two years later (he was too ill to go to Russia for the wedding). He reminded her of the traditional Jewish custom of remembering in moments of great happiness the souls of those who had passed into the eternal world. This is a good custom, my father said, it exerts a softening influence on the heart. And so now, he went on, remember on your wedding day your Grandmother Babushka, who sacrificed so much of her life for the welfare of our family, and who would rejoice for you at this time.

And in another letter, to the Berkowitzes, he refers again to Babushka when describing Numa's bar mitzvah in 1914. "I remembered," he wrote, "the Old Mother, how she once looked at Numchick and expressed her one heart's desire to live to see him at his bar mitzvah. I thought of it when he sang the blessings for the Torah, and his clear voice rang in my ears—and my eyes filled with tears. . . ."

For my father, Babushka's passing was more than the bereavement felt at the passing of a close member of the family. It was also a break with the past, with the last bond with Sofievka, where he had found his love and had had the happiest three years of his life. In a sense, he was orphaned by her death. We, too, felt her passing in both aspects—as a grandmother, and as the foundation of our past. We felt more uprooted after she was gone, and older.

Ironically, Babushka was buried in the Jewish cemetery in Geneva next to Mikhail Rafailovich Gotz, a famous Russian revolutionary, a man who had given his life to destroy the very world to which she had clung tenaciously all through her years.

XIV
Catastrophe in Baranovici

THE PROSPECTS my father brought from America were considerably augmented by others: a newspaper in Warsaw wanted a novel for serialization; a man in Berlin had an idea for the production of one of his plays; and there were possibilities in England and Latin America. My father himself had a plan for the revival of a defunct Zionist publication of which he might be the literary editor. If only a couple of these projects would materialize, our financial situation would be stabilized. The trouble was, however, that not a single one of them could really be counted on for actual cold cash; they were still hopes floating in the air. But the obvious demand for more writing from him, the anticipation that so many more people would be reading his works or seeing them on stage, was fascinating enough for my father to overlook the down-to-earth practicalities. He had only to write, he assured himself, and the rest would follow: he was writing, and already living in the realization of these prospects.

Influenced perhaps by my mother, he took the only decision which was practical under the circumstances: to settle as comfortably as possible in Geneva for at least an extended temporary period. We rented an unfurnished apartment on a three-year lease and bought our own furniture, thus creating a sort of home of our own, the first since we left Russia. There was no money, of course, for this undertaking, but relying on the money that would soon be due him, and which, indeed, was already due from the newspapers in New York, he borrowed from friends.

Still short of money, he arranged a few public appearances in Western European cities; a literary function where he read extracts from his works had always been the surest shortcut to income. But the audience in Western Europe for such appearances was, naturally, limited; besides, for all the pleasure he derived from meeting his admiring readers, these tours were physically exhausting and interfered with his writing. He resorted to a tour only when there was a real need for it materially—and also emotionally. Emotionally because he often needed the reassurance and inspiration he derived from meeting his readers face to face and feeling their warm response; all the more so when we lived in Switzerland, which lacked large groups of "his people."

Our apartment was a walk-up on the fourth floor of a house on Plein Palais, not far from where some of our friends in town lived. Simple and spare as the furnishings were, they were our own; no longer would the landlady come to check how we were treating her precious possessions, keeping her silver, handling her linen. We were filled with a sense of freedom, and our father was elated. He bustled about the rooms with hammer and nails, asking each of us where he should place a nail for hanging clothes (built-in closets were still unknown in those quarters). I think he had a particular liking for driving in nails, for he used to do the same in Boyarka when we moved into a new *dacha*. We enjoyed watching him drive the nails in for we sensed his own satisfaction doing it.

After a few days, however, a complication developed. On our first Sunday afternoon, the doorbell rang and in came a tall, shaggy man, with thick mustache and a husky voice, who told us in Swiss German that we were disturbing him by stamping our feet over his ceiling. Then, looking at our floor, he said: "Ah, no rugs! You'll have to cover your floors with rugs or move out of here. You're foreigners, and have no business renting your own apartment anyway. You should live in a furnished apartment. My name is Monsieur Koligé, I live right underneath you. Good day!"

We were stunned, but our father made light of it. He paused for a moment, as though he was trying to think up something, then he said, "If the worst comes to the worst, we can walk on all fours without the least sound," and he showed us how to get down and creep along on all fours. We had a good laugh, but laughing did not eliminate the Koligé problem. Every once in a while he would knock on his ceiling with a broomstick to warn us we were stepping too hard on our floor and his ceiling. We lived in this apartment for about a year.

The fall of 1907 and the winter of 1908 were a period of great expectation for our father. I say "for our father," because the rest of us could see all the prospects vanishing into the horizon. He could not, since he was working and writing at a feverish pace, and when he was fully absorbed in his writing the affairs of the real world about him receded far into the background. He lived with his characters, their problems, their environment. He laughed with them and cried with them. And we kept our doubts to ourselves, for what really mattered was that he was writing and happy.

For a newspaper in Warsaw he revised a novel he had written in America and published serially in a newspaper while he was there. He continued the stories of his beloved boy hero, Motel, the orphan son of Paysie the Cantor. Through Motel's eyes he described the tribulations of the late cantor's family and a couple of their neighbors, who set out with insufficient funds and less knowledge to get to America, wandering from one emigration center to another, knocking at the doors of the Emigrant Aid Committees, first in London, then in Antwerp. To describe the experiences of this group in Antwerp my father went there himself to meet the emigrants, and find out how they were helped on their last lap to the Land of Promise.

Most of his energy and effort, however, went into the writing of a new play, which he called *The Treasure*. Now he was writing for the stage like a professional, having a particular theater in view, Adler's in America, of course, and knowing the actors who were most likely to play the characters and the kind of audiences the play would have. To test the response of the public to the play, he read it at a public appearance in the Handwerk Hall of Geneva, a large meeting place where Lenin occasionally delivered his harangues against the dissident groups of the Russian revolutionary movement. The hall was packed, and his audience, mostly young people, Jewish students from Russia and other emigré elements, reacted to the play with tremendous enthusiasm, continually bursting into laughter and applauding the lines that had special meaning for them. My father was now doubly sure of the success of this play on the American stage. He sent it to Berkowitz, who was by then visiting his parents in New York and exploring the literary field for his own work. Berkowitz was to offer it first to Jacob Adler, but if for some inconceivable reason Adler should decline the offer, he would give it to one of the two other theaters on the East Side that might produce it.

Weeks followed weeks, ran into months, and the great expectations failed to materialize. The Warsaw newspaper did run the serial, but it made no payments, since it was struggling for its very existence. The newspapers in New York did not publish my father's contributions regularly, and what they owed for the stories they did print they did not pay, small as the amount was. After long, tortuous, exasperating negotiations with each of the three possible producers in New York, *The Treasure* was not accepted for production—and all the other chimerical ideas of half a year earlier had long evaporated into thin air. Now the only reality about our economic situation was overdue bills and growing debts.

What was to be done? There was no point in staying in Geneva without any basis for a livelihood. After the second mortifying experience with the New York newspaper publishers and the disastrous negotiations with the theater producers, what grounds could there be for moving with his family to America? Return to Russia? What could he do there, in regard to his writing, that he could not do from Geneva? It was too late, he was too miserable, to even think of returning to the exchange and brokerage.

Dark as the hour was, it could not entirely obscure my father's faith and hope. In a letter to Berkowitz after the fiasco of the *Treasure* negotiations, he wrote that he firmly believed a day would come when people would beg for *The Treasure*. His belief was well founded; his prophecy was fulfilled.

The Yiddish theater, he promised, would yet come into its own artistically, first in Russia and then in Yankeeland, and he was confident that his plays would one day dominate the scene, adding: "My eyes may not live to see this, but yours will." *The Treasure* was produced in 1927, eleven years after my father's death. Another Sholom Aleichem play, *The Great Win*, (*200,000*) brought to artistic prominence Moscow's State Jewish Art Theater in 1923; in America, the Yiddish Art Theater achieved recognition and financial success with Sholom Aleichem's *It's Hard to be a Jew*, in 1919. In Moscow and New York, whenever theater business slackened, both these theaters put on plays by Sholom Aleichem.

Whatever the future, the present was most distressing; a critical point had been reached in the family fortunes. In this extremity my father turned to his sole escape, his one refuge—his readers. He decided to go on a reading tour in Russia, revisiting the cities and towns in which he had appeared at various times before leaving that country, and hoping that other places might also invite him. This contact with his readers and admirers would be, as always, a restorative, and the income at least enough to pay off the loans and creditors and leave a little for the future until something came up.

What could come up?

There was nothing in view, as far as we could see, but in the back of my father's mind lay the possibility of returning to Russia. The political situation seemed to have become stabilized, a modicum of live and let live had been restored, and Jews, too, had a breather. Perhaps the lessening of tension would mean renewed literary endeavor and interest. A visit to Russia would allow him to size up the situation and see if return was possible.

However, such a tour required not only initial capital for expenses until the first returns from the readings came in, but also money for his family during his absence. If they were in want while he was away in Russia he could not have peace of mind. For this only a hundred dollars or so was needed, but the money was not there, and it was not easy to obtain. His public appearances were arranged by local cultural institutions or groups of readers and admirers formed for this purpose, which were themselves impecunious. Borrowing from friends would have been no novel experience, but he had already exhausted possible sources in order to keep afloat during the past months. In desperation, and against his own instinctive demurral, he asked a rich and famous professor at the University, supposedly an admirer of his writing, for a loan, and suffered the humiliation of a refusal. As a last resort my father did what he had doggedly refrained from doing all the years heretofore—he turned to a colleague, a close personal friend, from the days both had first appeared on the literary scene. This was the novelist Mordecai Spector, the only person outside the immediate family with whom he was on familiar *du* (thou) terms. Spector was at the time an editor on a newspaper in Warsaw, and he sent the amount requested by wire at once. It was in these circumstances that my father, accompanied by my mother, started out on his first tour of Russia since we had left that country, and it was to be tragically interrupted.

The tour was overwhelmingly successful, surprisingly so, even for those who knew his great popularity among the masses. In Warsaw he had five appearances on five successive nights at one of the largest halls in the city, the fifth being as packed as the first. Equally enthusiastic was his reception in the other cities, when a flood of invitations from all sorts of towns came begging for at least "just one appearance." It was not in my father's nature to refuse a call from his readers, and the result was a grueling, exhausting circuit, with one-night stops, night after night, hopping on and off trains to meet scheduled appearances. To top it all, the weather was inclement—bitterly cold temperatures which taxed his health. It would have been a miracle if he had endured such a timetable and such conditions for long. He did not. For over two months he carried on; then, in a town called Baranovici, he came down with an illness that nearly crushed him and left him ailing for a number of years.

Baranovici was typical of many towns my father had already visited in the course of his tour. Despite their sharp divisions on ideological lines, as was customary at that time in Russia, the youth of Baranovici united in the cause of bringing Sholom Aleichem for a reading in their city. Upon hearing that my father had accepted their invitation the young people at once began to organize his visit: a general reception committee was set up, and a hall committee for the box office and ushering; and a sort of bodyguard who would stave off the expected crashing crowd when the celebrated guest arrived and departed from the hall. Posters were put up, and my father's picture with headlines announcing his reading could be found all over the town. On the eve of his appearance the number of people clamoring to be admitted was more than twice as large as the hall could contain. Many remained outside, spreading around the building, crowding outside the windows, hoping to hear a word of his reading, waiting for a possible glimpse of him when he left the hall.

When my father came on stage, he was pallid and fatigued, and his back, always slightly bent, was even more so. But he went through with the reading, making an effort to raise his voice so that those standing at the back of the hall might hear him, too. He read more than the program called for, since his enthusiastic, excited audience would not let him leave the stage, and he read one encore, and another and another. Exhausted, he finally reached his hotel, and while he was preparing for bed, he coughed and brought up blood. As the night wore on he developed fever and suffered a hemorrhage. The local doctor was awakened and brought to my father's bedside; he prescribed a medicine, and the druggist came in the middle of the night to fill the prescription. Meanwhile the news of my father's illness had filtered out to the crowds that had stayed outside the hotel for hours —and soon the whole town knew of Sholom Aleichem's collapse after the reading. With the shock and grief came a resolve to do their utmost to help in the fight of their beloved writer for his life. Telegrams went to and fro, and early that morning two specialists were brought in from the neighboring cities, Vilno and Minsk. Their diagnosis was acute pulmonary tuberculosis, and they ordered the patient to bed for an indefinite period. Immediately an emergency committee was formed to help in the care of my father. They spread straw over the stone pavement in front of his hotel so that the horses and wagons passing by would not disturb the sick man. A corps of young men and women volunteers banded together to serve as nurses and helpers—professional nurses were then unknown in the town— twenty-four hours a day, and the druggist made himself available at any hour of the night in case some service from the apothecary was necessary. Regular medical consultation with specialists was arranged.

All this organization was, of course, under the command of my mother, who was with my father all through the dark hours, his guardian, his fighting angel, working for his recovery. The sickness had its ups and downs, but after a number of weeks he started on the long slow road of improvement, although the doctors indicated that at best he would need attentive care, a special diet, and a warm climate for years to come. For some seven weeks he had to stay in Baranovici—from early August to late September 1908—after which the specialists decided he could be moved. On the advice of the doctors it was decided that he go to Nervi, near Genoa, where the sun was warm even in the winter, and the high cliffs of the coast kept back the winds.

My father's departure from Baranovici for Nervi began a period of semi-invalidism that was to last, in various forms, for nearly five years. While he continued writing as before, except for the crucial weeks at Baranovici, he had to follow a regimen of diet and climate, winters in Italy, summers in Switzerland, falls and springs in other places of suitable weather, with some periods, when his health seemed to deteriorate, at sanatoriums. It was not until 1913 that the doctors pronounced him completely recovered and strong enough to function as before, even to resume his readings in public. This was only three years before his death.

My father felt he owed his recovery largely to the good people of

Baranovici, and he was grateful to them for their love and devotion during those fateful days. All through the years, the very name of the town evoked a pleasant smile, and anyone from there was a special person to him, like a distant relative. When some of his daughters had to return to Russia for a brief stay, he had them stay in Baranovici, and the good people received them as their own.

We in Geneva first learned about our father's illness from a close friend of the family, already mentioned earlier, Moshe Weizmann, a brother of the late President of Israel and likewise a chemist. My mother had written from Baranovici asking him to relay the sad news to the children. We were stunned and anguished, our hearts going out to our suffering father, yet we could do nothing for him, not even visit him. Only one of us, Lyala, saw our father and mother in Baranovici, and only because she was going to Russia to visit her future in-laws. For news from our father's bedside we had to depend on the brief, infrequent notes from our mother and the bulletins on the course of his illness in the newspapers.

With the Berkowitz family in a country place for the summer, there were only two of us, my sister Emma and myself, left in Geneva. We lived with our family friend, Moshe Weizmann. He had a large apartment in which he lived alone, as his wife had just left him, taking with her their young son, Herzl. We had little money, our mother being too troubled in Baranovici to keep us provided, and we would not ask our host. He was raising funds to send to our parents and we feared he might keep back some money to give to us. Too bashful to consume the scant food our host kept in the house, we often went hungry. Moshe Weizmann usually had dinner outside, returning late in the evening, when he would have only tea. He always asked us if we had had our dinner, and our reply, of course, was in the affirmative, although the tea and crackers we had with him were all the dinner we had in those days. On rare occasions he would tell us, on leaving, "Girls, don't have dinner tonight, I'll return early and bring food." We were both concerned that he should not detect that we often went hungry, but I could not repress my joy at the thought of having some dinner. I would stand at the window for hours waiting for Moshe's return with the food, my hunger growing by leaps and bounds.

Finally, a letter came from Mama telling us that Papa was much stronger now, but still unable to write us. They were hoping he would soon be able to leave Baranovici and return to Geneva whence we would all go to Nervi.

At this point, Moshe Weizmann thought up a plan that was to mean much more in solving our immediate problem, as well as our future, than all the prospects floating in the air upon our father's return from America. Moshe knew our financial situation better than we did. Perhaps our mother had communicated with him about it; she knew how to recognize a person who was a realist like herself. Perhaps Moshe had other sources of information as well. In any case, he knew that for all the uproar about our father's success on his tour, he had only forty rubles in his pocket when he fell ill; also that our father would now have to live abroad, with the family, naturally, at resort places, which would take much money. Consequently, some radical step must be taken now to solve the financial situation, while he was still in Baranovici and before the resort problem had to be confronted. The source for this radical step Moshe found in the calendar: it was now August 1908; just two months later, October 25, 1908, would be exactly twenty-five years since my father first appeared in print. This was an occasion for a celebration of the literary anniversary. He decided to write a letter—not as a friend of Sholom Aleichem or anyone special, but simply as another reader of Sholom Aleichem—to a newspaper, reminding other readers of this date. He would tell them the truth about the situation of Sholom Aleichem today, the physical and financial condition of their beloved writer, and call upon them to do something about it.

Anniversary celebrations of this nature, asking for gifts from readers to their author, were well within the literary tradition of Russian culture. On a similar occasion, readers of Maxim Gorki were called upon to send in contributions, however large or small, with which a villa could be bought for him at Capri, Italy, as a gift from his readers. (Gorki too at one time suffered from tuberculosis and had to spend his winters in the warm climate of Italy.) On another occasion, readers of the famous writer Henryk Sienkiewicz were asked to send contributions towards buying him a villa in token of their gratitude for the pleasure his writing had given them. What shocked the readers of the newspaper that first published Moshe's letter was that Sholom Aleichem, their idol, was a poor man struggling for existence, and that now, on his sickbed, he did not have the wherewithal for convalescence.

Any outsider must have assumed that with so many of his books selling in large quantities—individual stories in paperback form selling in the tens of thousands, and full-length books, too, in large numbers—Sholom Aleichem would be drawing a handsome livelihood from the sales. In fact, he was receiving nothing at all, having sold his works outright and forever to the publisher who first brought them out—and even these damaging sales had been for small sums of money. Over and above the legal publications of his works were the pirated ones: indeed, had he been receiving full royalties for all his works on the market he would never have been in such terrible straits. His publishers made fortunes, while Sholom Aleichem himself received nothing.

Moshe Weizmann's letter to the one newspaper was immediately picked up by others, by the entire Jewish press all over the world, even by those papers which printed my father's stories without paying him a penny. A famous Russian poet, himself a Jew, Simeon Frug, was so dismayed by Moshe Weizmann's letter that he wrote a piece for a Russian paper entitled "The Red Laughter," in which he told how the man who made a people laugh was now seeing blood, and none of his laughing readers spared a thought for him. Frug's article, accusing the entire Jewish community for its callousness and ingratitude, was picked up, published and translated by the press throughout the world.

The public responded immediately. In all major cities of the Jewish world, committees were set up to organize celebrations to mark the anniversary with public meetings, at which stories of Sholom Aleichem would be read and lectures delivered on the significance of his works. The proceeds of these meetings were to go to the author. Some of the committees had grandiose plans, which, of course, were not realized, like the Zionist Committee of Kiev's plan to build a home for Sholom Aleichem in Palestine with a balcony overlooking the Mediterranean. The readers in the small towns responded in their own ways, which touched my father's heart. Towns in the vicinity of Baranovici sent delegations to the Slavyanskaya Gostinitza, the hotel at which my father lay ill, to ascertain the condition of the patient and express their blessing and hope for a speedy recovery. One delegate brought a document, the blessing of the famous Rabbi in his town, who expressed confidence in the recovery of the sick man "because the children of Israel needed him." In some synagogues prayers were offered and psalms recited for his recovery. Some people went to the cemetery, to the graves of their forebears, appealing for their intervention in heaven for the sick author.

Some readers wrote or sent gifts directly to the sick author in care of the Anniversary Committee, or simply to the hotel in Baranovici, and later, as the date of the anniversary drew near, to Nervi, Italy. One telegram of greetings, forwarded to my father in Nervi, had been addressed with these two words, *Yubilaru, Kiev,* (Celebrant, or Anniversary Man, Kiev). My father was greatly amused that the gentile postman in the large city of Kiev knew who the *yubilar* was and had delivered it to the Sholom Aleichem Anniversary Committee. In the week before the day of the anniversary our mail was so heavy that the Italian postman did not bother to sort out our own mail; he brought the entire packet of foreign mail to our villa for us to pick out what was ours and leave the rest for him on his second turn of delivery. Some of these communications were from barely literate people, the address obviously written by a schoolchild—like one from a *treger,* a poor man eking out his living as a carrier of freight on his back, like a coolie. He told, in his curiously spelled scribble, that every Friday he bought a story of Sholom Aleichem's for five kopecks to cheer up his Sabbath, and now, on the anniversary, he was sending him a birthday gift, a ruble! My father was perhaps more moved by these letters than by those from his literary friends.

The anniversary date arrived. This was the eve when thousands of people gathered in many parts of the world to pay homage to Sholom Aleichem. Meetings were held in such far-distant places as Warsaw and Paris, New York and Buenos Aires, London and Moscow. But there was no celebration in the land in which he lived, there being no Yiddish-speaking Jews in Italy, nor in his own house. No one was in the mood. Perhaps the contrast between the celebrations abroad and his own condition was too depressing. He was alone with his immediate family that night, and he was sick. In his epitaph, which he had written several years earlier, he said of himself that he wrote for the plain people, and that when they laughed in joy while reading his writing, he was suffering and crying in private so that no one would see him.

On this night he wrote a brief note to his dear old friend and colleague, Mordecai Spector. The note said: "Brother Spector: You must feel, yourself, what is in my heart. At this time, when there, in the beloved Fatherland, Jews rejoice on my jubilee, I am here, lonely, sick, rootless, forlorn, crying bitter tears. Yours for nearly 25 years, Sholom Aleichem."

What were the practical results of the anniversary?

First of all, the gifts and proceeds of the celebrations. I do not know how much in all they totaled, for they were deposited in the local bank as they came in, and I do not recall ever hearing the amounts, or balance in the bank, mentioned in conversation. Secondly, the celebrations created a new demand for my father's works. Not only did people buy up the books and brochures published, but they were also anxious for any new writing by him. At that point in time this demand had special significance, for the Jewish press was expanding; there were new newspapers starting up and a resultant competition for circulation. A contribution by Sholom Aleichem, not to speak of a serial, or his regular appearance, could be measured in the number of readers and income.

Most important, however, was the achievement of retrieving my father's rights to his works, the "redemption of my children," as he called it. With his rights to his works restored, any enterprising publisher would not only pay royalties, but also guarantee a definite minimum amount, payable in regular installments during the year.

This did not come easy. The idea originated with a benign literary personality in Warsaw, Jacob Dineson. A popular writer in his own time, he had become a big brother to all writers, particularly the new ones, in their dealings with editors and book publishers. Dineson was a member of the Anniversary Committee of Warsaw, and he set the main objective of the Committee to be the recovery, or what amounted to copyright, of all the works of Sholom Aleichem for their author. This was the duty of this particular committee, he said, inasmuch as the majority of the guilty parties found themselves in that city.

There was no legal way to compel compliance since those who were most involved had legally valid contracts in which the author assigned to them all the rights to the particular works in perpetuity. However, there were various factors which, if revealed, might outrage public opinion. There was the unfairness of the original contracts in the light of the knowledge that the publishers had paid so little for the works in the first place and had made such big profits over the years. There was the position of the author, who had been struggling all these years to keep his head above water by continually producing new original writing, and who was now, because of his illness, no longer able to do so. At this very moment, when the Anniversary Committee was seeking funds to sustain the author in his illness, the publishers of his works had come out with new editions, having the audacity to call them "Anniversary Editions," which sold out on publication. And not one kopeck was paid to the author.

Public opinion was the weapon the Warsaw Anniversary Committee held against the publishers. If the Committee laid these facts before the reading public there would probably be such a popular outcry against them that people would not only discontinue buying the pirated edition of Sholom Aleichem's works but would boycott pirated publications of other authors as well.

The Anniversary Committee appointed a subcommittee to call upon the publishers to explain the situation and demand from them the return of the rights. One publisher appeared to be ready to cooperate. He said that he had originally paid Sholom Aleichem ten rubles for a binder's unit of sixteen pages, or about sixty-two kopecks per printed page for all the rights thereto in perpetuity, and that he had made so much money on this transaction that he was now ready to return the rights to the author—for a price, of course. Another publisher did not even have a contract. A brazen liar, he said that he had an understanding with the author, whom they paid five hundred rubles for every edition: the truth was that the understanding was to reach an agreement, which was never reached, and not a single kopeck had been paid on any of their editions. A third publisher said that, true, he had promised to pay Sholom Aleichem a share of the profits, but nobody could prove (by his books!) that there ever was a profit. A fourth made no bones about the matter. Sholom Aleichem was no baby when he signed his contract, a contract was a contract—and he would not change it.

My mother finally brought the matter to a head. She went to Warsaw with all the pertinent documents and masterfully presented my father's case from his first dealing with the publishers up to that day. The members of the Committee were stunned. They would never have believed that publishers, people of this caliber, with standing in the community, would stoop to such plain thievery and highway robbery for which, in other areas of enterprise, they would have gone to jail. Stern action was decided upon; the publishers were confronted with my mother, and threats were made to put the facts on public record. All the publishers except one agreed immediately to relinquish the rights without compensation and turn over the plates and the unsold books at cost. To forestall possible double dealing in the future, the plates for new editions were deposited with Jacob Dineson, and a stamp was devised which, when printed on the books taken over and on future editions, would indicate that they were authorized editions. Then my mother came to terms with the best of the publishers, Lidsky —the one who had offered at once to turn over the rights for a price —he was to be the sole publisher, taking over all the unsold copies, guaranteeing to pay two hundred rubles monthly against the royalties for the first year, increasing the amount as further volumes were published, and presenting full detailed reports of the sales at stipulated times. After a few years, the guaranteed monthly payment would be doubled.

We were all nervous when my mother left for Warsaw. We feared the effect her possible failure might have on my father's health, for retrieving the rights to his works had now become his paramount desire. His works were his children, and my mother's mission was to accomplish the redemption of his children; his works were captive, and she was journeying to redeem the captives—regarded as one of the great deeds of good men in Jewish tradition. So deeply did he feel about his books that it seemed to him that he himself was held captive by the publishers and was struggling for liberation. When a telegram came from my mother reporting the success of her mission, his joy was boundless. And on my mother's arrival he looked at her, and at the documents she brought, with the same admiration and amazement as he had regarded her when she returned from her graduation with her dentist's diploma. She was still a source of wonderment to him. In Baranovici she had saved his life; now she saved his soul.

This was spring 1909. My father had not been in so jovial and whimsical a mood since he first felt strong enough to reply to the congratulatory letters from his writer friends four months earlier. His first letter went to his closest literary friends—Grandfather Mendele, Bialik, Ravnitzky, and others. He wrote to them collectively in a characteristically playful mood, despite his condition. It ran as follows:

"By this handwriting you can see that Sholom Aleichem is more in this world than in the next. I feel improvement not by the day, but by the hour. During the few weeks that I have been in this God-blessed Nervi I have gained almost 4 kilos, which is ten pounds of flesh. As a practical man, once a man of affairs, I began calculating and came to the realization that if I continue at this pace, my business will soar higher and higher. The figures are right here before your eyes: the increase in weight of 10–15 pounds a month will add up to 180 pounds for the year. As my previous weight was 150 pounds,

I shall be weighing 330 pounds. At such weight I need write no longer, nor read my stories to the public. All I need is to be shown to the public. This is a much easier trade than writing or reading for the public. The public, too, is much more inclined to look at a big writer than to read his works, not to speak of America, where this would bring in a flood of gold. I even have in mind the text for a proper promotion of the enterprise:

THE GREATEST WONDER OF THE WORLD!

COME, SEE & BE STUNNED

THE GREATEST HUMORIST OF THE WORLD

SHOLOM ALEICHEM

HIS WEIGHT—330 POUNDS

ADMISSION ONE DOLLAR

DON'T MISS IT * TELL YOUR FRIENDS

"Now, let us have a quick look how much could be made on this. There are ten million Jews in the world. Let us not fly too high, so figure that only one in a hundred would want to see the biggest humorist. Would this not bring $100,000? With this amount there would be no need to look to the Jewish community for the purchase of an estate. For this amount the said biggest humorist could buy two estates by himself. You have known me not from yesterday, I believe, and you are well aware that I am not a dreamer, God forbid, going about with his head in the clouds. I am a practical man, seeing only what is before his eyes, with an affinity for figures. And according to my figures, with this amount I could spend more than one winter in Italy. There is nothing more I have to write to you, that is, I had much more to write to you, but they do not let me. In addition to the doctor, the Lord beset me with a family that watches over me like the apple of their eyes. (Not good when a man becomes an apple of an eye.) They watch over me as if I were the delicate glass at the Passover meal. They do not let me sit bent over my table for more than half an hour, and they drive me to go out into the sun, which dips into the sea all day, or urge me to eat. This eating will finish me off. Presses against my chest, squeezes the soul out of me, and all they know is eat, eat, eat! Yet, if you think that a man dedicated to stuffing himself is not writing at all, you are badly mistaken. May the Lord smite our enemies so many blows and grant as many thousands in gold to us all as the number of lines I have already written. Soon, God willing, you will read a little book of mine in three languages, Yiddish, Hebrew and Russian, and I hope you will enjoy it, and you will respond, saying, Sholom Aleichem is and will be. Sholom Aleichem."

My father was right about the family vigilance. We, the women in the family, formed a protective shield around him. He was not left alone at any time, one of us always on guard to prevent any disturbing or unpleasant occurrence; to see that all the prescribed care be faithfully executed; and that he be made physically and spiritually comfortable. The first winter in Nervi was particularly trying because improvement was slow and painful, and, as medicine was to learn only many years later, exposure to sun was just what tubercular people should not have. Indeed, my father felt better in the cooler, often cloudy, climate of Switzerland, and best in the rainy resort of Schwarzwald, while the cure, which was to be in the sun, aggravated his condition and only the special care and food prevented deterioration. The nights in Nervi were agonizing, for he could not sleep for coughing. So we took turns, one of us always on duty in case he should awaken and need something, and, primarily, to read to him, so as to occupy his mind or induce sleep.

I remember my own turn on those nights. We lived on the second floor of Villa Briand, which was situated on the top of a cliff jutting into the sea. At night the waves of the sea would break against the rock, and the spray reached our balcony. When it was my turn, I slept on the couch in the anteroom where I could hear the least sound in my father's room. The minute I had any indication that he was disturbed, I would throw my bathrobe over my shoulders—on winter nights, with the wind blowing in from the sea, the air could be quite cold—step into my slippers, and tiptoe into his room. On a small table near his bed lay the book which was placed there each evening, and a chair for the watcher to sit down and read to him until he fell asleep. The book was usually a collection of short stories by my father's favorite author, Chekhov, in the original Russian. I would read in a hushed voice so that the others sleeping in the room nearby would not be disturbed; often when I came to a humorous passage my father would laugh out loud. The wash of the waves could be heard everywhere, all the more loud because of the stillness of the night, and I learned to regulate my voice by the rhythm of the sea, raising it as the waves broke against the cliff and lowering it as the waves receded. My sister Emma, who was my only alternate—

Tissa being busy with her child, and Lyala away from home—had a low voice, which the waves would drown out. On nights when the sea was rough she would tell me, "Tonight you take over."

My reading would often be interrupted by a spell of coughing by my father, and after serving him something for that, I would resume. Occasionally, he would say, "My dear, didn't you skip something?" and sure enough, inadvertently I had skipped a line or two. When it seemed to me that he was falling asleep, I lowered my voice little by little until it was hardly audible; then I would hear my father say, without opening his eyes, "Maroussia, what was it you just read?" When he finally fell asleep, before returning to my couch I would make a mark just where I stopped reading. Strangely, my father knew the next morning exactly where we had left off when he fell asleep.

We also stood guard over him in the matter of receiving visitors. During the critical period it was, of course, taken for granted that he would see no strangers, but during the period of convalescence, which extended over years, visitors became a serious problem. There were many people at the resorts we were in who had the time and the ambition to meet celebrities, and then there were readers and admirers of my father who, being in the neighborhood, came to pay their respects. My father himself always wanted to meet people, all sorts of people. Whenever he stayed for an extended period in one place, he ran his address as an advertisement in the local paper, so that if any one wanted to communicate with him he would know just how to reach him. He could not be kept isolated from people, and it was not good for his morale to be so kept.

Our problem, then, was to select from the would-be visitors those who might be of greatest interest to our father, and to limit the time of the visit so it would not tire him. It required some ingenuity to ease out a visitor who ignored the prearranged time limit, and we had to keep an eye on our father, in cases like this, to gauge from his expression whether he was really interested in the visit or was showing signs of weariness.

There was the case of a Russian visitor, a journalist, who wanted to see my father while in Italy. We set the date and the hour and advised the young man that since our father was not well we must set a limit to the time he might stay with him. My father seemed to be interested in this talk with the journalist, and the visit extended considerably beyond the set time. We could see, however, that he was getting physically tired despite his interest, and we had to intervene with some excuse to terminate the visit.

This journalist later published a long piece in his newspaper describing how Sholom Aleichem was the captive of his monopolizing, overbearing wife and daughters, who did not permit him to move an inch without their surveillance, and how poor Sholom Aleichem was too weak to fight against the domination of his family. He all but suggested that a relief committee be formed for the liberation of Sholom Aleichem. He sent a clipping of this article to my father, who roared with laughter on reading it, then pasted it on a cardboard and hung it up on the wall of our living room. Whenever a guest came he led him to the wall to read that article.

This visit was well worth while.

XV
The Good Years

THE GOOD YEARS—this is how I would designate the period in my father's life between the time he began showing definite signs of recovery, in 1909, and the outbreak of the First World War.

Not that those years were entirely good, in every sense, since only in 1913 did the doctors consider my father fully recovered. For most of this period, four out of the five years, he was a sick man, struggling with a beastly cough and other ailments, too weak for any physical effort, occasionally having to enter a sanatorium for special care, and continuously dodging the inclemency of the weather by changing countries with the seasons, following the sun.

When he had almost completely improved, he developed a prostate condition; he was in excruciating pain and had a mortal fear of the operation which a urologist said was imperative. He was sure he would not survive such an operation (which at that time was extremely dangerous), and was determined not to undergo it. Fortunately my mother took him to a Professor Zuckerkandel, in Vienna, who saw no reason for surgery and assured him the condition would clear up. But he found my father generally run down, with a sort of nervous exhaustion and a weakening of the heart. (My father's version of the latter diagnosis was that the Professor had discovered he had a heart.) For this condition, complete rest—even writing was forbidden—was prescribed for two months. My father could accept the punishment of rest, but not to write was impossible for him. As soon as he felt a little stronger he resumed writing while resting.

Perhaps the most depressing factor in this period for my father and for all of us was my brother Misha's situation. He graduated from the Gymnasium in Kiev with honors and a silver medal, normally a certain guarantee of admission to the reputed Kiev University —but at this moment a new complication set in for Jewish applicants. This was a regulation that for them a silver medal was not sufficient (for non-Jews just a diploma was good enough), and only a gold medal would insure entry. Our father asked Misha if he wanted our mother to come to help in the matter, and although at first his reply was that this was unnecessary, a few days later we received a wire that she had better come. We were certain that this was in connection with his admission to the University, but, in fact, it was Misha's health that made her visit a necessity. He had had an attack of tuberculosis, like his father, and my mother brought him back to us in Nervi.

Misha had grown handsome during the years in Kiev, tall—a head taller than his father—and like him he was blond and blue-eyed, with a pleasant voice, and a sense of humor when he was not thinking about his condition. Our father was proud of Misha, loved to walk with him, look up to him and marvel. But all this was wrapped in the tragedy, and perhaps in a sense of guilt, of having passed on the dread germ to his son. It was sad to have both father and son, in two sanatoriums, each fighting for his life with the same enemy. During this period my mother also came down with a physical ailment, a painful phlebitis, which confined her to a hospital under the shadow of a possible operation, the very word striking terror in my father's heart.

There were hard, trying, heartrending times during those years, but they were good years in the sense that the desperate struggle for existence was gone, and this made even those ordeals easier to bear. For the first time since my father lost his fortune, there was no concern for the basic needs, no fear for the morrow. The great dream of living on his writing, and actually drawing a living from it, toward which he had been striving even when he was doing well on the exchange, was at long last realized. To the money left from the anniversary celebrations, and the steady, rising income arriving from the publisher of his books in Yiddish, was soon added almost an equal amount in royalties from his works in Russian translation. The publication of my father's works in Russian opened the Russian literary journals to him, and he was now invited to contribute to the outstanding highly paying Russian literary monthlies. One of these serially ran my father's new novel, *Wandering Stars,* the story of the life of the early Jewish theatrical troupes. All this created a modicum of steady comfort, enough to make it possible for the family to concentrate on his health alone, and for him to think only of his writing.

It was sad that all this had to come with the "Red Laughter," when he was broken in health, not when he was well and could fully enjoy and utilize the release from economic strain and delivery from desperation. He was only fifty years old then! But how miserable the situation would have been without this material security. Who knows if he would have survived the dread disease if he had not had the means with which to fight it?

The strain of the literary marketplace had likewise been eased. There were always disappointments, frustrations and heartaches in dealings with publishers and editors of newspapers and periodicals, who were long on promises and short on fulfillment, humble when asking for the literary contribution and arrogant when the copy was in their hands. Still, it was easier to bear, to negotiate, to protest, in the knowledge that one was not dependent on them for the basic living.

The translation of his works into Russian was an additional justification for the designation of "the good years." This was a great and happy moment in my father's life: it had long been his dream to see his work translated into a principal European language, and so emerge onto the scene of world literature. Every author who is proud of his own work no doubt has such dreams, but in my father's case it was more than a dream; it was an ambition based on the firm belief that other peoples, too, would enjoy his writing, if it were properly presented in their own language. As in other highlights of his literary career, his concern was for Yiddish literature as well as for his own work. Just as at the beginning of his literary life he was much concerned about the recognition and prestige of Yiddish literature among the Jews themselves, he now had in mind the recognition by the non-Jews of Yiddish literature as part of the world scene over and above the acceptance of his own works.

There had been translations of his stories into Russian and other languages long before then. But they were done by amateurs, people who believed that knowledge of the two languages was sufficient equipment to make a translation; and since these translations were published in the local Jewish periodicals, whose readers mostly knew Yiddish, the character of the translation did not really matter much.

Above all, these translations reached only the Jewish readers. But this time the offer came from a reputable Russian publisher, whose lists contained both leading writers of Russia and famous foreign authors. Moreover, the publisher intended to follow up this first volume with others.

The pressing problem was to find an able translator. Those who knew my father's works in the original had always maintained, as some still do, that his writing was untranslatable. His Yiddish was so rich, so idiomatic, earthy, folksy, allusive, that no equivalents for it could possibly be found in another language that would carry the same shade of meaning, association and mood. My father, who knew several languages, a couple of them perfectly—and had a special sense for Russian—was not pessimistic about the possibility of translation. He had his own notion of what a translation ought to be, a rendition not of the same words or phrases, but of the idea and mood the original sought to convey; he explained this in detail, with examples, in a letter to my brother Misha, who wanted to try his hand at translating our father's stories into Russian. So the Yiddish idiom, "From hurrying comes no good" (*Fun eilenish koomt kein goots nit arois*) becomes, in Russian, "The quieter you ride, the farther you get" (*Tishe yedesh dalshe budesh*); and the (ironic) Yiddish, "Some jump!" (*A folg mir a gang*), becomes the Russian, "He hit the spot in the sky" (*Popal palchem v nebo*).

The Russian publishing house tried out several would-be translators, checking with my father, of course, and finally engaged a young medical student at Moscow University, U. Pinus by name, who had a thorough knowledge of Russian, with a sense for literature as well as an appreciation of Yiddish literature. U. Pinus was only a mediocre translator, whose work cannot compare with the excellent Russian translations in recent years, but he was good enough at least for the time, and soon my father's works became very popular with the readers of Russian literature.

In Leningrad, in 1966, we visited the Literary Museum of the Academy of Science, and were shown a new acquisition of their Sholom Aleichem collection, a considerable number of letters in his own handwriting in Russian, which have been practically unknown heretofore. Many of them were part of his correspondence with his translator, in which he helped him over some difficult passages in the original. The assistant curator, a Jewish woman who processed these letters, told us that Sholom Aleichem not only possessed a perfect command of Russian, but evidenced a deep, delicate sense for that language. She was sorry he did not write in Russian.

The translation of my father's work into Russian met with an enthusiastic reception, not only from reviewers, but also from leading lights of Russian letters.

Maxim Gorki wrote to my father: "I received your book—read it, laughed, and cried. A wonderful book. The translation seems to me to have been done by an industrious hand and with love for the author, even though occasionally it can be felt that it is difficult to render into Russian the sad and hearty humor of the original. I liked the book very much. Again, I say, an excellent book. It sparkles with true love, goodness and wisdom for the people, a sentiment so rare in our day."

Other Russian writers repeated the feeling expressed by the then most popular novelist, Alexander Kuprin, who wrote to my father: "Others laugh at your sad humor, I cry."

The literary reviews were all favorable and enthusiastic, comparing Sholom Aleichem to that classic humorist of Russia Nikolai Gogol. Most eloquent was the outstanding literary critic of the time, Alexander Amphiteatrov, whose literary articles were reprinted in many publications. He wrote:

> Laughter through tears is a great delight, and praised be the man who can give it to mankind. I have just read the first volume of the collected works of Sholom Aleichem [the stories of *Motel, Son of Paysie the Cantor, The Flag, On the Fiddle*]. No other book in a long time has given me so much laughter, such good and wholesome laughter, and I will confess, without any feeling of shame, that many a time I had the feeling that a little more and I would not be able to hold back—one more stroke of that great master's pen, and from my old eyes, which have seen so much good and evil, will come tears. A great humorist! A spirited artist!
>
> Once I wrote on Sholom Aleichem that in his talent I can hear the breath of the characters of Dickens. Now, after reading these stories, I hold even more to this view. Of all the humorists Sholom Aleichem comes closest to Dickens: a writer psychologist, who is able to laugh and cry with children with that hearty simplicity which springs from purity and sanctity, and which touches the heart. I urge all Russian parents who want the young generation to grow up with a sense of justice, and love for human friendship and equality, to let their children read the works of Sholom Aleichem.
>
> Sholom Aleichem is an artist in the full sense of the word, and a

nationalist in the good and deep sense of that word. Nationalist like Maupassant, Dickens, Chekhov; his Jewish types we can see just as we see the French described by Maupassant, the English described by Dickens, the Russians as described by Chekhov.

I come back to what I said above, my desire that the Russian adults read his works with attention, and after they have read them themselves, give them to their children to read.

The reception the first volume received encouraged the publishing house to issue two more volumes in the same year, and within a few years my father saw twelve volumes of his stories, the cream of his works, translated into Russian, and enjoying a steady and considerable sale.

In time we adjusted to a sort of life that depended on climate, following the sunshine and warmth through the seasons in various lands. Winters, October through March, in Nervi, Italy; spring, April through May, in Lugano or Montreux, Switzerland; summers, June, July, August, in the Black Forest resorts of Southwestern Germany. September was a problem month, spent, according to the weather, in one of these places. Everywhere we were only temporary residents, living in rented furnished quarters, or *en pension* strangers in a foreign land, without the possibility, reason, or desire to become part of any place. Only the mail, letters, newspapers, periodicals, books, connected us with our own world, which remained Russia and the Jewish communities elsewhere. The arrival of the mail was the great event in our life, the echo of the real world, where people were rooted in their own soil, contending, struggling, with achievement or frustration. Ours was a life in a hothouse, nurturing a precious flower that could not withstand the winds outside.

During my father's illness the entire family was around him, even the Berkowitzes, who had been set to return to Russia and build their life there. As my father's condition improved and as he began to convalesce, our family began to spread out. The Berkowitzes went to Warsaw, where Berkowitz took an editorial position on a newspaper. My sister Lyala married and joined her husband, who was studying medicine in Berlin. My brother Misha for a time continued his studies, living with Natasha's family. Only my sister Emma, my younger brother, Numa, and I remained at home to move about with our father, following the seasons. This irregular sort of existence normalized itself for us almost into a routine.

Every October we came to "our" Villa Briand, perched on the cliff protruding into the sea at Nervi. Upon our arrival, "our" Rosina came to work for us, young and pretty despite her being already toothless, overjoyed to be with us again. Rosina was engaged to Alfredo, the young fisherman of whom she loved to tell us, and whom we saw at times from our window. Did she ever go for a walk with him? *"O Mama mia,"* of course not; this was forbidden by custom. But he would walk by the kitchen window, wave to her, and receive a smile. Every winter Rosina was about to be married to her Alfredo, but Alfredo seemed to be in no hurry. Rosina kept her spirit, however, and her fine voice could be heard singing in the kitchen, *"O cara mia."*

We learned other mores from Rosina, such as that it was improper for me to wave to the Italians who, working with the boats at the foot of the rock, would look up at us on top. A girl must not respond to such overtures. The Italians knew us as "Russos," and were heartily friendly, and we in turn loved Italy and the Italian people; my father said that the Italians reminded him of the Russian people, warm and devoted. He had personal friends among the native population—storekeepers, peddlers of cheap jewelry, and others who just sat and basked in the sun. He could not carry on a conversation with them, but he would exchange a few everyday words and beam at them, and they returned his speechless good feelings. There was, for instance, one woman on the marina who sold various things made of seashells, some useful and some not. Among the piles of oddments my father spotted a small shell box, which fascinated him. There was really nothing unusual about the box except the way it opened—only by pressing one corner of it with the thumb—but for a week or so, every time we passed the woman's stand my father had to stop and admire it. The woman did not mind my father's examining the box and handling it without buying it: his pleasure was so great that she was proud of the box. One day, passing her stand, my father noticed immediately that the box was gone. As soon as the woman noticed my father, she produced the box from underneath her stand and put it right in front of him. This happened again and again. Apparently she did not want anyone else to buy the box, so in the end my father bought it, and for many days he would display its wondrous quality not only to us, but also to friends who visited us. Anyone who did not share his enthusiasm for the gadget would mortally disappoint him. The popularity of this box outlived many other "toys" he had bought, but when I packed his things before leaving Nervi I found it in one of the drawers of his desk, all the way at the bottom.

In summertime in the Black Forest, our life was altogether different. Our father stayed at a sanatorium, usually at Badenweiler, and the rest of us lived in a pension at the foot of the sanatorium grounds so that we might see him every day. This climate was the opposite of sunny Italy, for the days always seemed to be cloudy, with intermittent rain. Yet my father felt better in the Black Forest—he would gain weight, look healthier, and become more hopeful of finally recovering completely. He would even project plans for the future, when he would be well and could go back home. And by home he still meant Russia. "I might even take a reading tour, what do you think, Olga?" He would look at my mother, and she would smile and agree with him.

The sanatorium was kept spotlessly clean, in spick-and-span order; doctors visited their patients every day, even those who needed it least and who were about to be discharged. The director of the sanatorium knew that my father was a famous man, and at once bestowed on him the title of Doctor. "It's too bad, Herr Doktor, you have so little sun; another cloudy, rainy day today." But my father would disagree on the forecast. "There—" he would point to a parting of the clouds—"over there the sky is blue, it will clear before long, and the sun will come out." The director would gloomily shake his head; he could not be so hopeful. But I, for one, seconded my father's optimism, and when we walked together on a misty day and he discovered a break in the clouds, he would say so positively that the sun would shine before long that I really believed it.

It was a strange life for the rest of us in the Black Forest, healthy people in a health resort for tuberculars, with nothing to do or any place to go except the Kursaal to hear the orchestra, and nothing to occupy our minds with save reading. Occasionally it was even embarrassing to be healthy. The forest air and solid German food did not disagree with me, an adolescent with a good appetite and little exercise, and I gained weight and a blossoming apple complexion. Running up the hill to see my father on a misty morning made my cheeks a flaming red, and the director would stop me, look at me amusedly and say: "You, Fraulein, do not exactly need a sanatorium," which made my cheeks burn even more.

The long hours of emptiness were more than compensated for by the precious hours with our father. We would take walks with him, and watch him write, for he spent most of his time writing. To ease the physical effort, and to have the writing paraphernalia always at hand, he had his ever-present little book, smaller and narrower than his palm, this one backed with a silver plate, and with a leather cover. At the top was a silver clip to hold the paper, whose like for its unusual thinness and firmness I have seen nowhere since. He would hold up his hand and write on it with his sharp-pointed fountain pen—these were then first coming into use—and after he had written for a while, the little book would go back into his coat breast pocket. But only for a short space of time, for soon there would be something else to write in it. The fountain pen was an endless source of delight, but fountain pens were not really dependable in those days, and my father discovered a new sort of pencil. This was called an *agat*—again, I have never seen such a pencil since—that came in a golden case. But since this pencil required a special kind of paper, which he was not always able to obtain, my father's enthusiasm for it soon waned, and I received it as a gift on my birthday. His preoccupation with his fountain pen and his *agat* was characteristic; he was always keenly interested in the mechanics of writing, in the "tools" of his trade, and ready to try new gadgets. When the Anniversary Committee of New York sent him as a gift a Hebrew typewriter, the first to make its appearance, he was fascinated by it and wanted to learn how to operate it, but he tired of it and passed the typewriter on to Berkowitz, who did some copying for him on it.

An average convalescent day for my father would begin early in the morning. As soon as he opened his eyes my father would reach for his little book and fountain pen lying on his night table and begin to write. My mother would be the first to come to his room, and work would then be interrupted for breakfast, which he took in bed. After breakfast he called for his only grandchild, whose parents lived with us at the time, and perched her on his bed and taught her to sing various songs, which the little girl obligingly and pleasantly learned. (Tamara Berkowitz grew up to translate her grandfather's works into English.) Later in the morning Emma and I would go out with our father for a walk, usually only as far as the first unoccupied bench, and there my father would stop, sit down, and bring out his little book and fountain pen. Friends would stop to talk to us, but my father would be undisturbed, and although some of our friends felt uncomfortable talking to us, fearing they might disturb our father in his writing, I am sure he did not even notice them. This was the first draft, which later in the day, in his easy chair, or in bed, he would rewrite, revise, cutting out a piece of the tiny page and pasting the other parts together, or adding a small section to the paper he wrote on.

To watch our father writing had always fascinated us. Used to his habit of biting his nails, which transferred to all his daughters, we paid no attention to this. What we loved to observe was his own amusement at his writing, for if the passage he was writing happened to be humorous, as it so often was, he would laugh out loud, even stopping to have a good laugh, and then continue.

I particularly recall how my father laughed while writing one of his series of stories of the New Kasrilevka. The series described what happened to the poor, simple, good folk of the East European small town, frozen in medievalism, when modernity burst upon it like a bolt from the sky. Before the people realized it, their town had a trolley, hotels, restaurants, theater, newspaper, all like the modern towns, but of course Kasrilevka-style. Instead of bringing the people of Kasrilevka to the modern town, he brought the modern town into Kasrilevka. This was a natural for a situation comedy. But my father went much farther and deeper: the incongruity was there, to be sure, built in, so to speak; but his concern was with the human situation, with the relationship of man and man, with the conflict of social values between the old and the new.

That particular story dealt with the trolley. At the beginning of its route, people get into the trolley and, being in Kasrilevka, naturally talk to one another. When the conductor attempts to collect the fares, he runs into difficulties. First he approaches a passenger who is obviously poor, but the man ignores the conductor completely, does not even look at him. The conductor insists he either pay his fare or get off the trolley. At this point a woman peddler, carrying two large baskets of fruit, comes to the defense of the poor passenger. "What do you want of this man?" she argues with the conductor. "You see he has no money for the fare, what do you expect him to do? Go on foot when there is a trolley? What do you lose if he rides? The tram is running anyway." The conductor turns to her: "Nobody appointed you as this man's advocate, you better pay your own fare!" The woman is in consternation, and now she is talking not to the conductor, but to the people in the trolley: "I knew it, I tell you I knew he would be after me, too! He has put on a hat with a visor, and a button at the top, and thinks he is the czar. Where would I get the fare? A woman struggling for a piece of bread—and he wants me to pay the fare!"

The conductor turns to the visitor-author, and says, "Did you see it?" One passenger after another has an argument—not a fare is collected. But how can a trolley function if people pay no fare? However, he puts out neither the poor man nor the woman, for, basically, were they not right? Why should a poor man walk if the tram runs in the same direction anyway? How was a poor woman peddler to pay fare?

In the end, as the trolley finally starts, something breaks, and a mechanic has to be sent for. There is a long delay. The indignant woman peddler gets off the trolley in a huff: "Some trolley! Some communication! and they want fare yet!"

While writing this story my father laughed most when he told about the woman screaming: "I knew it! I knew he'd be after me, too!"

Berkowitz's return to Russia to accept an editorial position there, which I spoke of earlier, was not a simple matter. Since he had originally left that country without the special passport for going abroad, he was subject to a stiff penalty upon his return. He could avoid it by obtaining certain documents from friendly officials in some locality. Tissa went to Baranovici for this purpose. Like the rest of us she felt kinship with the good people of Baranovici because of their solicitous care of our father when he fell ill there. Her mission took much longer than she expected.

I, too, had to return to Russia to prepare for my entrance examination to the University, since all my schooling until that time was in the Russian language. I joined Tissa in Baranovici, taking along Tamara, whom she had left with us in Geneva. The border authorities saw nothing amiss in a seventeen-year-old girl mothering a three-year-old child from one country into another. I lived with Tissa for a while, then took a room with another Jewish family, tutoring two girls in Russian for their entrance examination to the Gymnasium. Then I moved to another, better place, on the Chaussee, as they called the high road, or boulevard.

Since it was my first experience living away from home, I shared with my parents every detail of my life there. In one letter I told them that the new room on the Chaussee cost fifty kopecks more a month. To this my father replied with an amusing letter:

"Dear Maroussia: Inasmuch as you have rented a new apartment on the Chaushee [here he imitated the Lithuanians who mispronounce the *s* as *sh*] and are now paying fifty kopecks more a month, it is no more than right I should address my letter directly to you, and you will turn it over to Tissa, instead of the opposite as heretofore. But, dear Maroussia, how could you get yourself to undertake such a risk as paying fifty kopecks more a month? Did it occur to you that this adds up to six rubles a year, and in one hundred years it will amount to 600 rubles? I am not saying you are a spendthrift, only reminding you that one must be frugal; 600 rubles is a handsome sum. The hundred years will flit by fast, and money (600 rubles) is capital. True, living on the Chaushee is worth something. But I think Tissa is still living near the Chaushee, or is your Chaushee a different one? If so, it is another matter.

"You can tell by the tone of this letter how I feel, and the state of my health generally. Regards to you from our Rosina and the fat fruit lady. Her weight is now 132 kilo, last year it was 114. Give Tamarka a kiss on her muzzle. Papa."

The Berkowitzes were finally together in Warsaw, and I joined them later, renting a room in the same apartment house. I continued writing home frequently and at length, and my father, in his joint letters to us, held me up as an example for Tissa and Berkowitz, who did not write as frequently. In a postscript to a joint letter to us, he wrote: "Maroussia, all my praise to you. You are a great girl. You are more considerate of me than the others."

Of those who remained home, Misha entered the University of Lausanne, attending lectures even while in a sanatorium nearby. Emma attended an institute, but mostly stayed at home, assisting our father with his correspondence and generally helping to take care of him. Little Numa entered a Swiss school. Only our father found it difficult to adjust, and the more his condition improved, the more restless and fidgety he became, except when he was writing.

After a while the doctors suggested he try a cooler climate for the winter, in order to acclimatize himself to the normal European winters and, as he still hoped one day to return "home," those of Russia. But he made only a feeble effort to stay in Switzerland for the winter, and at the first October winds went back to Nervi, with us when we could accompany him, and when we could not, he went alone, waiting for us to come later. As the news went out that Sholom Aleichem was better, overtures for possible public appearances began to come in from various cities. He was gratified, but reluctant to make commitments. Possibly he was still too unsure of his strength to undertake anything that might bring on a recurrence of his malady. On the other hand, he was now too well for his invalid's regime. He had always been active in two spheres: the one was his Republic, his entire family, living their lives with them as they did with him, and the other the literary marketplace, with its throbbing, however often disappointing, flurry. Now, he was frustrated in both.

His family was broken up into three parts; his beloved Tissa and Berkowitz, who had become intimately involved with his writing during his illness, were now living in Russia; Lyala and her husband in Germany; and he, with us, in and around Switzerland. He realized that as children grow up they leave their parents' nest to build one of their own. But he could see no reason why these nests must be so far apart instead of close to one another. He strove toward bringing them together but could not succeed. And as for the literary world, during his sickness the loving letters from his literary friends and occasional echoes of the turbulence in the Yiddish press and literary journals had sufficed. But now he wanted to be in the deep waters with the rest of them.

He yielded enough to take half a loaf: each year there had to be an extended family reunion—all the children and the grandchildren were to spend the summer months together with him. And this prevailed throughout the entire period of his illness. There was no happier man in the world than he in the midst of all the members of his family, the entire population of his Republic, enjoying every word said by everybody, playing games with his grandchildren, and delighting them all with his joviality. No field marshal marched out with greater pride at the head of his host than our father when he took Numa and Tamara by their hands, with the declaration: "We're going into the woods to write."

As to the literary world, he sought to involve himself with newspapers, although no longer dependent on their income. Disliking association with cheap and sensational sheets, he was vitally interested in any new newspaper that promised to be clean and literary. Even in isolation he sought contact with his readers, his people, trying to show his awareness of their situation, conscious of how they had expressed their concern for him when he was ill. So, for example, when he read in the papers that due to dry winds there was nearly a mass conflagration in the small towns in Russia, one little town after another being burned down—with most of the victims carrying no insurance, either for their houses or their household effects—he published an open letter to his fellow literary men to organize mass affairs, the proceeds to go for the victims of the fires.

1913 was a great year in my father's life. His doctors assured him that he was now absolutely cured, with no sign of the illness, or its effects, detectable. He was urged by them to proceed as before he fell ill, living in any climate he might want to, undertaking any chore, just as he had done before his illness. Now he felt like a prisoner released from a long confinement: he wanted to go about, visit cities, as though to see how well people lived. This coincided with other happy developments in our family life—Numa's bar mitzvah, for example, about which he was very sentimental. It may have reminded him of his own bar mitzvah, and his mother crying for joy in the woman's wing of the synagogue, of the happier days when Numa was born, and of the dark hours when he did not believe his eyes would see this day. Then, too, Misha's health improved, and he was able to fully pursue his studies at the university, due to graduate, like myself, the next year. And the Zionist Congress, set to open at Basel in the summer, offered a perfect occasion to realize his desire to see old friends and to be seen by them in good health and spirits.

We all came to the Zionist Congress as if to the house party of a close friend. That Congress, being the tenth, was a gala affair for the Zionists, and no less for us. For there my father met not only his closest personal friends among the writers, but also his old Zionist friends. From these friends my father received a special welcome for he was remembered for his activities in pre-Zionist Congress days. In those days a brochure, similar to that of Dr. Herzl's, which was written for the occasion of the first Zionist Congress—Dr. Herzl was the father of the Congresses and of the entire modern political Zionist movement—was prepared by my father. Dr. Herzl's brochure, written in German and translated into Hebrew, sold only 2,000 copies whereas my father's, written in Yiddish, had enough popular appeal to sell twenty-five thousand copies. The Zionists rejoiced to see Sholom Aleichem in their midst again, and took us all to their hearts like their own kith and kin.

In the spring of 1914 my father and mother made the longed-for tour in Russia, but this time it was managed by an impresario. He wanted my father to appear in a hundred cities and towns, but remembering his last trip, my father limited it to twenty places. The response was fantastic, far beyond the tremendous enthusiasm on the earlier tour. It seemed that his popularity had grown in the meantime, not only among the literary elements and the younger generation, but among all classes of people, from the ultra-Orthodox to the Socialists, from the intellectuals to the common laborers.

Although, in keeping with his request, my father's arrival in a town was kept secret, each time his train pulled in not only the railway station, but all the streets around, would be filled with people. His appearance would evoke an outpouring of Hurrahs and *Heydods,* and he was not only presented with bouquets but literally sprayed with them. Even in so large a city as Warsaw he could not walk the streets, for the suspicious police might have thought that the large crowd which would certainly congregate around him, was an illegal demonstration. Once my parents took a stroll in the city park of Warsaw. Word spread that Sholom Aleichem was in the park, and people began flocking there from all sides. The park authorities informed the police, and as the police used not words but whips to disperse people, my father retired to a nearby restaurant to prevent such an incident. The people massed around the restaurant for so long that he had to stay there until dark, when he went through the back door into a waiting carriage. Everywhere he appeared, the hall was filled to overflowing, and the crowds outside who could not be admitted were larger than those inside.

The most touching incident that my mother told of this tour, on their return, was of two pious, Hasidic young men, in their special garb, long side curls, and short visor caps (the special headgear of the Hasidic young men then), who kept passing back and forth across the street from the veranda of the Bristol café in Warsaw, where my father and mother and a friend, a writer, were sitting. The young men, with little beards that seemed only recently to have begun growing, were agitated, arguing between themselves. Then one of them, highly flushed, came across the street, walked over to my father, and said: "May I offer *sholom aleichem* (meaning, "May I greet") to our dear Sholom Aleichem?" My father extended his hand to the young man. "I have been praying for this moment a long time," the young man said, and kissed my father's hand, "You are our comforter, you sweeten the bitter exile for us." Tears came from the young man's eyes, and he quickly turned away.

Whether it was the tremendous increase in his popularity, or simply that the times were ripe for it, various offers now began pouring in upon him. All seemed tinged with fantasy.

One such offer was from a new newspaper, which offered him four thousand rubles a year for a contribution once a week, plus 5 per cent of the net profit of the newspaper. This made him a sort of partner in the newspaper, certainly someone who could influence policy decisions. His contributions to that newspaper at once raised the circulation of the paper by thirty thousand.

He had been an early admirer of moving pictures, having seen their great cultural possibilities at their very first appearance. At one time my father had planned to contact film producers in Berlin to film some of his stories. Now he had an offer from apparently serious entrepreneurs to make records of his own readings of his works and to make movies of his novels and short stories. For this he was to receive one thousand rubles a month for helping with the scenarios, and 10 per cent of the net profit of the company.

The film offer fascinated him. He was intrigued by the idea of seeing his works in a new medium that could reach millions of people everywhere, while the percentage clause had an echo, perhaps, of his early days on the stock exchange, or of another "treasure" of his childhood friend Shmoulik. Yet he could laugh at the Menachem-Mendelian aspect of the film offer, while pursuing the negotiations seriously.

In a letter to the Berkowitzes in Berlin, in which he reported this offer to them, he wrote jestingly: "The plans are so tremendous that they make your head turn. . . . Pathé [the famous French film company at that time] also began quite small. Now they are worth 40,000,000! Multiply by 20 per cent and it runs up eight million. That is, we shall have eight million in hand. I will buy Tamara a piano, Bella a giant doll; Tissa a villa, Lyala, a medical office outfit for Michael [her husband] and some shares in Wertheim & Co. [a department store in Berlin]; Misha an automobile, Emma and Maroussia 250,000 each as dowry, Numa a gold chessboard, Berkowitz a newspaper with its own printing press, for Mother a hat she would be proud of [Mother had just bought a hat he could not stand], and for me some writing tools. . . ."

XVI
Cataclysm

THE GOOD YEARS came to an end at their most exalted peak with the crash that brought down the world as we knew it—for us and for the whole of Europe.

The summer of 1914 our entire family was to spend together at a resort, as in previous years, but this time it was to be under the happiest circumstances. For not only was our father now fully recovered, but due to return, with our mother, from his triumphant tour in Russia. The resort chosen was Albeck, on the Baltic coast of Germany, selected primarily because part of our family, the Berkowitzes and Kaufmans, were then living in Berlin. So, there we were, ten of us, all six of the children—two grandchildren, and two sons-in-law—awaiting the arrival of our parents at our villa on the beach.

Those happy days of late July 1914 stand out clearly in my memory. The sun was shining powerfully in this northern bathing spot on the neat, solidly built houses clustered perhaps a little too near to each other, as if the people in them felt the need to be close together in the face of the cold northern sea spread in front of them. Even the dunes separating the sea waters from the little gardens around their houses seemed too puny to give any feeling of security. The sea was almost always rough, and bathing was permitted only from the bathhouses on the dunes. Stepping out of a bathing house to walk on the dunes was most pleasant, but the pleasure of walking barefoot was forbidden.

This was the respectable Germany of 1914, the good old solid foundation stone of European culture and civilization, which seemed as solid as the rocks on the shore.

Our fortunes seemed equally solid. The Kaufmans lived comfortably in Berlin on the income of a property in Odessa which his father had assigned to Michael on his marriage to Lyala. Soon he was to receive his medical diploma, after which he would return to Odessa to practice his profession. Berkowitz was weighing two literary offers, one to edit a Hebrew publication for youth in Palestine, the other as the literary editor of a Hebrew publication in Warsaw. Fresh from graduation, Misha and I were relaxing, Misha not worrying for the time being about the future. Our father's income was now ample and steady, and new plans were being discussed for greater opportunities of reaching mass readership. All seemed to be well in our own little world.

All seemed to be well in the world at large. There was a general feeling of well-being and stability on the continent based on economic progress and spreading prosperity. The two major powers, Britain and Germany, were at the height of their power and importance. Britain, ruling the waves, was gathering riches from its political dominance, while Germany was becoming increasingly affluent through her industrialization. The two lesser powers, France and Austria-Hungary, seemed relaxed, complacent, never having been so well off in a century or more. Even in Russia, the poorest and most backward of the powers, my father found a new tempo of enterprise, a new spurt of industry and spirited commerce—in which, he was happy to add, the Russian Jews, despite the czarist restrictions, managed to share considerably. The abject poverty and hopelessness that was so prevalent on his earlier visit were now only rarely evident, and, in addition, the improvement in the material conditions reflected itself in increased cultural activity. Yiddish newspapers were appearing in provincial cities, often good enough to compete with the metropolitan press; literary evenings, with author guests, were becoming a usual affair; culture had become a substantial part of living.

Little had it occurred to anyone that total war was imminent and destruction looming on the horizon. Yes, there were rumblings in the Balkans; but, then, when were there no rumblings there? The Crown Prince of Austria-Hungary had been recently assassinated, but the assassination of ruling monarchs was not historically a rarity, and history did not show that international complications necessarily followed. Diplomats were sending notes, naturally, this was their trade.

. . . So ran the minds of those who followed the newspapers carefully —which most of us did not, preferring to lounge on the sand in the daytime or, in the evening, listen to the soft music at the casino and watch the couples dancing the new daring dance, the tango. (My sister Emma and myself had already danced the tango at college in Lausanne, but now we hesitated, not knowing how our father would regard this new craze. It was not a case of being afraid of him, but a matter of displeasing him.)

Our parents returned from Russia on July 22, 1914, only ten days before the outbreak of the first World War. Yet we heard no war talk. We enjoyed the days we had together perhaps more than during the preceding summers. Our father was with us on the beach, sitting in a shaded chair, writing in his little notebook, while at his feet his two little grandchildren, Tamara and Bella, built sand castles. Occasionally, he would stop writing and close his eyes for a moment, perhaps also creating his own castles—in the air. After the day on the beach we returned to our comfortable villa and to the delicious meal which our maid had ready. There was no housework to be done, the one maid cleaned all the rooms, cooked and served till all hours of the evening, and was pleasant and agreeable—even in this respect the era was due to end.

In two days the atmosphere completely changed, like a black squall rushing in to darken the sky and freeze the air. Scareheads in the newspapers screamed that Russia had ordered mobilization, and, of course, exhorted Germany to do the same. There was a call to eliminate the enemy from within, which at the moment meant the Russians living in Germany, particularly those in the sensitive areas like the seashore. Then the scares became official. Germany declared war on Russia, and the Social Democrats threw their Socialist internationalism overboard and voted for the high war budget. . . . This was how it happened, as it looked to us afterward.

All twelve of us sat down for our last meal in Albeck, which was to remain unfinished—our last meal together.

Herr Gruber, the German from whom we rented our villa, appeared with a face strangely unfriendly and forbidding. Previously he had always been cordial, and particularly respectful to our father, since he knew he was a prominent author. He liked to talk to my father, and was fascinated by his vest-pocket watch, a gift from the tea magnate Wissotsky after he had met my father at the Zionist Congress in Basel. This watch was most unusual in two respects: its dial contained not the Roman numerals but Hebrew letters, number one being the Hebrew *aleph,* the first letter of the Hebrew alphabet, number two the second letter, *bet,* and so on, down to twelve; the other feature was its music box—small as it was, the watch chimed on every quarter hour a piece of a melody, continuing the melody to completion through the four chimes of the hour. My father liked to watch the expression on the face of a visitor, hearing the chimes so close by, yet unable to determine their source.

Now Herr Gruber came to tell us that an order had come forbidding all aliens to be near the seaside; moreover, at any hour now, all Russians would be expelled immediately from the country, because Russia and Germany were now at war. In short, we should leave at once, but not before we paid him the full rent for the season. We were tempted to argue that inasmuch as we had to leave Albeck not by our wish but because of an act of God, so to speak, we should not be held responsible for the contract for the entire season. But one glance at Herr Gruber's countenance now disabused us of the success of any such argument. My father told Herr Gruber that since we had no German money he could pay him only in Russian rubles. "Nein," said Herr Gruber. "Your rubles are not worth a pfennig now. It's got to be German money."

But how could we pay him in German money if we did not have any?

This seemed to be the question Herr Gruber was waiting for. Yes, you have no German money, but you have valuable *schmucksache,* jewelry, particularly the watch. He would take the watch in place of money, he said, pointing to my father's vest pocket. But my father would not think of it. My mother had Russian money in gold bullion —it was customary at that time to carry money in gold coin, particularly when traveling abroad. This saved us from the clutches of Herr Gruber, as it came to our rescue at other points in our desperate efforts to escape from Germany.

At the railway station we found a multitude of people, crowding, pushing, trying to get into a train that was already overfilled, while another mass of humanity pushed in another direction, seeing there a different way to get out of Germany. These were terrified, desperate and hysterical people, talking agitatedly, each involved with his own plight, as though it were unique or as if anyone cared. We had never realized there were so many foreigners about Albeck—surprisingly they were practically all Russians, and mostly Russian Jews at that. Finally we managed to squeeze inside a train going to Berlin, for there, we thought, there might be more ways to get across the border. Only poor Berkowitz remained behind. He was not permitted to get on the train with the large wooden case containing the files of father's archives. He was, hopefully, to arrive by the next train.

The situation of the Russian subjects in Germany was growing worse by the hour. Now that war was declared, they were, under international law, enemy aliens and subject to internment for the duration of the war. The men, particularly, were liable to be drafted for nonmilitary labor, according to the will of the state. Naturally, every Russian subject was anxious to get out of the country in the general confusion of the first day at war, before the situation hardened.

When we arrived in Berlin at the Stettin depot, the crowd was much larger and much more frantic than at Albeck. Stettin was the only remaining depot from which trains were leaving for abroad, to Denmark. By nightfall all the other borders of Germany had closed: France and England had declared war against Germany; Switzerland, trying to observe strict neutrality, closed her borders to all countries. As my father stepped down from the Albeck train, the waiting people at the station noticed him. They surged toward him, imploring him to save himself by getting on the train to Copenhagen right there, that minute. My father hesitated; we had all planned to remain in Berlin until we would pick up the balance of our belongings, and, most important, exchange some of our Russian money for German money with our German Jewish friends and wait for the return of Berkowitz. But my father's admirers did not even wait for his answer. They began to push him through the crowd, toward the train, with my brother Misha and brother-in-law Michael beside him, while we, the women, were left behind in the confusion. Despite our distress, we were glad that the men would be out of danger, for we knew the situation in Germany would be worse for them. But the train was so crowded that my father was actually pushed off the platform just before the train took off. Only Misha and Michael went to Copenhagen, and the rest of us, with our father, returned through the streets, darkened by military orders, to where the Kaufmans and Berkowitzes had lived before they left for Albeck. But the landlord refused to accommodate us, and only after great trouble did we manage to find shelter for the night.

The next day we could not go to Copenhagen. We did not have enough German money for the fare, and we did not want to arrive there penniless. It was a hard decision, but we decided that as soon as Berkowitz returned from Albeck, he and our father would set off at once for Copenhagen, leaving us to follow as soon as possible. After all, the Germans were human, we thought, and they would let women and children who were separated from their husbands and fathers rejoin their families abroad. No sooner had Berkowitz arrived than my father and he hastened to the Stettin depot to get out of Germany. The crowd there was as large, if not larger, than on the day before, but now there were uniformed police driving the people into the train—as though they needed prodding. Apparently the local authorities wanted to get rid of these people as quickly as possible and clear the place. Once again my father, with Berkowitz as his bodyguard, was pushed into a car of the train by the surging crowd around them. Nobody knew exactly where the train was going, where it would finally land them, or what was to happen to them there, while the presence and the interest of the police aroused suspicion that they might be on their way to a military camp for internment. Actually, the train let its passengers out at the port city of Sassnitz, across the water from the Swedish city of Malmö, which connects by ferry with Copenhagen.

There was a boat in the harbor of Sassnitz when my father and Berkowitz alighted from the train, near the pier. But that boat was already overcrowded, and there were thousands of people standing on the dock gazing enviously at the hundreds of fortunates who had managed to wedge themselves on board. Still, there was hope that, as the run was short, the boat might return for more passengers, or that other boats might be procured. But in the minds of all the fleeing people lay the overwhelming anxiety as to how long the two states involved would permit this mass escape to go on. Would Germany continue to allow the people to depart? Would Sweden keep its frontiers open to so many refugees? For my father and Berkowitz the immediate problem in Sassnitz was to find accommodations for the night, and in this jam-packed town it was not easy. Next morning came the repeated rush to the pier to follow up leads for a possible boat to Malmö.

Ironically, caught in this nightmare situation were two of the worst and the most powerful anti-Semites of czarist Russia: there was the leader of the Rightist, and openly anti-Semitic, party in the Duma, Roman Dmovsky, and the Minister of the Interior, Kasso, who had only recently promulgated new and more oppressive laws against the Jews. Both were trapped in the maelstrom of their victims, crowding with the Jews, pushing along with them toward the narrowing aperture of escape on the train to Sassnitz and on the ferry to Malmö. Maybe they had even said to themselves, Better stick to the Jews— leave it to them, they will find a way out, they are used to finding escape routes. Some of the Jews recognized them but pretended to take no notice of them. Kasso, who had ordered the local police in a number of places to refuse permits for my father's literary affairs and who was now in the same pushing line as my father, spent the night at the same inn in Sassnitz, and went on the same boat from there to Malmö. Indeed, on board ship, on the overcrowded deck, Kasso came over to my father and politely asked if he could take the free space next to him. On my father's polite but not overfriendly reply, he sought to engage him in conversation.

There was no problem for my father and Berkowitz in getting to Copenhagen from Malmö; as for us, we had even more trouble and torment in reaching Copenhagen than our men had, for all their ordeal. We were five women and two little girls, nine and three years old. It took us five days to get to Copenhagen. Every day our men waited at the station there to meet the incoming train, and every day they returned in disappointment and anxiety, not having had any news of us during all this time. We spent two full days at the station in Berlin. Instead of being considerate of women and small children, the Germans acted in the most brutal, sadistic manner. I recall the conductor coming over to us, eying us hatefully, and saying, Ah, we must be *verfluchte Russen* (damned Russians). My sister Lyala, having lived for some time in Berlin, tried in her best German to tell him that we were not really Russians, we were Jews, to which his remark was: *"Verfluchte Russischen Juden."* He could be mollified only by a gold coin slipped into his hand. At another time, an officer came to tell us that we were to take the train to Kiel, where we all would be put in jail. It was the magic of another gold piece that kept us from going to Kiel—if indeed we were supposed to go there—and permitted us to wait for the Copenhagen train. On the train, not the least consideration was shown us, helpless women and children in a strange land; even the most elementary services normally accorded passengers

273

were unavailable to us, except when handsomely rewarded by gold in advance. An entirely different Germany was unraveling before our eyes, a different type of German, previously unimagined. It was as though he had at once shed all his culture and civilization, and all his humanity, and had become in place of a fellow man a hard, brutal machine. However, for all the torment we were subjected to, our luggage and belongings arrived in due order—the baggage car was a baggage car, delivery was delivery—Germans were efficient, no human nonsense there.

What a different world we found in Denmark. The Danes had never had such a sudden influx of so many diverse strange people, none of them arriving at their best. Most were haggard, flustered, frantic, oddly dressed from lack of time to pack proper clothing, having only limited funds, if any, absorbed in their own immediate problems of how to get in touch with relatives, what to do next, where to turn. In consequence, social amenities and manners were jettisoned. But the good Danes took the sudden influx of visitors in their stride, exhibiting vast tolerance and great sympathy for suffering fellow humans, trying hard to understand, anxious to extend a helping hand. I have often thought since what warm hearts these people from the cold north possess.

How did my father take this catastrophe?

It depressed him utterly; all trace of his usual conquering optimism had vanished. His joy of life was gone; his playfulness disappeared. Silent and withdrawn, he kept himself apart, and, worst of all, he did not even write! His own personal world had collapsed, his world that had just a few years earlier come into bloom. The entire Yiddish press in Russia was closed at once; Jewish publishing disappeared; whatever income there might still be due him from the Russian translations was now beyond reach; and the money that he had in his possession, the income from the tour and the last payments from the publishers, was now worthless. Once again he was homeless and helpless, with a family of twelve, without means or basis for existence. The only prospect seemed to be America. On a happier occasion, when there was no dependence on the opportunities there, he might have envisaged a return to America; but remembering his previous experiences the thought of return under these unhappy circumstances was more than disheartening.

Also he began to suffer from an annoying disability, an insatiable thirst. It began, in a mild manner, while still in Albeck. In our ignorance and our desire to reassure him, we said it must be due to the salty air to which he was not accustomed, but it became much worse during the strain of the flight, and in Copenhagen the doctors told him he had *diabetes insipidus*. To a friend he wrote: "Now I am sure I will not die of hunger; I'll die of thirst!" This continuous physical distress, in addition to his mental anguish, overwhelmed him.

What depressed him most, I believe, was the world situation. Like other men of genius, he had a special sense for the historical process, a subconscious presentiment, a foreboding of what was to come. Naturally, he did not foresee the events that were to come out of the First World War; but unlike so many others in those days, he did not believe that the war would soon be over and all would be well again. He felt in his bones, as some do the forthcoming weather, that a period of woe and evil was opening for mankind. In time he recovered enough composure to renew his writing, and some rays of hope broke through the darkness of his sky; but he was never his carefree, jolly self again.

We were not alone in Copenhagen. A considerable number of Jewish writers, mostly journalists, and other intellectuals, all admirers of Sholom Aleichem, were among the refugees. There was also a local Jewish community of Russian Jews who had emigrated there from Russia at the turn of the century whose dramatic circle had often produced sketches of my father's. They were all proud to have Sholom Aleichem in their midst. Even the assimilated Danish Jews, for centuries estranged from their brethren in Eastern Europe, learned about Sholom Aleichem—the local newspaper ran a story about "the Polish Mark Twain" who had escaped from Germany and was now residing in the city. Professor Simonsen, the great light of Danish Jewry, a descendent of an old aristocratic family, had once read some stories of my father's, and a committee representing the Danish-Jewish community called upon my father to bid him welcome and offer assistance. A few young enthusiasts from the Russian Jewish community (locally known as "Polish") began looking for an apartment for Sholom Aleichem, hoping he would stay with them for the duration of the war. My father appreciated these efforts, but the thought of staying in Copenhagen for the duration was abhorrent to him. We moved into a furnished apartment, but his mind was elsewhere. Again the premonition: America is bound to become the heart of the future;

Jews from all parts will stream to America; the American Jews are destined to assume the leadership. And my father wanted to be among the first to tread this new path into the future. But was American Jewry worthy of this new destiny? The doubt, based on the earlier experience, weighed heavily on his heart.

Fate seemed to drive my father toward America, although he was reluctant to go. He knew he should, according to his own analysis of the situation, but he shrunk from what he might have to undergo there. We, the children, certainly had no enthusiasm for the idea; the reports of our parents and of Berkowitz on his return from New York were not encouraging. As for my mother, she was definitely opposed. She knew what it took to get a start in America, and she had no illusions about the Jewish publishers and theater directors there. Her husband was not strong enough, she thought, to undertake the trip now.

Yet the current of life has its own way of bypassing a block in its course. The days were long and the nights lonely in Copenhagen. Those who could trickled out of the city to seek tortuous roads back to their homelands. Even Lyala and Michael decided to return to Russia via Sweden and Finland, although this meant medical service for Michael, possibly at the front. After all, their future was in Russia. It was a blow for my father, but he could understand the sense of this step. Of the Jews who remained, some became destitute and my father agreed to appear at a benefit program—a large public meeting, which turned into a hearty, enthusiastic reception, the laughter amid tears of homeless people torn from their own flesh and blood as well as from their own world, trapped on a barren island of peace in the raging sea of war.

My father asked Berkowitz to write to one of his friends and admirers from the first visit to America, James Faller, then on the staff of a Yiddish newspaper, and tell him of the plight of Sholom Aleichem and his family, and of his desire and need to come to America. This time the response was immediate and generous, without any of the heartaches and humiliation of the similar approach before the earlier visit. Mr. Faller at once organized a Reception Committee which included the editors of all the newspapers and other prominent people of the city, and found a private banker—there were still a few about on the East Side then—to advance the necessary money against the income of the first public appearances. A very short time after my father's message had reached Mr. Faller, first-class steamship tickets arrived for all of us. My father was deeply moved. The fact that the

Committee should send these tickets rather than cheaper ones in second class meant more to him than the comfort this entailed; and the idea of borrowing from a bank rather than turning here and there for advances impressed him. The American Yiddish community had gained a different level since his visit. It had grown up during the past eight years.

After four months in Copenhagen we left for America.

XVII
In America

THE GOOD PEOPLE of Copenhagen tried to make our departure for America as pleasant as was possible under the circumstances. The warmth and tenderness of the farewell function on the eve of our sailing and the crowd on the pier comforted us on the cold, bleak days that followed. The literary evening was arranged by the Russian Jewish community, but the leaders of the Danish Jewish community were present as well, their own glory and pride, Professor Simonsen, being the principal speaker. The physical proximity and genuine love of his readers raised my father's spirits, and when his turn came to read he was almost his old self again. He read one of the stories, "Say, We're Going to America!" from his series *Motel, Son of Paysie the Cantor,* telling of the tribulation and distress of a poor Kasrilevka family trying without means to get to the Promised Land.

Every word that he read struck home to every heart in the hall. Were not they all, like the family in his story, stranded abroad, the bridge to the road back home burned, the road ahead uncertain, strewn with all sorts of blocks? True, the gates of the United States stood wide open then, and no passport or visa was required, but there were psychological as well as material impediments. They knew America was the refuge, but there was always the deceptive hope that so big a war could not last long, that it would end any day now, and then they could return to their own nests and live as before. They laughed heartily because they would not cry, and only occasionally and shamefacedly dropped a tear.

We also were looking forward to a speedy end of the war for our own personal interest as well as for the sake of humanity. Our hearts were perhaps even more depressed, for our father's moral support lay in his Republic, and his Republic was now sundered into three parts, each in a different part of the world. Not only had the Kaufmans gone their own roundabout way to Russia, but we had had to leave Misha and Emma behind in Copenhagen. Misha was not well, and while he stayed in a sanatorium near Copenhagen, one of us must remain with him. He could not be taken along for several reasons: the roughness of the voyage at this time of the year, the problem of a suitable sanatorium for him in or near New York, and the uncertainty as to whether we would have the means to keep him there at the high American charges. Misha and Emma would be sent for after we were settled in America.

There was a large crowd at the pier to see us off, many of whom had been at the literary function the evening before and had heard my father read. Then someone in the crowd shouted jubilantly to us across the upper deck, "Say, we're going to America!" There was applause from the assembled people on the pier, and another took up the phrase but amended it to "Say, Sholom Aleichem's going to America." Others repeated the shout, adding the word "our" and so it was that to these exultant salutes from the pier of "Say, our Sholom Aleichem's going to America," that our ship, *Frederick the Eighth,* put out to sea.

The voyage took longer than usual, a full fortnight. Four days, and especially during the dark nights, the ship moved slowly, barely creeping along its circuitous lane through the North Sea, which was extensively mined. We passengers knew the situation and spent many sleepless nights as our ship threaded its way slowly until it reached the open Atlantic, where the danger was less but not entirely eliminated. During most of the time the ocean was rough, with tempests that kept many passengers to their cabins, including my sister Tissa and myself, who were seasick practically all the time we were on board. My father took the crossing in his stride, while surprisingly my mother, who had been a poor sailor on her first crossing, now stood the bad weather well. Bored in first class, my father went exploring the other classes, and found large numbers of Jews, "his Jews," who recognized him at once, who had heard him read his stories, and who now surrounded him in great excitement. He visited frequently with these people, listening to them more than he talked.

As we neared America a wireless came for my father from New York. It was from a man he had met on his earlier visit to America in 1906—Herman Bernstein, an Anglo-Jewish newspaperman, close to the German Jewish Establishment, and the self-appointed guardian of the poor Jewish immigrants from Russia. On the earlier visit, as told in the preceding part of this book, Bernstein had been assigned by Hearst to take my father for a stroll on the East Side and write down his impressions of America for an article in the Sunday *New York American*. (Years later Mr. Bernstein was appointed by President Hoover as American Minister to Albania.) In his telegram Bernstein advised my father that he had recently established a new Yiddish newspaper, *The Day*, and requested my father not to tie up with any other newspaper until they could meet.

For my father this was a good omen. Inevitably it recalled the wireless from Hearst's new Yiddish newspaper as he was nearing America in 1906. But what a difference! Hearst's *Jewish American* was an election gimmick—it folded soon after the election; this one was a genuine Yiddish journalistic undertaking, and with such an intelligent and worldly editor as Herman Bernstein it was an indication of the cultural development and maturity of the East Side. Evidently, he thought, his second coming to America was arousing the same strong interest, if not a stronger one, as his first.

Sadly, this hope was not borne out. As in other turns in his life, my father was now again due for disappointment. But for the present he was ebullient with expectation, while my mother, the inveterate pessimist, kept her misgivings to herself.

It was a cold, gray, windy dawn when our ship reached the Narrows, the entrance to New York Bay, where it dropped anchor for quarantine. Soon the revenue cutter came to the side of the ship bringing medical inspectors and a flock of ship reporters over a rope ladder on board.

I was still in bed, though awake, for who could sleep that last night on board ship? I heard a knock on the door of my cabin, and before I could respond, the head of a man with bushy disheveled hair and silver-framed glasses on his bumpy nose appeared through the doorway, demanding without ceremony, "You're Sholom Aleichem's daughter? Where's your father?" As I later learned, he was the exuberant, Americanized—a typical reporter, in fact, out of *The Front Page*—and politically active Yiddish newspaperman Joel Slonim, a poet of note in his off hours. I gave him the number of my father's cabin. Slonim was accompanied by a flock of ship reporters, some Jewish but mostly non-Jewish, who covered the incoming steamers with their loads of immigrants. They stormed through the corridors and decks, like marauders raiding a helpless vessel on high seas, in search of the story of the Jewish Mark Twain.

Finally, the Jewish Mark Twain met the press, and before he knew where he was, Slonim had taken over, appointing himself as the interpreter, not bothering overmuch to translate, but himself answering the majority of the questions directed to my father, for he assumed he knew in advance what the answers would be. The questions dealt mostly with the war in Europe, what my father thought of the Germans, of the position of the United States, which was still striving to remain neutral in the conflict. When Slonim did translate both the questions and answers, they bore only a slight resemblance to the original. By the time we arrived at the pier and cleared our baggage, someone brought us a newspaper that was being sold in the street and which contained my father's interview with the press. We were all amazed at the speed with which American newspapers operated, and my father was especially amused when someone translated the interview for him, most of which was news to him.

Only two officials of the Reception Committee had boarded the revenue cutter with the reporters, the journalist James Faller, who had organized the committee, and Honon J. Minikes, its secretary. A quiet, modest man, immaculately dressed, soft-spoken and polite, Mr. Faller was on the staff of *The Jewish Morning Journal,* but a frustrated playwright. (In time he retired from the newspaper to devote himself entirely to playwriting. None of his plays ever reached the stage. Whenever he was asked how he was doing, his reply was, "We live and hope.")

Minikes was a small, slight, nondescript person, who spoke in a low voice and swallowed half his words. Yet he was a most interesting character. Although only an usher in one of the Yiddish theaters, he was a pillar of the literary establishment. He put out a special literary magazine for the Jewish holidays, mostly of reprints, which he called *Minikes' Holiday Magazine;* but more importantly, he was the organizer of all the literary benefits for writers, old and new, on such occasions as their arrivals or departures, anniversaries, appearance of new works, etc. Minikes was always involved in at least a couple of such affairs at once, and always occupied, during his evenings at the theater and through the days, with these activities. He served every literary person of any importance, but nobody knew much about Minikes, whether he had a family or how he lived, and nobody cared. He was simply taken for granted. Only when he died did the literary people feel their obligation to him, and they organized a memorial service for him, which ran most haphazardly—people said you could see Minikes was not managing. My father was to be the chairman of the memorial meeting, but he died shortly before, and the chair was draped in black at the meeting.

As our ship pulled into Hoboken harbor we noticed a crowd, mostly of young people, on the pier. Hats were thrown in the air, and shouts of "*Sholom aleichem,* Sholom Aleichem" could be heard on our ship. A group of children were waving Zionist flags. As we reached the pier, the crowd rushed toward my father to lift him up in the air, with the accompanying excitement and confusion. Those were my father's readers, most likely themselves recent arrivals in this country. But the Jewish notables who had come out to meet my father on his first visit eight years earlier, the editors of the Yiddish newspapers, the directors of the Jewish theaters, the union leaders, etc., were conspicuously missing.

My mother's reaction to this comparatively subdued reception was one word, "Americhka," which meant, What could one expect from these people in America? All their concern is with sensation; the second coming of Sholom Aleichem to America could not be as sensational as the first, and one's value in America is commensurate with the amount of sensation produced in the masses. However, my father was more concerned with those who did come to welcome him than with those who did not. He never forgot that a crowd, however large, consists of individuals, and he always sought contact with individuals in the crowd.

In the eight years that had intervened between his two visits to America, great changes had taken place in the immigrant Jewish community. Some eight hundred thousand additional Jewish immigrants from Eastern Europe had come to the country. Most of the new generation had at least a smattering of worldly knowledge; a number of them had been Socialists and revolutionists against the czarist regime. These became the articulate element on the East Side. Indeed, *The Day,* the newspaper that Herman Bernstein started, was an expression of the changing times, a revolt of these new elements against the existing Yiddish press, which was either too primitive or too yellow-sensational for their taste. By making a clear appeal to sophistication and intelligence the new newspaper won a circulation of one hundred thousand almost immediately.

Then, too, the war in Europe caused tension and schism among the Jewish immigrants in America. America still being neutral—it joined the war only in April 1917—people took a position on the war in accordance with their general inclinations. Ordinarily, because of its liberal tradition, the East Side would have been wholeheartedly with France and England and against the divine right claimed by the arrogant Kaiser and his Junkers. But the involvement of the czarist regime in the war on the side of the democratic powers complicated the matter. A defeat at the hands of the Germans might undermine the czarist regime (as indeed it did), while victory at the front would only further entrench the reactionary forces. There was little sympathy for the Kaiser on the East Side, but there was a burning desire to see the collapse of the czarist regime.

Moreover, there was hardly a week that did not bring some Jewish celebrities from abroad, leaders of political parties, heads of movements, scholars, noted writers of Russia or Austria, who had been outside their own countries when the war broke out. It seemed as though the entire intellectual and political Jewish leadership of Europe was concentrating in America, injecting a new vibrancy, push and drive into the American Jewish community.

It was a different Jewish America now, and under these circumstances the attention given to my father's arrival was considerably greater than that afforded to other celebrities.

From the pier we were taken to the apartment of a Mr. Finn. Used to renting furnished apartments in Europe, I assumed that this apartment was meant for us, and I inspected the apartment as though we were renting it. The lady of the house apparently was complimented by my close interest and showed me every room and convenience. In my mind I figured who of us would occupy which room, and had everybody comfortably settled. Then we came to an additional room, when I said more to myself than to the lady of the house, "And who will sleep here?"

The lady replied, "What do you mean who? I sleep here, this is my bedroom." Then I realized we were only guests, here for a rest.

We were put up at the Hotel Theresa, on the corner of Seventh Avenue and 125th Street, in the heart of today's Negro Harlem. The Negro community then occupied only the northeast patch of Harlem, from Madison Avenue and 129th Street to the River. One Hundred and Twenty-fifth Street was one of the better business streets of the city, a sort of uptown Yorkville; the Hotel Theresa was then a "modern" hotel, and like the modern hotels of later years its rooms were very small, and the rates high. We occupied two rooms, each containing one double bed, a small table and chair. My parents were in one room, Numa and myself in the other; the Berkowitzes had gone to stay with Berkowitz's family in Brooklyn. Since Numa was now a boy of fourteen, he slept on the floor, on padded bedding beside my bed. This was about the most crowded accommodation we had ever had, and we did not know what to do about it. None of us spoke a word of English, and could not look for another place, preferably an apartment of our own, while the two active people of the reception committee, Faller and Minikes, were either too busy with their own affairs or too occupied with arranging my father's reception meeting to bother with our living quarters. We felt as though we were trapped in a coop, helpless and speechless and far from home.

The late afternoon of our third day at the Theresa, a young Columbia College student, whom we called Ben, came to our rescue. He had come for quite another purpose, to invite my father to read his works on the campus of Columbia University. It was very much within the tradition of the East Side of the time for intellectuals to organize courses for the ignorant immigrant masses, and Ben had brought together a group of students who could speak Yiddish to form a Jewish Students' Lecture Committee. They were available to give free lectures to any organized group on such topics as history, literature, and science. A notice about this service had appeared in the Yiddish press, and invitations were coming in from various elements on the East Side. It was under the auspices of this group that the young student invited my father to speak.

My father was much impressed by this invitation. It meant that there were Jewish students in America with some knowledge of and interest in Yiddish literature, as in the continental universities, a situation which could not have been imagined eight years earlier. He loved to meet such young people, but he was in no hurry to accept the invitation. Perhaps he wanted to learn more about the group from other sources; possibly he hesitated to make any commitments before his official reception would take place, in two weeks. He wanted the young student to tell him first of all about himself, who he was, what he was studying, how he came to know Yiddish so well, what he had read of his works and of the works of other Yiddish writers; then about the other students of the group. As to the invitation, my father said to him; "You ask me to come to read to your students when I do not even have a roof over my head."

Ben didn't understand what my father meant by this.

"We live here," my father explained, "in two cages, no place even to move about, and we cannot find an apartment of our own."

Ben was puzzled. "Can't find an apartment? I could find you any kind of an apartment in a jiffy."

My father looked him over, smiled and said, "You say you can? Take my daughter with you and go out and find an apartment."

Ben smiled back and said, "With pleasure."

Finding an apartment proved not to be so easy. There were plenty of apartments to be had, certainly, but not filling our requirements, which were exacting. My father wanted the Berkowitzes to live with us, so that we were really two families requiring five bedrooms; furthermore, the rooms were to be separate, with doors, off a corridor or foyer, to assure privacy. In addition, the rental had to be moderate as our income was as yet uncertain, and not very large at best. Walking with Ben in the attractive, leisurely streets between our hotel and the northern end of Central Park was very pleasant, but we had no success in finding an apartment. When the next day my father himself went with Ben to see what could be rented, they, too, came back without finding anything. Only one apartment, on the corner of 110th Street and Seventh Avenue, was close to what they were looking for, but when my father heard how much it was—one hundred and fifty dollars a month—he said, "Let's run away, quick!" Finally, after some hard searching, Ben and I did find an apartment of eight small but separate rooms, at 110 Lenox Avenue on the corner of 116th Street, at a rental of less than one half the sum that had made my father say "Let's run away, quick."

We bought furniture on the installment plan and settled down to some sort of life in America. At least, those of us who were in this country were now together again. My little niece, Tamara Berkowitz, was registered in the neighborhood public school and Numa was enrolled in the nearest high school—all by Ben, who gladly took over the chores of our family affairs that required a knowledge of English. He began to teach me English, for which I, in return, was to help him with his French in college; this was, at least in part, an excuse to spend more time with me. He seemed to grow naturally into our family, and my father accepted him cordially—he was a young man after his own heart.

New York impressed all of us as a most interesting city and unlike any of the cities we had visited in Europe. Its tempo overwhelmed us, even though there were still two horsecar lines and comparatively few automobiles in the streets, particularly in our section. Ordinarily we would have been elated to explore the great metropolis, but we lived under a lengthening shadow of anxiety. Our father's health was not good, and we could see him making a conscious effort to put on a bold front. What depressed him most was the splitting up of his family. He could accept, though not quite approve, the return of the Kaufmans to Russia; after all, Michael's parents and large family were there, as was also a property given him by his father, and his professional career was naturally adjusted to life in Russia. But only lack of money kept my sister Emma and brother Misha in Copenhagen. My parents realized quickly that there was no prospect of earning a large enough income to maintain Misha in a proper sanatorium in America. Indeed, the necessity of providing for both children in Copenhagen was an unremitting factor in my father's desperate efforts to earn more money here.

Discouraged by the comparatively modest reception on landing in America, the Reception Committee arranged my father's first appearance not at Carnegie Hall, but at Cooper Union, which has a capacity of 1,400 seats. But the outpouring of people toward the hall was tremendous; for blocks around the streets were packed with people who failed to gain admittance. The editors of the newspapers now came to bid him welcome, as on his first visit to America, and the audience was exuberant in its enthusiastic applause. The Reception Committee at once announced a second appearance two weeks later at Carnegie Hall, which proved just as successful and also sold out. With the money from these appearances, the loans for the passage were paid, and enough money was left for immediate needs. The next morning my mother was able to send money to Copenhagen.

At the first reception my father read one of the war stories he had written on board ship, based on what he had heard from some of the passengers in third class who had been caught by the war in their small towns, and who, only after two or three horrendous months had managed to get out. In that story a small-town Jew tells about his son Yechiel at the front. Yechiel had been recruited, briefly trained, and sent into battle. At the firing line the sergeant noticed

Yechiel shooting up in the air instead of ahead; he poured a flood of curses and abuse on his head, with all the worst names for Jews in Russian, to boot, and showed him where to aim his gun. A little later the sergeant again saw Yechiel aiming up in the air. This time he was flabbergasted: What, he wanted to know, was the matter with that crazy Jewish soldier? Hadn't he told Yechiel where to aim his gun? "Yes," Yechiel replied, "but there are people there!"

Just as the schoolteacher in my father's story "If I Were Rothschild," epitomized the attitude of the Kasrilevka Jews toward war and the craze for gain, so did Yechiel exemplify the stance of the Kasriliks toward the killing entailed in war.

As on my father's first visit to America, the German-Jewish elite took due notice of his arrival. This time they had him as their guest of honor for their annual public meeting at the Educational Alliance. None of their earlier meetings had drawn any such crowds. My father was introduced by Judge Samuel Greenbaum, chairman of the meeting, and the speech of welcome was delivered by no less than Jacob H. Schiff, who was moved to eloquence in the presence of such a large, enthusiastic audience.

Even while these receptions were under way my father had to make the agonizing decision of which newspaper to join as a regular contributor, thereby excluding the others. The two conservative, Orthodox newspapers, *The Tageblat* and *The Morning Journal,* with which he had been connected on his earlier visit and some years subsequently, had now dropped out of consideration. The large influx of young men and women, with modern, secular, and mostly Socialist views, had given preponderance in circulation, prestige and enterprise to the radical newspapers, while the conservative, Orthodox papers, dominating the scene years earlier, were now relegated to the background. There were three radical newspapers: the oldest and largest in circulation was the Socialist *Forward,* edited and dominated by Abraham Cahan, himself a literary figure in this country. The second oldest, originally also Socialist, but lately merely radical, was *The Warheit,* edited and controlled by another picturesque character, Louis Miller, popular with his readers for his personal, bombastic style. The third was the new liberal-bourgeois and Zionistic paper *The Day,* edited by Herman Bernstein, who had telegraphed my father on board ship.

Of the three newspapers, *The Warheit* was in no position to bid for my father's connection; it was undergoing a circulation crisis because of its pro-Allied, and thus also pro-Russian, stand in the European war (the United States was still neutral). The other newspapers exulted in the defeats of the czarist armies at the front without aligning themselves with the audacious Kaiser. So the choice was narrowed to the two others, *The Forward* and *The Day*. *The Day* offered a weekly salary of one hundred dollars for two contributions a week, which was a large sum in relation to the salary scale of the Yiddish press. *The Forward* could not go above seventy-five dollars a week; this was the salary of its editor, Abraham Cahan, and no one could receive a higher pay. (In time Cahan's salary was increased to four hundred dollars a week in order that the salary of the manager and other employees could be raised accordingly.)

This decision was important, for according to the mores of Jewish newspaperdom then, the moment an author, however well known, joined one newspaper, other papers ceased to mention his name for fear of giving publicity to their competitor. This was called the "silent treatment." One such incident greatly amused my father. A reception was given for him, after he had joined *The Day,* by the elite of the Jewish community at the Educational Alliance. Among those present were such outstanding Jews as Nathan Straus, Felix Warburg and Jacob H. Schiff. One Jewish newspaper could not bypass such a gathering of German Jewish celebrities on the East Side, despite its competition with *The Day,* so it reported the reception fully, quoting the laudatory words of Schiff, and the others, but leaving out the name of the person who was praised and to whom the reception had been tendered.

My father's friends and advisers had been divided on his choice of a paper, the partisans of each warning him not to tie up with the other paper. My father himself was inclined to accept the offer of the *The Forward* for several reasons. First of all, this was the paper with much the largest circulation, so that he would be reaching a much wider audience. Possibly the fact that its readers were plain workers, who were everywhere his staunch admirers, was also a factor in his consideration. Above all, its editor, Cahan, was a literary man, with a knowledge of Russian literature. My father knew Cahan from the earlier visit, and believed they would have a language in common if not a common standard of literary values, Cahan's taste being somewhat sensational—and the latter difference between the two men was just the one which partisans of my father's joining *The Day* strongly emphasized.

A frustrated novelist, despite the success of one of his novels in English, and an intemperate, self-conceited critic, Abraham Cahan was a dangerous editor for a writer. He was anxious to have great literary figures on his paper, which meant his entourage, and when he engaged a new writer he exerted every effort to popularize him among the readers of his newspaper, using all the promotion tricks he had learned while working on an American journal. When his new writer was on the pinnacle of his popularity, Cahan would turn against him—subconsciously jealous, perhaps, of his literary position —and try to involve himself in the writer's work—in the selection of the topic or its treatment. And if the writer resented it, Cahan would make his life miserable—as was the case, in later years, with Sholem Asch.

The literary atmosphere at *The Day,* all agreed, would be more congenial, and there he would be sure of peace of mind in his writing. The objection of the *Forward* patisans that the duration of *The Day* was by no means secure was answered by pointing out that my father's contributions would decisively tip the balance in making the paper a success. Of course, the financial difference in the two offers was a great consideration, the needs of the family here and in Copenhagen being what they were.

So my father accepted the offer of *The Day,* and a contract was drawn up, limited to one year and subject to renewal. It had great spiritual satisfaction for my father, for he would be writing his autobiography, *From the Fair,* regularly, a chapter a week, as a part of his contributions to the paper, without the interruptions that had blocked his earlier efforts.

With his health failing, and so much writing to do, particularly on his autobiography—which he intended to be the crown of his literary creations—my father might have been expected to retire to some quiet, comfortable place in a salubrious climate, like Florida, Arizona, or California, and devote himself entirely to writing. Who knows if such a step might not have improved his health and prolonged his life by many years? But this was beyond our dreams, for we barely managed to live from hand to mouth. Even a change and rest at Lakewood, New Jersey, a pine-wooded winter resort some forty miles out of the city, was a cherished dream that took time and a loan of one hundred dollars to realize. Besides, it was not in my father's nature to isolate himself "from the fair," from his people anywhere, and all the more so in America.

As in Europe, my father ran his home address in the newspaper so that anyone who wished could contact him—and many did, all sorts of people. Some were just bores, and our problem was how to hasten their departure. Others had information to offer, what America was like, how people lived here, and the stories of their own experience in the land of Columbus. Still others came with plans for my father, grandiose plans in keeping with the size of the country and the zest of its enterprise. My father absorbed it all in amazement, with the delight of discovery.

With some of these people he visited such places as a modern laundry—modern for fifty years ago—a grocery, a tailor shop. At each place he would want to know how it operated, the working process as well as the working conditions, what was the character of the people he met there, what had brought them into that line of business, and how they felt about it all. A few of these visits were later reflected in such stories of American life as "The Laundry."

One of the projects proposed to him was a lecture tour by an American non-Jewish impresario, Ben H. Atwell, then connected with the Hippodrome Theatre. The terms of the contract were attractive enough: an extensive tour through many cities from New York to California, at two hundred and fifty dollars an appearance, plus expenses for my father and mother both. Atwell apparently expected everywhere a turnout like the one he had seen in Carnegie Hall. The sort of promotion he had undertaken might have been suitable for a tour of Mark Twain, but not for the "Jewish Mark Twain," as he persistently called my father. He did not publicize in the Yiddish press; neither did he contact Jewish organizations in the particular localities. He publicized his visit just as he would have publicized a circus at his Hippodrome, depending on huge posters with a grotesque figure of my father. His first bookings were in the least promising places, comparatively minor cities with small Jewish communities composed of the older, more sedate elements, of shopkeepers with long hours at their place of business, unconcerned and uninvolved in matters outside their immediate personal affairs; and there were very few new immigrants. Many of them had not even noticed the posters; those who did were only confused by them. They had never been called in that way to a Jewish meeting before. The result was a poor turnout. Much as my father had been mortified by the kind of promotion and by the mismanagement, he did not want to break the agreement with Atwell, the financial pressure being what it was, but to his great relief Atwell himself broke the agreement.

Now, Berkowitz took over the arrangements for readings in the traditional Jewish way, contacting certain individuals active in the cultural field, who organized appearances in their cities either directly by the organizations themselves, or by local entrepreneurs. The result was not only packed halls, but also a heartening experience for my father, who needed the warm receptions to strengthen and raise his spirits in those difficult months. Wisely, Berkowitz limited the number of such engagements so as not to tax my father's health.

An American Menachem Mendel brought another project, a movie of stories by Sholom Aleichem. He had talked with the "people higher up," and they were very much interested—who they were, if indeed there were such, he did not say. But it was urgent, and he needed a scenario, in English, of course, and at once. As usual we turned to Ben, and I shall let him tell this story, as he described it in his memoir of my father that appeared in *Dos Sholom Aleichem Buch*, in 1927:

A Wednesday, in the spring of 1915: I come home from college and find a message: Sholom Aleichem's servant, a Polish woman, had come in the afternoon, barely found the apartment, and delivered a letter from Berkowitz. The letter said that Sholom Aleichem was in Lakewood, and it was urgent to prepare at once a scenario of *Motel, Son of Paysie the Cantor* in English, and that it was a very important matter, so I simply must drop everything and go to Lakewood. Sholom Aleichem is expecting me. I happened to have a test the next morning, but if Sholom Aleichem was expecting me nothing mattered. So, a wire was sent that at eleven the next morning I would be in Lakewood.

Sholom Aleichem awaited me at the railway station and took me to his hotel. But first of all I had to see the lake. He took me to a small wooden bridge at the corner of the lake, set against the pine wood, the best spot from which to view the beauty of the entire place. It was beautiful indeed, but I did not show any special enthusiasm.

Sholom Aleichem took me around to show me other most wondrous spots, unusually beautiful villas, of which he was enraptured. But, again, I took it coolly. The climax came at dinner. He lived in a fine hotel. The food was excellent and served with exquisite taste. I do not know if he had especially ordered the menu, but it was a great feast. He sat at the table placidly, eating the food, as though he were not looking at me at all, but I felt he was watching me closely at the arrival of each new course to see if I was impressed. Naturally, I could not enjoy the meal.

One course consisted of stuffed young squabs that seemed as though they had just lost their feathers. The tiny legs were wrapped in fringelike paper. I watched Sholom Aleichem to see how he went about it, and did likewise, but he acted as though he didn't notice it. For a moment he raised his eyes to look at me, and I acted as though unconcerned. After the peach melba, which I accepted as a matter of course, Sholom Aleichem lifted his head, looked at me for a moment, and said; "You are a frozen Litvak!" [Lithuanian Jews had a reputation of being dispassionate.] I laughed, but he was serious.

After dinner we went to his room, a large, bright parlor with an oversized writing table, and began to talk about the work for which I had come. He was telling me, in Yiddish, how the stories of Motel should be told on the screen, while I took notes in English. He dictated a scenario of every story of Motel in great detail, as though he were telling me of an actual movie he had seen. I saw him now in the great combination of his talents, acting the roles of his characters, as though he was performing before the lights in the studio, and yet being the observer of it, enjoying it all immensely. When he turned his forefinger into the air to indicate a hand moving over the screen, writing the words "Elihu, the Inkmaker," I could see the screen and had the complete illusion of a movie scene.

We both roared repeatedly as he improvised the action on the silent screen. He laughed fully, freely, heartily. I have never seen him laugh so much and so boisterously. I have never laughed so much on one occasion in my life. If a stranger saw us then he would think we were touched in the head. Two men sitting and bursting into laughter, like two kids at a Charlie Chaplin movie.

Nothing came of this project. I do not recall hearing the matter discussed in our house, and I never learned why it failed to materialize. My father preferred to get involved with a new and hopeful project rather than dwell on the failure of an old one.

In early summer of 1915 we had an unusual problem with our father. Our apartment on Lenox Avenue was quite noisy, with the clang of two streetcar lines crossing underneath our windows, and the small rooms were confining, particularly for my father, who had been used to the warm sunny outdoors abroad. He longed for a change, a rest in the countryside. A friend recommended a small boardinghouse, maintained by an intelligent woman of Russian background, an admirer of my father's, at Pine Hill, in the foothills of the Catskills. My father went there for a stay of a few weeks, but after the first enthusiastic letter there was a perceptible letdown in the tone of the others. He did not complain of anything, but we could tell that something was wrong: he simply was not happy there. It might be possible to find another place in the neighborhood for him, and so my mother decided that I and Ben should go to Pine Hill to visit my father, see what the situation was, and do what was necessary.

When he met us at the railway station, he seemed to be in good spirits, jesting playfully, pointing out the natural beauty of the place, boasting of it as if it were his private estate, and wanting us to admire it as he did. But he looked haggard and worn. The place was fine, he said, except for its steepness; wherever he turned, it was either up or down a hill, which made walking difficult. The food was not so good, either, but the landlady was now trying to prepare the food he liked. Subsequently we learned of another irritant, a vulgarian boarder who ate at the same table with him; coarse-looking, gruff, his table manners were even worse, and my father in his weakened state could not bear to watch him take a big thick slice of bread, pile on it a heap of butter, and push it into his mouth. Clearly, we had to move him to another hotel.

But my father hesitated; he would stick it out there, and all our persuasions could not change his decision. Why stick it out? asked Ben. In a couple of hours we would find a more suitable place, move him over, no trouble at all, and he would be settled there in a moment. My father's face darkened with suffering. We could see that he realized he had to move, for the hills alone, if not for the other inconveniences, and he wanted to, but there was something inhibiting him. What could that be?

We soon discovered the source of his hesitation. The landlady's five-year-old daughter was a beautiful child, with big blue eyes and a captivating smile: she had fallen in love with Mister Sholom Aleichem, and he returned that love. Early in the morning—my father would rise at six—she was there in his room, saying, "Hello, Mister Sholom Aleichem." Sometimes she would crawl into his bed, and double over, like a kitten, at his feet. When he was writing she played near him, not disturbing him, watching to see when he would stop writing. If he sat down on the veranda she would appear at the arm of his chair, and once when she overheard a remark that Sholom

Aleichem might go away for a few days, she cried so that it was hard to quiet her. How could he break her heart?

Our problem was not my father, but the little girl. I befriended the sweet thing, had her on my lap while talking to my father on other matters, and then, when we were alone, I confided a secret to her: we would all surprise Mister Sholom Aleichem and take him to another place; then she would be coming to visit him, he would come out to meet her, and it would be so much fun. She joined the conspiracy, but manifestly not without misgivings. When we left to find another place, my father stood outside, stooped, forlorn, with an expression of pain on his face, looking at Ben like a patient at his doctor who had just ordered him to go under the knife.

We soon found in Fleischmanns Station a more suitable place and in a couple of hours we were back. The bread-and-butter eater helped bring my father's luggage down to the car, and my father had already taken leave of his little sweetheart, who stuck to her part in the conspiracy. She stood on the veranda, finger in mouth, but without tears, watching us depart. With his head lowered, my father slowly paced to the car, and as the chauffeur stepped on the gas a childish outcry came from the veranda. My father was startled; the car tore up the hill. Not a word was passed between us all the way to the new hotel.

The new place pleased him very much. He had not expected to find such a beautiful spot in this part of the country. His mood improved, especially after he heard that Misha and Emma were planning to arrive in New York in August (Berkowitz had managed to obtain a loan for their passage). A letter to Misha and Emma, dated Fleischmanns Station, July 7, 1915, reads as follows:

"My dears: So, you have decided to come in August. We will be praying for a benign breeze, for this is the most pleasant time of the year to travel by boat. Emmachka, do not forget the beer (a special sort of Danish beer my father's doctor in Copenhagen prescribed against his persistent thirst). Bring along a whole case, although I am not sure it will have the same taste, since my thirst is decreasing. And you, Misha, have become absorbed in commerce? I am afraid you may become a Morgan and tie up with the Entente, and then some fanatic German will get to you and fire bullets through your white waistcoat and flannel trousers.

"You complain we do not write you about our life in America. That is not easily done since we are all so busy. I will tell you exactly about everybody. Myself—I write. Twice a week for *The Day*, and—principally—a comedy for the theater (it is called *The Great Win*). I hope to have it produced in the fall by Adler or Thomashevsky. I think its success is a sure thing. Then, for mother it is very difficult to write. She still is troubled with her leg. The hot baths [she had been to Mt. Clemens] helped only the hotel where she lived and the railway. The injections have done more for the doctor than for her. Berkowitz hammers away at the typewriter copying my, and his own, writing. Tissa is preoccupied with the cinema, which she frequents very seldom, no more than once, and occasionally twice, a day. That is why she is not eager to go to a country place where the cinemas are few. Maroussia would love to write to you, but first of all she would have to go and get the paper, secondly, she would have to go to drop it at the post office, or into the mailbox, and the devil knows where this might be, perhaps in the lobby. Numa has three occupations: 1) he reads Verbitskaya [a popular light novelist in Russia], 2) he bites his nails, and 3) plays chess. Would you expect him to write letters, too? 'I think, if it is not too hot for you,' as Soloveichik, the matchmaker, says in my new comedy, under the circumstances, I alone remain to describe American life for you, but where can I find the time? Think of this, if it is not too hot for you. I give this writing to Maroussia—perhaps she will roll up her sleeves and write you a long letter, not just, 'Kisses, Maroussia.' I kiss you."

The hot summer months of 1915 we spent at Belmar, a small, quiet, not yet commercialized resort in New Jersey on the Atlantic coast. For its exceptional qualities—proximity to New York City, and by no means least its moderate rentals and inexpensive boarding —Belmar became the favorite vacationing place for the new emigré elite: writers, artists and other intellectuals, refugees from the first World War. There was the novelist Sholem Asch, the dramatist Peretz Hirshbein, and Pinhas Rutenberg, a leader of the terrorist Social Revolutionary party under the czars, later to become ruler of Petrograd (earlier, St. Petersburg, subsequently Leningrad) under the Kerensky regime, soon thereafter a refugee again (from the Bolsheviks) in New York, where he promulgated the idea of a World Jewish Congress. An engineer by profession, he designed and successfully carried through plans for the introduction of electricity into Palestine. These, and others like them, constituted the social milieu of my father in Belmar.

A local carpenter constructed a contraption like a pulpit for my father, a crude piece compared to his desk in Europe, but serviceable, and at this he could stand and write on the porch of our bungalow.

It was not a happy summer. He wrote much, but under disheartening conditions. His health was not good; he had no specific complaints, but his strength was ebbing. The family situation, too, was depressing; my mother was bedridden with acute sciatica, for which the doctors had no relief, and worst of all was the news from Emma and Misha in Copenhagen. Originally we had planned for them to come here in early summer so that Misha would be with us at Belmar during the summer months, and then we would see where he could live in the fall and winter. All was set for them to come, but Misha fell ill and could not make the voyage. Once again they were about to come, in August, and again a relapse. Emma's letters, always brief, were now laconic. Then she stopped writing altogether, so we did not know whether they were coming, or whether, possibly, Misha had had a relapse again.

Again, I quote from *Dos Sholom Aleichem Buch*, in which Ben, by then already an expected member-to-be of our family, described the atmosphere in our house in Belmar:

End of Summer, 1915. Came for a brief visit to Sholom Aleichem in Belmar. Arrived in evening. After dinner Sholom Aleichem invited me for a walk. It was dark; thick branches, overgrown with leaves, hang down from the trees overhead. We walk briskly, arm in arm. First he inquires about my immediate plans, what I am expecting to do this fall, and of my plans for the future. Then he speaks of himself.

He had just finished the chapter in his autobiography, *From the Fair,* in which the boy had fallen ill—because of an ill-fated love affair— and while he was running a fever, in delirium he makes the transition to youth. He was impressed himself by his thought of having the changeover during such a physical crisis. Then he spoke of the chapters that would follow, not yet written. He was so youthful that evening that the curtain of separation between us—my awe and adoration of him, the realization that I was in the presence of the greatest genius of Jewish literature, not to speak of the age difference, he coming "From the Fair," myself only just preparing to enter there—faded away in the bracing evening air. We were two romantics, walking arm in arm, dreaming dreams of the morrow.

In America

Two days later. Terrific heat. Mrs. Sholom Aleichem in bed with excruciating pain. Pesky flies give no let-up. A bad letter from Copenhagen. Misha ill again. Money needed, but there is no money. Atmosphere nerve-trying, depressing, distressing. Sholom Aleichem not well. Suffers terrific headaches. Keeps an icebag on his head. He sits in his easy chair; I stand beside him, holding the icebag on his head. He is writing. He writes as usual, serenely, in his clear, concise hand, except for an occasional jerk of the finger getting a letter out of line. One week later people will read in the newspaper what he is now writing—a funny, jolly story, and they will laugh.

A couple of days later. We are all at the railway station, waiting for the train. Sholom Aleichem walking on the platform with his little notebook in the palm of his left hand, writing in it with his right. In the train he sits in a corner by himself writing. Stuffy. Humid warm air making people drowsy. I look at Sholom Aleichem. His eyes closed, pen in the right hand, notebook in left. Is he napping? A bit of breeze coming through the window, or a jerk of the car, and his eyes open, and he writes again. No, he was not napping.

Later, a most trying hour. Mrs. Sholom Aleichem incapacitated by her sciatica. Still no money. No word from Misha, not even a reply to a cable.

Sholom Aleichem is silent. Keeps away from people. Whenever he is not well, or in a bad mood, he withdraws to his room. Hearing me come in, he emerges from his room to talk to me. What can be done? A ship from Copenhagen is due this noon. Maybe the children are on it? Possibly an acquaintance who may have a word from them, or know something about them? We decide to go to the pier to see the passengers disembarking.

We take the 9th Avenue elevated train. No thought of going by taxi; or no money. A long, tedious, uncomfortable ride. Sholom Aleichem does not even write. Just sits, silent, his glance straight, sharp, strained. A long walk, amidst rushing trucks, to the pier. We find the ship, due at 1 P.M., will not arrive before 3 or 4. We have no choice but to wait.

The pier is of tremendous size. You can hardly see its end; must crane your neck to see the rafters. No place to rest, nothing to sit on except an empty barrel far off in one corner. I help Sholom Aleichem perch on it. He takes out his little book and writes. An uncanny sight that I still can conjure before my eyes:

An immense structure, bare, dark, drafty. Far out in a corner, a speck, like a fly. This is the great Jewish humorist, waiting in the greatest anxiety for a possible word about his dying son, meanwhile writing for his people to cheer their spirits with hearty laughter.

The ship finally in harbor. We stand at the gangplank, Sholom Aleichem scrutinizing the disembarking passengers for a possible familiar face, still hoping against hope the children might come out after all. No sign of them, or of an acquaintance. Then a gleam of hope in the dark, an acquaintance, a well-known journalist, whom Sholom Aleichem used to meet in Copenhagen, coming down the gangway. The man seemed surprised and confused by the meeting, and terribly nervous. No, no, he knows nothing, he heard nothing, he is terribly sorry, in a terrible hurry.

We are left with a still greater anxiety. Sholom Aleichem hurt by the abrupt manner of the man. Subsequently it occurred to me that if that man could not have told the sickly Sholom Aleichem what he knew about Misha he might have been more considerate and friendly.

It is pitch dark when we leave the pier. A terrific snarl of traffic. One huge truck seemed to have come right upon us, its lights blinding our eyes, a terrific blare of the horn, a sharp grating of the brakes. Sholom Aleichem recoils, like a wounded bird. I grab hold of him with all my might.

We returned home silently. What was uppermost in our minds was, What will we tell the mother?

Even in this dark hour he managed to put on a bold front. Two days later he wrote an encouraging letter to the children in Copenhagen, dreaming up new dreams for them and the family. It was dated New York, 15 September, 1915:

"My dears, Emma and Misha: I had a mind to describe to you what we have lived through during these past two weeks, that is from the moment we began waiting for your arrival till our great disappointment, when I went (the 13th) to meet *Frederick the Eighth,* and instead of meeting you I met that ———. But then I reconsidered, as my pen appeared to be too weak. Let us talk instead about what is going to be rather than of what was. I cannot accept the thought that we might not realize our set plan to spend the winter with you in California. I am thrilled with this prospect. We have decided that right after Yom Kippur, Mother should go to you in Copenhagen and come back with you here by the end of October. During the summer I might go myself to Copenhagen, as it would be a pleasure voyage, but just now my work is starting (the theater, the newspaper, the recording and lectures). The climate here is much better than in Scandinavia. In addition, there are warm and cold climatic sections. Too bad you did not come with the first ship. If Mother is unable to come, I will send you two first-class passages for the sailing of September 22, so that you could leave, with *Frederick the Eighth,* on October 12. You will also receive additional money for whatever expenses you may need. It is hard, indeed impossible, to send money by cable, but still I will try. In a month or five weeks we shall see each other. It is time. The heart is torn into pieces, as it is. Almost a year that I did not see you, Misha, and I do so want to see you. And you, too, Emma! We have suffered enough. We have been looking for an apartment, and every one we saw we planned, Here would be Misha's room, and this for Emma and Maroussia. Also a writing table for Misha. Already we are imagining our meeting with you. Even Tamara—she, too, is asking, When will Misha come to us? And the main thing—California, Los Angeles, et cetera. No, get the next ship and come here! I embrace you, mentally, and kiss you both. Papa."

Alas! none of these dreams were to be realized. My father's vision of a renewed better, brighter, happier life with his family in America was suddenly blacked out by a grim catastrophe. The pillars of his world collapsed, crushing him underneath. When he wrote the above letter Misha was no more, and the sad news had been kept from us. Three days after my father mailed that letter was the austere solemn day of the Jewish year, Yom Kippur, the last in his life. He dressed formally, with a stovepipe hat on his head, and walked to the synagogue to hear his favorite cantor, Yossele Rosenblatt, chant the prayers. He returned home with the blessings of a happy New Year. The next morning, as fate would have it, the cable breaking the tragic news was delivered right into his hands. Shocked, anguished, crushed, he sought to comfort my mother, himself unable to suppress his wailing. "What can be done? Misha will not come to us, we will go to him. . . ."

We were grieving, weeping together, and then we separated to mourn each by himself. My father was the first to leave and retire to his room, closing his door behind him. As he did not emerge from his room for hours, Berkowitz became concerned and he quietly opened the door slightly to see what he was doing. He saw my father standing at his pulpit, as though absorbed in deep prayer, writing, not as usual in his little notebook, but on long white paper. This was, as we later came to learn, his last will and testament, which he began with these words:

"Today, the day after Yom Kippur, a new year has just begun, and a great calamity has befallen my family—my oldest son, Misha (Michael) Rabinowitz, passed away, and carried off with him into his grave a large portion of my life. . . ." Two days later he wrote, in a letter to Lyala in Odessa: "I carry a dead coffin in my heart, and I will take this coffin with me into my grave. . . ."

He began to stoop, he aged overnight, and the cloud of sadness never left his countenance, although he still wrote much that was humorous, read his writing to other people and made them laugh.

My father was only fifty-six years old when the tragedy of Misha shattered his life. My mother had just turned fifty, their youngest, Numa, was going on fifteen, and there were two unmarried daughters. Poor Papulia! He must have staggered under the terrific responsibility of being our provider, and he had to brace himself to pick up the pieces and carry on. But he was like a slight, wearied swimmer in midstream trying to reach shore with an overwhelming current against him. Fate continued to batter him mercilessly. He bowed his head beneath each blow only to raise it again, until he fell, defeated but not humbled.

On October 14, 1915, he wrote to Lyala in Odessa:

". . . A misunderstanding: instead of the son saying daily the *Kaddish* for his father, the father is doing this for his son. And even though considerable time has passed our tears have not dried, and the wound is fresh. . . . Expect no letters from Mother. She is hardly in a position to write—not because of her physical condition, this has improved—but her spirit is crushed. She is mortified, hurt, terribly hurt. . . . As to my spiritual creative life, I cannot complain. I keep writing continuously, as is my wont, running two serials besides other work. The inspiration to write has not forsaken me even in these hard days. Perhaps it is this that gives me the strength to bear the blows of fate. . . ."

With the activity of writing came a glimmer of his old self. Responding tenderly to Lyala's cable telling how Michael, her husband, had passed the medical boards examination, and how he was now a full-fledged military doctor, he added: "Your cable arrived punctually on the 31st day after you sent it" [the delay was due to war conditions]. When he sent regards to his dear friend Hayim N. Bialik, in Odessa, he wrote Lyala: "When you meet Bialik shake his hand for me, I almost said give him a kiss, then I thought of Michael, and got scared: a military doctor, with saber, epaulettes and braids—better not provoke him! Numa has stretched out beyond recognition; Tamara is growing like a cucumber; Maroussia is an American girl or an English lady. . . ."

Like a mortally wounded eagle trying to soar to his earlier heights, my father was desperately seeking to reach the goals for which he had persistently been striving. He was writing feverishly, as though in a race with time, trying to get his works translated and trying to get his plays produced. Not for one moment did his efforts slacken; he was chasing the rainbow to the end.

The comedy *The Great Win,* which my father wrote in 1915, is today a basic play of Jewish repertory everywhere: of Habimah, in Hebrew, in Israel; of the Ukrainian theater in the Soviet Union; the late Erwin Piscator produced it in German in Berlin; and it was recently produced in Czech at Prague. But in 1915 no director of a Yiddish theater in the United States could find any interest in it, to my father's great chagrin. Not until six years after his death, was it produced for the first time by Maurice Schwartz in New York, where it had a great success, and within the year also staged in Vilno, Bucharest, and Moscow, where it was turned into a musical—it is almost a natural for that.

To his bitter disappointment at the rejection of the comedy was now added distress and anxiety at news from *The Day.* The new newspaper had met with financial reverses and was not able to renew its contract for my father's contributions. This blow knocked the very bottom of our livelihood from under our feet; without the weekly check from the newspaper we simply could not exist. It fell to my lot to accompany my father on a humiliating mission, the like of which he would never have thought of doing had he not been in desperation —to call personally on one of the publishers in an effort to retrieve his position on the paper.

The founding editor, Herman Bernstein, had been dropped. The two publishers, involved in other businesses, engaged an intellectual as an editorial executive (I almost said executor). This was Leon Moiseyeff, a rare professional in those days, a Jewish construction engineer, noted for building bridges, who wrote Yiddish literary criticism in his spare time. We might as well have saved ourselves the steep climb of four flights of stairs to his office, for Moiseyeff, who impressed me as a hard, unfriendly person overwhelmed by his own new importance as arbiter in the literary community, said, Yes, it was up to him to decide, but his decision must be no. My father's face was ashen when we returned home, and he retired immediately to his room.

In a letter dated December 2, 1915, to my sister Lyala in Odessa, he wrote:

". . . What can I write you? The year is coming to its end, and so is my contract with the newspaper to which I contribute—But we have an almighty God! And America is a large country. We'll see, maybe we won't be stranded. One consolation. In Europe it's even worse. We are sighing for the end of the war. Will we then rush back to Europe! But don't breathe a word, for the peace might be delayed. . . . And Bella is already reading. Before you turn around she'll be married. My Tevyeh says: 'Girls have the bad habit of eating in the daytime and growing during the night. . . .' "

The Jewish literary community was outraged by what had happened to Sholom Aleichem, their pride and glory. Some tried to intervene with the publishers, but to no avail. A personal friend of my father's approached Abraham Cahan of *The Forward*, but he would not consider Sholom Aleichem now after he had preferred another newspaper a year earlier. This was, according to his lights, tantamount to treason. Finally, a deal was worked out with *The Warheit*, at that time the weak sister of the Yiddish press. Financially it was a comedown, a weekly salary of forty dollars, instead of the hundred paid by *The Day,* but an additional weekly payment of twenty-five dollars was to be an advance on the publication by that newspaper of two volumes of the published installments of *From the Fair*. Emotionally, the new connection turned out to be gratifying to my father; the new publishers and editors were most gracious to their celebrated new contributor.

Happily, too, just at this point, one of my father's fondest dreams was, at least in part, realized. Some of his stories, in English translation, were to reach a vast number of American readers. *The New York World*, then the largest newspaper in the city, boasting of a circulation of one hundred thousand more than any other paper including *The New York Times*, began the publication of my father's series *Motel, Son of Paysie the Cantor* in its Sunday Magazine. The Magazine was circulated with many other Sunday newspapers in the country so that its readership reached into the millions. The series was promoted on a large scale, both within the Sunday Magazine and through large posters on all stations of the elevated railway of the city.

On Sunday, December 26, 1915, *The World* ran an announcement right across one of the pages of the Magazine headed INTRODUCING SHOLOM ALEICHEM OF NEW YORK, with a subhead, "He is one of the world's greatest writers. He is called the Jewish Mark Twain. *The World* Magazine will publish the first of his new series of humorous stories next Sunday." The lengthy biographical sketch began as follows:

> One of the world's greatest writers lives in New York. He is unknown to the larger community of Manhattan, though to his compatriots of the East Side he is a figure of light and learning.
>
> He is a humorist. He has been called the Jewish Mark Twain. His fame is international, for his stories and sketches and dramas are read and quoted and laughed and wept over in Russia, in Poland, in Austria and Germany, a genius of whom we know little or nothing and acclaimed one of the brilliant figures of the day.
>
> Impossible, you may well say. It is true nevertheless. Solomon Rabinowitz, called Sholom Aleichem, writes in Yiddish. It is difficult adequately to translate his works into English, and though his name and fame have been recorded in the press, the writing on which his reputation is founded is unknown to the great majority who cannot read the Jewish papers.
>
> Readers of *The World* Magazine are now to have the opportunity of knowing Sholom Aleichem. Next Sunday we begin the publication of sketches, *Off for America,* in which he describes the exodus of a family of Russian Jews from their little home village to this land of prosperity and peace across the Atlantic. . . .

After describing the characters in the stories to be published, the announcement concludes with this paragraph:

> And while you are laughing at the foibles of Motel, and Elihu and Pini and Brocha, you catch glimpses of their souls. From beneath their strange cloaks and prayer shawls their real selves struggle to the surface. You sense the utter helplessness with which the Russian immigrant faces the gap between the life and thought of the Russian Pale and the Golden Land. You learn why "the children of the ghetto" are really children, groping toward the light of freedom, dazzled after the darkness of oppression. Travel with Motel and his

family from the little Russian village to the gates of America. Sholom Aleichem will make you laugh—and love.

The promotion was continued during the week, with the final statement, "For genuine humor do not miss this remarkable series," and on Sunday, January 2, 1916, *The World* Magazine carried on its front page a large reproduction of a noted painting, *The Immigrant in America*, by Tony Well, with a legend underneath saying that *Off for America* began in that issue. The *Motel* stories were elaborately illustrated by an artist, Samuel Cahan.

My father was sick in bed when the series began appearing in *The World*. He enjoyed looking at the page containing his story, at the way it was featured, and particularly the illustrations. I remember him laughing, obviously pleased, when he saw Samuel Cahan's drawing of Motel. So, this is how Motel looks, he mused in delight. The publication of the series meant much for him, materially as well as spiritually. Not only did additional income make it possible for him to go to Lakewood for a rest and recuperation, but he now saw the possibility of his works in English in America becoming as popular as the Russian translation was before the outbreak of the war.

His mood of the time is reflected in his letter to Lyala, dated January 29, 1916:

"Firstly, I long awaited your letter, which did not come. Secondly, I was laid up for six weeks with influenza, but not severely, even though I was in bed all this time, lying and writing. On the first of January, I left the newspaper *The Day* and transferred to another, *The Warheit*. The conditions are not bad. I am to contribute twice a week. I feel much better about working for this newspaper: a veritable prima donna. In addition, since January 1, I am appearing in translation in the English newspaper *The World*, and its syndicated newspapers. This means that every Sunday my *feuilletons* appear in twenty or more newspapers in various parts of the United States, with a combined circulation of some 5 million readers, or more. They run *Motel, Son of Paysie the Cantor*, with illustrations. The promotion is colossal. Example: in New York, on all the stations of the elevated train, there are posters, in large letters: 'Read Sholom Aleichem, the Jewish Mark Twain, in *The World* Magazine! Original! New! Humoristic! Read Sholom Aleichem!' This is a good beginning. This opens the possibility of entering into the broad stream of English literature. Already there are publishers willing to put out a complete edition in the English language. The trouble is there are no good translators. Bunglers. We try and try. I am seeking translators. For good money. Perhaps. The first two volumes of my autobiography, which is dedicated to you, children, will appear any day now. *The Warheit* is publishing it. To this paper I also contribute the third and fourth volumes. In addition, I appear there weekly with the second volume of *Motel* [*Motel, Son of Paysie the Cantor in America*], and other *feuilletons*. Generally, I cannot complain about unproductivity. On the contrary, diametrically opposed to the condition of my health, the spirit is growing stronger. And thank God for this. . . ."

There were, in fact, no publishers willing to put out my father's complete works in English, or even a selection of his writings. But there were people who assured my father that such publishers could be found, and offering to find them: these people were not liars; they only mistook their own reasoning for reality. There had been so much publicity in the general press about my father, so why should a publisher not be willing to publish his works in translation? My father had always attracted such people, well-meaning, devoted, with grandiose ideas and fantastic plans, mistaking fancy for fact, incorrigible Menachem Mendels. They did not even wait for one plan to fizzle out before they proposed another. One of these characters was dubbed by members of our family as the *vsemogustchi,* a Russian word with a meaning between all-powerful and all-effectual. There was not a thing the *vsemogustchi* could not do, not a plan he could not devise to accomplish some fantastic idea. With every problem he would touch his forehead with his two fingers, as though extricating something from his brain, and say, "I have another idea. . . ." While my father recognized these people as kin to his own Menachem Mendel, he still listened to them and went along with them for a time. But afterward he tried to reach the same goal on his own, in the frame of his own reality. Characteristically, he never held the failure of their plans against these people; instead, he commiserated with them. No wonder Tevyeh's resentment against Menachem Mendel for the loss of his savings, which Menachem Mendel had induced him to invest with him in some stock venture, soon turned into compassion, Tevyeh consoling Menachem Mendel rather than scolding him for it.

I do not recall much negotiation with commercial publishers. A couple were approached, to be sure, and no doubt they were interested in seeing some material in English translation. A few stories were translated for this purpose, but whether the translation was so poor— Heaven knows what passed for translation from Yiddish then—or the publishers simply were not interested in the stories, or could not see a market for them, no contract materialized. The first serious effort by a commercial publisher to bring the works of Sholom Aleichem to the American readers came thirty years later.

I remember much ado about a subsidized publishing venture to bring out the works of my father in English. This was to be a sort of independent undertaking by what we might call today a foundation, with my father doing the selection of the stories and their revision for the American readers, and the foundation doing the publishing itself. Those who urged this plan were perhaps more interested in improving my father's situation than in seeing his works in English. They must have realized that his health was failing, and his economic state, on the completion of his series in *The World*, once again meager and precarious. The publishing enterprise would at once begin paying my father a salary for his services, and he would thus be assured of an adequate income, while not having to drive himself to do so much writing. At the same time he could proceed with his autobiography for the newspaper, for he had a driving anxiety to make progress in this as though he were racing against time. But as to the rest, he could do as he pleased and at his ease.

For my father this arrangement would have meant the difference between need and comfort, strain and relaxation, and it might even have prolonged his life. But comparatively small as the required amount of money was, even for that time—and it would have been an investment which would eventually have paid off—no money was in sight. Possible financial sources for such a purpose were unknown in the Russian-Jewish community: most of the Jewish immigrants were still poor, and the few who had attained a degree of affluence had not yet learned to part with any of their wealth for a social, not to speak of a cultural, purpose. The recourse, therefore, was to the few German Jewish millionaires, who, for reasons of *noblesse oblige*, and for the prestige of Jews in the country generally, assumed the guidance of their poorer and lesser brethren from Eastern Europe— brethren who, in fact, did not care to be guided, yet were flattered by the attention of their big brothers. This group was headed by their venerated leader and elder statesman, Jacob H. Schiff.

Since Mr. Schiff and his closest friends, the Warburgs and Strauses, had participated in the receptions for Sholom Aleichem, it was deemed proper to approach Mr. Schiff for an advance of the working capital for the project.

My father had to initiate the project himself by writing directly to Mr. Schiff, and his opening move was to be followed up by Dr. Judah L. Magnes, a great and pathetic figure on the New York scene. A native of San Francisco, of German Jewish parents, a Reform Rabbi ordained by the Hebrew Union College of Cincinnati, with a doctorate from the University of Berlin, Dr. Magnes married into a prominent rich German Jewish family and embarked on a spectacular and storm-ridden career which has already been briefly mentioned. Tall, handsome, and a master of rhetoric, he duly became the Rabbi of the leading Reform temple in America, Temple Emanu-El of New York, only to become a thorn in the side of his congregation by calling for more Jewish tradition when this was most distasteful to his congregation, and pronouncing himself a Zionist when this was anathema to them. Leaving the Temple, he betook himself to organize the Jews of New York, whose activists resisted union, into a community; picketed along with the striking waistmakers when the police locked up pickets; called for peace amidst the maddening cry for war; and, becoming founder and President of the Hebrew University in Israel, settled with his family in Palestine, where he outraged the Zionists by agitating for a binational state. For all that, Dr. Magnes was highly regarded by the leaders of the German Jewish community, as their great, if wayward, pride, and since he had learned Yiddish during his years in New York, he was the bridge between the German and East European Jews. And to my father he was always a good friend.

The matter hung fire for a couple of months, my father taking a close interest in the financial details of the plan, the cost of production, etc. Then Dr. Magnes wrote to my father, giving him Mr. Schiff's final word: "As I promised you," he wrote, "I talked the matter over with Mr. Schiff, who, I regret to say, does not feel inclined to go into the proposition you laid before him. His main reason is, as I understand it, his doubt that a good business venture can be made of the undertaking. He also is of the opinion that in these difficult times an attempt should be made to do something, perhaps on the basis of a publishing house conducted along commercial lines, that will be of assistance to more than one writer." This man who managed loans in vast sums for foreign governments could conceive either of business or of charity, but not of anything in between.

It took time to recover from this setback, and for a while it seemed as though the matter was dropped, particularly as we were becoming increasingly concerned for our father's health. But another effort was made, again with Mr. Schiff, perhaps more to raise my father's spirits than in expectation of practical results. Another friend of my father's, who was personally close to the great financier, was to approach Mr. Schiff, with a better explanation of my father's situation and a modification of the original plan. This was Professor Israel Friedlaender, of the Jewish Theological Seminary, an institution established largely with the aid of Mr. Schiff. Although born and raised in Poland, Israel Friedlaender was a graduate of the Rabbinerseminar of Berlin, and held a doctorate from the University of Strasbourg, where he served for a time as a *privatdozent* in Semitics. This German background gave Professor Friedlaender exceptional prestige with the leaders of the German Jewish community in New York.

I accompanied my father on his visit to Professor Friedlaender. It was not easy to get to his office at the Seminary on Broadway and 123rd Street, and twice we were misdirected. By the time we climbed up the steep stairs to the Professor's office, my father was exhausted. Professor Friedlaender was an amiable man within the limits of the meticulousness he had acquired through his years in Germany. He spoke Yiddish to my father, and by his allusions to some of his characters, he seemed to be well read in my father's writing. I could not follow the details of their discussion, but the gist of it, as I understood it, was that a small committee should be formed—"One did not need a *minyan*" [ten persons], he said—and that he would write to Mr. Schiff explaining the entire situation. There were two handicaps, however: one, that for the next several weeks he would be out of town most of the time, and the other, that he had no secretary to whom to dictate the letter to Mr. Schiff. But he did have a typewriter in the office. We immediately thought, of course, of Ben, who knew how to type, with two fingers, that is. He would be at the Professor's service, and would contact the Professor.

Ben called the Professor and made an appointment which proved a painful experience and ruined whatever future the project may have had.

As he told me later, writing the letter to Mr. Schiff was for Professor Friedlaender like a performance of a supreme rite by a priest in the Holy of Holies. He nervously paced back and forth the small room, flushed, hesitant in speech, forming and reshaping a sentence, which Ben copied in longhand and read back to him, only to have the Professor strike it out and dictate another in its place. This took, it seemed to Ben, an eternity. Then Ben had to struggle with the old typewriter and copy out the letter properly, poor typist as he was. Finally, to the great relief of the two men, the letter was done, and the Professor ceremoniously settled himself comfortably at the table to go over the letter very, very carefully. But no sooner did he glance at the first lines than he screamed, "What have you done? What have you done?"

Startled, shocked, Ben looked about him to see what he could have done. Noticing the young man's puzzlement, the Professor pounced upon him: "You don't know how to spell Mr. Schiff's name?" This seemed as improbable to the Professor as it would be if a priest did not know how to spell the word Bible. Ben shrugged his shoulders. Frankly, Jacob H. Schiff meant nothing in his world, and he had inadvertently put an "e" after the "i."

It was too late, as the Sabbath was approaching, for Professor Friedlaender to wait for the retyping of the letter. The following two weeks he would be out of town, and Ben was to contact him after his return. But he never did. During the two weeks my father's physical condition took a turn for the worse. We were much too worried about him to bother about Schiff and the project.

This was the last project in my father's life. In the short time he lived to survive this disappointment he was too ill for enterprise and too depressed for ambition. His last public reading was another sad experience. Early in the winter, two men from Philadelphia, representing themselves as acting for the community, arranged for my father to come to their city for a reading at a small hall for the moderate sum of two hundred and fifty dollars. As he could not keep that date because of illness, they changed it for another in March, 1916. When he arrived with my mother for the appearance, he learned that the small hall had been changed for one of the largest houses in the city, the Metropolitan Theater, with a seating capacity of over four thousand, and that every seat in the house was sold out. But he received the same small amount, a check for two hundred and fifty dollars.

The check was put through the bank, and was returned marked "payment stopped." It was then that my father learned that those two men represented no organization, but were simply entrepreneurs with

a shady reputation in business. When my father's admirers in Philadelphia learned of this, they tracked down the two men and ordered
them to make good the check or they would be run out of the city.
They did make it good.

Shortly after his appearance in Philadelphia, my father fell ill
again. The doctors told us nothing about the nature of his illness,
simply saying to Berkowitz that he was a very sick man, but holding
out some hope for him. My father's mood was changeable; he was
depressed when confined to his bed, but brighter when he was able
to be up and about. As I now look back upon those hard days I have
a feeling that his moods were due not only to his physical condition.
His belief in fate, bordering on superstition, was a psychological factor. In March 1916 he reached the age of fifty-seven, which was the
span of his father's life, and also that of his grandfather's. In a letter
quoted elsewhere in this book, his father, then ill, wrote him that he
had reached the age of his father, and that he now felt like his father
before him, that he too was being called to his fathers. On the other
hand, he had already been through the experience of being on the
verge of death, and had recovered. So there was hope that he might
not have to heed the "call," and his optimistic nature tended to cling
to the last shred of hope. At the slightest recovery of strength he
cheered up, and if he was at all able to do so, he dressed and took
a lively interest in all that went on about him.

Late in March a great event took place in the life of the American
Jewish community in which my father was emotionally involved. This
was a grand bazaar for the relief of the Jewish war victims in Europe.
For the first time East European Jewish immigrants participated in a
joint communal effort with the elite of the rich German Jewry in
America, who until this time had looked after the relief of needy
Jews abroad, mostly in the East, on a small scale and on a personal
basis. This, too, was the work of the indefatigable Dr. Magnes, seeking to amalgamate the diverse elements of the Jewish community.
Some weeks earlier Dr. Magnes had chaired a relief meeting at Carnegie Hall, also the first of its kind, which attracted all the Jewish
elements—who responded to his eloquent emotional appeal with near
mass hysteria, women removing rings and earrings to drop into the
collection boxes. The meeting brought in $650,000, one half of which
was given by three German Jews sitting with Dr. Magnes on stage.
Now, the grand bazaar was to raise a corresponding amount from

the Jewish masses, with the planning and management entirely in the hands of the Jewish intelligentsia from Russia and the more intelligent of the rising Russian Jewish middle class.

The huge space of Grand Central Palace was subdivided into a central open space with alleys containing all sorts of articles, from precious stones and works of art to books and clothing. All the goods were donated and all work was done by volunteers. The Jewish writing profession was particularly active, primarily the wives and daughters of writers. Mrs. Sholem Asch headed the art booth, my sister Tissa was in charge of the book booth, while my sister Emma and I spent much time relieving the volunteers at various booths.

My father was stirred by the fervor about the bazaar. He loved to see enthusiastic mass action on behalf of a good cause, and here was the cause of his own people, his Russian Jews, who were being helped by their own brothers and sisters in America. He was proud that his own children were taking part and he wanted to participate himself. One day, as he felt better, he came to the bazaar himself, not on a ceremonial occasion, but just as another visitor. He was recognized, of course, as soon as he entered accompanied by my sister Emma, and was thunderously applauded by all present. I joined him and Emma, saw to it that he removed his coat, and we walked from booth to booth, seeing what was for sale, and meeting the salespeople. Before leaving he made his own contribution, an old manuscript of his and an original letter to him from Leo Tolstoy, to be sold at auction at a later date. At one of the booths they asked him for his autograph, also to be sold at auction. The autograph was sold for ten dollars, and Tolstoy's letter brought one hundred and fifty.

This visit may have been too much of a strain on my father, or it was perhaps another phase in his illness that sent him to bed again, feeling that his strength was ebbing. Nevertheless, he kept writing while in bed, continuing his chores for *The Warheit,* and even writing a special story for the forthcoming Passover issue of the newspaper. It was one of his very funny stories, about a lad who was a poor student and having a hard time learning the *kiddush* (the evening holiday meal prayer) which he would have to recite on his first visit to his future in-laws in another town—the match had recently been arranged. He botched up the *kiddush* and lost his bride, whom he had now seen for the first time, without regrets for himself, but to the chagrin of his father.

The arrival of Passover, in April, was another occasion for my father to muster all his strength and assume the role of the master of ceremonies. Probably for our sake he wanted to give the Seder ceremony at least some semblance of its joyousness in former years. He concerned himself about the wine, laid out the Haggadoth, and put together the special plate of symbolic articles of food, as he had always done through the years. We had invited a number of guests, refugees like ourselves, including Dr. Leon Motzkin, a noted Zionist leader who served as presiding officer at all Zionist Congresses, and Pinhas Rutenberg. As the guests began coming, my father was almost his old self, the charming host, making everybody immediately feel at ease and evoking much laughter by his playful mood at table.

Yet I could not say that we of the family were happy at the Seder. We looked at our father and saw the open wound in his heart, which he was trying to cover—the first Seder with Misha not among the living; and the lengthening shadow of his illness which was ever before our eyes.

We raised our glasses and drank *Lehayim,* to life, yes, to life that was hanging by a thread. . . .

April, which had come in with warmth and sunshine, now left in a spell of cold and rain. The dreary, miserable weather befitted the atmosphere in our house. Soon after Passover my father was in bed again, now with abdominal pains, which reinforced his suspicion that his end was due. He had not only reached the departing age of his father and grandfather, but he had also developed the symptoms of his father's mortal disease. He did not speak to any member of the family about this, only occasionally to some close friend visiting him, so that we knew of his dark fears at second hand. There was, for instance, a young woman from Baranovici who came to see him when he was ill in bed; he confided to her that he felt "they were calling him," yet the good people of Baranovici had pulled him out of the valley of the shadow, and perhaps she was an emissary of the people of Baranovici now coming to his rescue.

It was no longer a matter of mood, however. His actual physical condition was alarming. His face had grown thin and haggard, its color yellowish. The doctors were depressingly silent. But whatever he thought of his condition, my father was fighting hard to hold onto life; he kept writing continuously, and even when he dozed off or was under sedation, his hand on the bedcover moved as though he were writing on paper. When he regained some strength he would get up from bed, dress as when he was well, and go about the house as though he were recovered.

We tried to divert him in various ways. When he was confined to bed we had some of the people we knew he was fond of pay him short visits. Yehoash, the famous poet and translator of the Bible into Yiddish, a sick man himself, would visit him and read to him from the newspapers. Ben, a poor hand at cards, would come into his room for a game of "1,000," a sort of Russian pinochle. He told me of a whim of my father's on his sickbed. One day my father asked Ben to get an envelope from his desk, and read the clipping it contained. The clipping, so carefully kept by my father, was a short story by a man who regarded himself as an important literary person but was considered by real writers to be a hack. Ben read the story very carefully, trying to find what there could possibly be in it for Sholom Aleichem to clip it and keep it so carefully in an envelope. When my father asked him for his true opinion of the story, Ben said, "Frankly, I think it is just rubbish." My father exploded in hearty laughter. He, too, regarded it as trash, of course, but he wanted to see who would be taken in by this ruse, would think that the story must be good because he, Sholom Aleichem, had kept it.

My father did well at cards, although he played very seldom. A game of cards was a special occasion, particularly during a visit by his old friend Avrom Lubarsky, who regarded himself as a master at cards and could not bear being beaten by my father. Ben was a poor proxy for Lubarsky and was almost invariably beaten by my father, the question being only how badly he would be beaten. We felt that playing cards would take our father's mind off his condition so he and Ben played. In their last game Ben saw my father losing the game, and this time Ben was anxious to have my father win as usual. He carelessly disposed of his aces, neglected to hold on to his kings, but my father played even worse. In the end, as Ben counted up the score, he could not help telling my father apologetically that he had lost. "Yes, lost," my father repeated, and a wry grin appeared on his face. It seemed to say that he had lost more than the game. Ben never forgot that grin, and he never played cards again.

On the days that our father was up and about we often invited guests for the evening, so that he might sit with us at least for a time and be distracted from his trouble. Our guests were made up of old friends from Europe, now refugees here, and some new friends made in this country. Among them were a few well-known writers, particularly those who were good raconteurs.

The last visit made by guests was on April 29, my sister Tissa's thirty-second birthday. My father had been in bed the day before and could not prepare the customary birthday surprises he loved to arrange for the members of his family. He did not feel too well on her birthday either, but he would not spoil Tissa's day. So, toward evening, he rose, dressed, and when the guests came, sat with us at the table.

That evening was not unlike the others. Bertha Kling, an amateur singer, sang in her passionate manner the same romantic folk songs that my father always enjoyed, but somehow they sounded hollow. The famous Yiddish dramatist Peretz Hirshbein told an amusing story in his inimitable, if elaborate, style, as he did on other evenings, but it did not call forth the usual levity.

Hirshbein told of a play he had seen once on the Russian stage about a Jewish shoemaker in a village who derived his sustenance for the winter months from sewing a new pair of boots for the landlord of the village. Every year he lived in anxiety that the landlord might not order new boots this year, or might get them made in the city; and when the landlord did order his boots, there was the problem of getting the leather on credit until the landlord called for them. In the last act, the landlord called for the boots to try them on. But he could not get his foot into the boot; apparently, one part of the boot was too narrow. This was the moment of dramatic tragedy. For if the boots did not fit, the landlord would not pay for them, and the shoemaker was ruined. He would not only lose the expected income, but he would have to make good the cost of the leather.

At this crucial moment of the play, a voice from the balcony shouted "Powder, sprinkle some powder into the boot!" This came from a shoemaker in the audience who knew his trade, and who for the moment forgot it was a play he was seeing.

Hirshbein related his story act by act, as it appeared on stage, with all the minutiae and mimicry, asking his auditors at the end of each act if they had heard enough or if they wanted to hear the next act. Naturally, he was asked to continue. On another evening the punch line, "Powder, sprinkle some powder," would have brought an ex-

uberant response. That evening the people around the table reacted
only politely. My father was straining to be attentive and at times
seemed to be mildly amused, but he was obviously disturbed or in
pain. At the end of the story he rose from the table and excused
himself. I followed him into his room.

He sank into his chair at his desk. He opened a side drawer, took
out an envelope to show me, and said, "This is my will; it will be
in this drawer, so you'll know."

I came closer to him, kissed him, and said, "Oh, Papulia, you must
not be thinking of this. You will be with us for many many years."
He smiled wryly and said nothing.

He never came out of his room.

He died two weeks later, early Saturday morning, May 13, 1916.
Radio being still unknown, and the morning papers already out, the
Yiddish newspapers issued extras, all in black borders, the huge letters SHOLOM ALEICHEM DIED occupying most of the front page,
the rest given to a picture and the sad news. Newsboys ran through
the streets of the Jewish districts with their packs of extras, holding
one of them unfolded over their heads, and shouting on top of their
voices, "Sholom Aleichem dead," so that those inside the houses
might hear and come down for an extra. Many did, congregating in
the streets, shocked, grieved, gesticulating, crying. The afternoon and
Sunday English papers carried the news and special feature stories
about the passing of the Jewish Mark Twain.

For two days and nights the body lay in state in the living room
of our apartment at 968 Kelly Street, the Bronx, with a changing
guard of all the Jewish writers in the city, while a continuous stream
of people kept passing the bier all through the night as well as during
the day, the line outside, even at night, stretching for blocks around
the house. They came from all boroughs of the city and from Jewish
communities outside.

The funeral was possibly the largest the city had seen. While the
estimates of the numbers of followers varied, the generally accepted
figure was "over 100,000." A couple of newspapers, counting the
people who came out to meet the procession at various points on its
route, gave the number as "well over 200,000." The funeral was arranged by the Kehillah, the United Jewish Community of Greater
New York, which had recently come into being, and was led by the

founder and leader of the Kehillah, Dr. Judah L. Magnes. Despite the inclement weather there were thousands of people at the cemetery. What was most touching was the number of people in the crowds weeping bitterly as if the deceased was a close member of their own family, a father, a brother. The afternoon papers carried streamers about the funeral, with four-column pictures of the procession.

The day after the funeral *The New York Times* reproduced my father's will, calling it "one of the great ethical wills in history," and Congressman Bennett of New York spoke of it on the floor of the House and had it printed in the Congressional Record. The first provision of the will read:

"Wherever I die I should be laid to rest not among the aristocrats, the elite, the rich, but rather among the plain people, the toilers, the common folk, so that the tombstone that will be placed on my grave will grace the simple graves about me, and the simple graves will adorn my tombstone, even as the plain people have, during my life, beatified their folk writer."

Another provision was:

"At my burial, and throughout the first year, and thereafter at the annual recurrence of the day of my passing, my remaining son and my sons-in-law should say Kaddish for me. But if they are not so inclined, or this be against their religious convictions, they may be absolved therefrom only if they all foregather with my daughters and grandchildren, and with good friends generally, and read my will, and also select one of my stories, of the very merry ones, and recite it in whatever language is more intelligible to them; and let my name be recalled by them with laughter rather than not be remembered at all."

The final paragraph read as follows:

"My last wish for my successors and my prayer to my children: Take good care of Mother, grace her age, sweeten her bitter life, heal her broken heart; not to weep for me, on the contrary, to remember me with joy, and most importantly, live in peace together, bear no hatred for one another, help each other in bad times, think occasionally of the other members of the family, take pity on the poor, and when circumstances permit pay my debts, if there be such. Children, bear with honor my hard-earned Jewish name, and may God in Heaven sustain you ever, Amen."

I may say for four of the children who joined him in the beyond, and for the two of us who are here, that we have tried to live up to his will. On the anniversary of his death, all through more than a half century, we have foregathered, all of us, with his friends and admirers, and have read his will and some of his merriest stories, and remembered him with laughter and love.

Works of Sholom Aleichem in English Translation

Jewish Children, translated by Hannah Berman. London, Methuen, 1920; reprinted 1922 by Alfred A. Knopf, Inc., 1937 by Bloch Publishing Co.

The Old Country, translated by Julius and Frances Butwin. New York, Crown Publishers, 1946

Inside Kasrilevke, translated by Isidor Goldstick. New York, Schocken Books, 1948

Tevyeh's Daughters, translated by Frances Butwin. New York, Crown Publishers, 1949

Wandering Star, translated by Frances Butwin. New York, Crown Publishers, 1952

Adventures of Mottel, the Cantor's Son, translated by Tamara Kahana. New York, Abelard-Schuman, 1953; paperbound, Collier, 1961

The Great Fair, translated by Tamara Kahana. New York, Noonday Press, 1955

Selected Stories of Sholom Aleichem, introduction by Alfred Kazin. New York, Modern Library, 1956

Stories and Satires, translated by Curt Leviant. New York, Thomas Yoseloff, 1959

The Tevyeh Stories and Others, translated by Julius and Frances Butwin. New York, paperbound, Pocket Books

Old Country Tales, translated by Curt Leviant. New York, G. P. Putnam's Sons, 1966

IN COLLECTIONS

Ausubel, Nathan, ed., *A Treasury of Jewish Humor*. Garden City, New York, Doubleday, 1951. Includes "Menachem-Mendel, Fortune Hunter"; "Aphorisms According to the Hebrew-Yiddish Alphabet"; "Rabchik: A Jewish Dog"; "My Brother Eliyahu's Drink"; "Gy-ma-na-si-a."

Goodman, Philip and Hanna, eds., *The Jewish Marriage Anthology*. Philadelphia, Jewish Publication Society, 1965. Includes "In Haste"; "The Marriage-Broker"; "Modern Children."

Grafstein, Melech W., ed., *Sholom Aleichem Panorama*. London, Ontario, *Jewish Observer,* 1948. Includes essays about Sholom Aleichem, as well as a large, rich anthology of his stories and plays.

Howe, Irving, and Greenberg, Eliezer, eds., *A Treasury of Yiddish Stories*. New York, Meridian Books, 1958. Includes seven stories by Sholom Aleichem.

Bellow, Saul, ed., *Great Jewish Short Stories*. New York, paperbound, Dell Publishing Co. Includes "On Account of a Hat"; "Hodel."

PLAYS

Goldberg, Isaac, translator, *Six Plays of the Yiddish Theatre*. Boston, J. W. Luce and Co., 1916. Includes *She Must Marry a Doctor*.

White, Bessie F., translator, *Nine One-Act Plays from the Yiddish*. Includes *Gymnazie*.

SHOLOM ALEICHEM IN OTHER LANGUAGES

The works of Sholom Aleichem have been translated into all European languages as well as a number of Asian languages, including Chinese and Japanese.

Index

Gorki (*cont.*)
  health of, 240
  on Russian translations, 254
Gottheil, Richard, 186
Gotz, Mikhail Rafailovich, 231
Grand Central Palace (N.Y.C.), 311
Grand Theater (N.Y.C.), 186–87, 190
Great Britain, 157, 166, 232
  prosperity of, 268
  in World War I, 271, 283
  S.A.'s reading tours in, 173–79
  See also London
Great Win, The (also called *200,000*)
  (drama), 210, 235
  rejection of, for production, 301
  writing of, 295
Greek Orthodox Church, *see* Russian
  Orthodox Church
Greenbaum, Samuel, 187, 287
Gruber, Herr (landlord in Albeck),
  269–70

Ha-Melitz (Hebrew magazine), 82,
  83, 92
Handwerk Hall (Geneva), 234
Hannah (custom peddler), 120–22
Harbinger of the Folks Bibliothek, The
  (literary journal), 91–92
Hearst, William Randolph, 187, 209,
  280
Hertzen, Alexander, 72
Herzl, Theodor, 263–64
Hirshbein, Peretz, 295, 314–15
Hoboken, N.J., 282
Hotel Theresa (N.Y.C.), 283–84
Hughes, Charles Evans, 187

"If I Were Rothschild" (short story),
  287
Imeninik, imeninitza, 22
Imperial Hotel (Kiev), 160–61
Israel (Palestine), 241, 268, 301
  electricity introduced in, 296
  Magnes in, 307
Italy, *see* Nervi, Italy
It's Hard to be a Jew (drama), 235
Ivanoff affair, 229–30

Jacobs, Joseph, 186
Japan, 155–56
Jewish American, The (newspaper),
  184, 185, 209, 280
Jewish Morning Journal, The (newspaper), 214–15, 287
Jewish customs, 72, 222, 245, 300, 316
  bar mitzvah, 34–35, 231, 263
  of burial, 85, 231
  of cutting bride's hair, 19
  of education, 45
  kosher eating habits, 116–18
  observance of Passover, 312
  observance of the Sabbath, 32, 36,
    50, 151
  observance of Simchas Torah, 68–69
  observance of Yom Kippur, 299
  prayer vigils, 36–37
  slaughter of animals, 142
Jewish Morning Journal, The (newspaper), 216, 221, 281
"Jewish Robinson Crusoe, The" (short
  story), 41
Jewish Students' Lecture Committee,
  284–85
Jewish Teachers' Institute (Zhitomir),
  45, 51
Jewish Theological Seminary (N.Y.C.),
  308
Jews, 47–48, 146, 165, 182–83, 252–
  53, 272–73
  Austrian, 167–68, 170–72
  British, 174–79
  celebrate S.A.'s 25th literary anni-
    versary, 240–44
  as chosen people, 145
  Danish, 275, 278
  Jewish concentration-camp survi-
    vors, 16
  proposed world congress of, 295
  Russian, 61, 98, 132, 153–62, 184,
    236, 311
    community life, 30–33, 78, 158,
      189
    czar's edict regarding, 156
    expelled from Germany, 271,
      275–76, 278